The Illustrated Book of
CHRISTIAN LITERATURE

The First Two Millennia

The Illustrated Book of
CHRISTIAN LITERATURE
The First Two Millennia

ROBERT VAN DE WEYER

Abingdon Press

Nashville

The Illustrated Book of Christian Literature

Copyright © 1998 Hunt & Thorpe

Text © 1998 Robert Van de Weyer

Abingdon Press edition published 1998

Designed by

THE BRIDGEWATER BOOK COMPANY LTD.

ISBN 0-687-08243-9

Cataloging-in-Publication data is available from the Library of Congress

Original edition published in English under the title
The Illustrated Book of Christian Literature
by Hunt & Thorpe, Alresford, Hants, UK.

98 99 00 01 02 03 04 05 06 -- 10 9 8 7 6 5 4 3 2 1

COVER AND TITLE PAGE ILLUSTRATIONS (FROM LEFT TO RIGHT):
St. Luke, from an 11th-century Greek gospel (e.t. archive).

St. Gregory writing with scribes below, c.850–875.
(Bridgeman Art Library/Kunsthistorisches Museum, Vienna).

Julian of Norwich, detail from the Benedictine window in Norwich Cathedral,
England by Moira Forsyth, 1964 (Sonia Halliday Photographs).

Albert Schweitzer at his desk (AKG London).

PICTURE ACKNOWLEDGMENTS
Archiv für Kunst und Geschichte, London: cover br, 8, 11 (Schatz der Kathedrale), 12
(Scuola Grande di S. Giovanni Evangelista), 68, 129 (Museo del Prado), 155, 169, 171.

Bridgeman Art Library, London: 2 (The Hermitage), 5, 18 (Kunsthistorisches Museum, Vienna),
22 (Albertina Graphic Collection, Vienna), 40 (Museo di San Marco dell' Angelico, Florence) 43 (Noortman),
52 (Bolton Museum and Art Gallery), 56 (Palazzo Barberini, Rome), 61 (State Russian Museum, St. Petersburg),
67 (The Hermitage), 74 (Bibliotheque Nazionale, Turin), 78 (Kunsthistorisches Museum, Vienna), 81 (Biblioteca
Medicea-Laurenziana, Florence), 84 (St. Florentin), 86 (Whitford and Hughes), 113 (Tretyakov Gallery, Moscow),
117 (Phillips), 123 (Victoria & Albert Museum), 124 (Museo dell'Opera del Duomo, Prato), 131 (Pinacoteca di Brera,
Milan), 145 (Fitzwilliam Museum, Cambridge) 156 (Museo del Castello, Sforzesco).

Bridgeman Art Library/Giraudon: 25 (Unterlinden Museum, Colmar), 88 (Musée des Beaux Arts, Caen).

Bridgeman Art Library/Index: 46.

Cameron Collection: 73, 83, 98, 100, 137.

e.t.archive, London: 16, 20, 28, 30, 39, 54, 69, 92, 95, 140, 141.

Sonia Halliday: 36.

Fine Art Photo Library: 118.

Manufactured in Hong Kong/China

CONTENTS

Prologue

From what we can infer, Jesus Christ never wrote anything down, he relied entirely on the spoken word. But within a few years of his death, collections of his sayings were circulating among Christians, and these were soon included in larger accounts of his life and work, which came to be called "gospels." At the same time, Christian preachers, led by Paul, started to write open letters, intended to be read aloud to congregations.

Thus began the stream of Christian literature which, by the third and fourth centuries, had turned into a mighty river and has continued to flow right down to the present day.

In one of the earliest Christian books, the Gospel of John, Jesus Christ is described as the Logos—the Word—and there is no doubt that Christianity is a very verbal faith. Over the past thousand years it has nurtured every form of art—painting and sculpture, music and architecture—but it is in the written word that it has most excelled. So at the end of the second millennium, as we look back at the achievements of Christianity, special attention should be given to Christian literature. And admiration for past literary genius is the greatest stimulus to even greater work in the third millennium.

The New Testament, the founding collection of Christian literature, contains broadly three types of writing.

The first and most striking may be called the testimony. The four gospels are testimonies of the life of Jesus himself, and the Book of Acts is a testimony of the life of the early Christian community. While appearing similar, a testimony is quite different from a historical record. It does not attempt to be a balanced, objective account of events, and may even be quite casual about factual details. Rather, it strives to convey the other spiritual meaning of those events.

The second type of writing is spirituality, in which the reader is given guidance on how to grow closer to God. In the first three gospels, Jesus gives surprisingly little spiritual guidance; the most notable piece is the Lord's Prayer, given at the direct request of the disciples. The letters of Paul are also quite reticent on this subject, apart from severe warnings about the disorderly use of certain spiritual gifts. But the writings of John, both his gospel and his letters, are a treasure house for those who wish to pray and meditate more deeply.

The third type of writing is philosophy. Jesus offers numerous moral insights, but they do not amount to an ethical system. Paul, by contrast, is gripped by the challenge of turning his new-found faith into a coherent structure of ideas. Over the centuries many devout Christians have felt daunted, and even affronted, by the philosophical complexity of some of Paul's writings and they have wondered wistfully whether Christianity could be confined to the more simple wisdom of Jesus himself. Yet without Paul's intellectual efforts, as well as his missionary endeavors, Christianity never would have emerged as a distinct religion, and Paul is the origin of most of what we regard as basic Christian doctrine.

From the second century onward, when the New Testament canon was formed, every Christian thinker has been immersed in its writings, striving to relate them to present challenges and problems. Thus, the three categories of testimony, spirituality, and philosophy, are roughly applicable to the literature that has flowed subsequently from Christian pens.

Naturally some writers wrote more than one type of book. Augustine of Hippo, for example, is a major figure in all three areas. But lack of space compels each writer to be confined to one category. Lack of space has a compensating advantage, enabling the reader to see clearly the development of Christian literature over such a vast span of time.

There are some obvious differences in style and approach in response to varying circumstances and concerns. But the similarities are far more remarkable. The underlying spiritual and mental challenges that human beings face from one era to another remain the core. Hence the literature of long ago is as fresh and vital today as it was when it was written.

Those who are already well-versed in some or all areas of Christian literature will regret that some favorite authors have been omitted. But this book is primarily directed to those who wish to see this vast field as a whole.

In the brief introductions to the writers, the book offers a simple historical sketch, and through the extracts, the readers may behold some of the choicest jewels. And if readers are thereby stimulated to open the treasure chest fully, studying great books in their entirety, they will find spiritual and intellectual wealth that can never be exhausted.

ABOVE *Tapestry page from St. Luke's Gospel (Lindisfarne Gospels)*

Part One

❧

SPIRITUALITY

*God is love: those who live in love
live in God, and God lives in them.
There is no fear in love; perfect love
banishes all fear. Love has not been
made perfect in anyone who is afraid,
because fear implies punishment.
We love because God first loved us.
Christ has given us this command:
those who love God must also love
their fellow believers.*

FROM 1 JOHN 4.

Introduction

According to Luke, the disciples on one occasion asked Jesus how to pray. Jesus instructed them to address God as "Father," and gave the words that came to be known as the Lord's Prayer as the model for prayer. Since that time, Christians have continued to have the same yearning for a closer relationship with God. And Christian spiritual teachers have written numerous books and treatises in reply. None of these teachers, of course, has tried to gainsay the instructions of Jesus himself. In effect they have been supplying their commentary. The greatest of these teachers, by general consent, was the writer of the gospel and epistles ascribed to John.

Among later spiritual teachers there have been some variations in emphasis, the most important of which concerns the relationship of the human soul to the body.

From the earliest decades many Christians have accepted the view common in Greek philosophy, and most famously expressed by Plato, that the soul is imprisoned within the body, and is tainted by bodily desires and pleasures. Thus a major purpose of spirituality is to purify the soul from these desires, and hence liberate it; and this is usually seen as involving rigorous asceticism, in which bodily sensations are suppressed.

Other teachers, however, have stressed that material needs, as well as spiritual, are created by God. Thus, while bodily desires may become distorted, and hence sinful, unity with God involves an appreciation of his material gifts. Moreover, through prayer, natural and Christian beauty become windows into the divine beauty.

Yet the differences are far outweighed by the common themes that can be found in spiritual writings of every period and in every part of the Christian world.

Christians should be honest in prayer, expressing all their feelings and emotions to God, negative as well as positive. Christians should practice moral virtue, not only for its own sake, but also as the root of spiritual growth; only by showing love toward one's neighbour is it possible to enter a loving relationship with God. Pride, especially spiritual pride, is the most deadly enemy of prayer, and humility is its vital ally; there is no place for spiritual rivalry between Christians.

Above all, Christian spiritual teachers speak of the pain as well as the joy of prayer. Many describe the darkness into which the soul is plunged as it realizes the falsity of its former goals and aspirations. They tell of the temptations besetting the soul, which grow stronger, not weaker, as it moves closer to God. And they warn of periods of dryness experienced by every devout soul, when spiritual satisfaction drains away, to be replaced by listless boredom.

The way of prayer, they unanimously agree, is not easy and hence requires great and constant self-discipline—but its rewards are infinite and eternal. Naturally phraseology and imagery change from one Christian tradition to another. Yet all spiritual writers are aware that they are pressing words into service beyond their capacity, since true spiritual experience is beyond words. And two words in particular cause recurring anxiety.

The first is prayer itself. Literally it means asking God for favors and blessings, and this is how the word is commonly used. Yet most of the great spiritual teachers regard this as a crude and even invalid spiritual activity. Christians are called to trust God completely, submitting to his will, and accepting whatever occurs with humble gratitude.

The second word is mysticism. To the writers of some traditions, this implies something esoteric, in which only a tiny minority can engage; and it also suggests a kind of religious selfishness, in which individuals pursue their own spiritual pleasures. Yet every Christian tradition teaches that in Christ all human beings may have a direct encounter with God—and this encounter may be described as mystical.

Taken together, the writings in this section are a manual of how anyone can become a mystic, and a description, as far as human language can go, of meeting God face to face.

ABOVE *God as creator of the world.*
(From the Bible moralisée
c.1230, Toledo Cathedral).

"Every Christian tradition teaches that
in Christ all human beings may have a direct
encounter with God—and this encounter may
be described as mystical."

John

The writings of John in the New Testament contain themes and metaphors that have remained central to Christian spirituality. In the opening verses of John's gospel, he identified Christ with the Logos, the Word of God, who is the agent of all creation. Thus we are invited to see God mirrored in all living creatures. And later, in the mouth of Christ he emphasized the presence of God, in the person of the Holy Spirit, within the souls of all faithful disciples. Thus prayer is a divine act in which we are unified with God: the Holy Spirit inspires our prayer, the Word of God guides our prayer, and God the Father is the focus. John described the experience of unity with God as light, and separation from God as darkness.

John was eager to stress that unity with God in prayer is not the preserve of a select few, but is open to all people. Yet equally, he warned that learning to pray requires constant effort and self-discipline.

THE WORD

In the beginning was the Word. The Word was with God, and the Word was God. He was with God at the beginning.

All things were made through him, and nothing was made except through him. In him was life, and that life was the light of all people. The light shines in the darkness, and the darkness has never overcome it.

A man came, sent by God, whose name was John. He came as a witness to testify to the light, that through him all might believe. He was not the light, but came to bear witness to the light. The true light that enlightens every person was coming into the world.

He was in the world; but the world, though it was made through him, did not recognize him. He came to his own home, and his own people did not accept him. But to all who accepted him, to those who put their trust in him, he gave power to become children of God, born not of human stock, by the physical desire of a human father, but of God.

So the Word became flesh; he lived among us, full of grace and truth, and we saw his glory, such glory as befits the Father's only Son.

FROM JOHN 1

LEFT *John sees the four horsemen of the Apocalypse (Venice, Scuola Grande di S. Giovanni Evangelista).*

GOD'S LIFE AND LIGHT

Our message is the Word which gives life. The Word existed from the beginning. We have heard it; we have seen it with our own eyes and gazed on it; we have touched it with our own hands. When this life became visible, we saw it and now we bear witness to it. We speak to you of the eternal life which was with the Father, and was revealed to us. We declare to you what we ourselves have seen and heard, so that you may share the common life which we enjoy with the Father and with his Son Jesus Christ.

This is the message we have heard from God's Son and pass on to you; God is light, and in him there is no darkness at all. If we claim to be sharing in God's life, yet continue to live in darkness, we are lying in both word and action. But if we live in the light, as he himself is in the light, then together we share God's life; and the blood of Jesus his Son cleanses us from all sin.

FROM 1 JOHN 1

THE COMING OF THE SPIRIT

"I have much more to tell you," Jesus said, "but now it would be too much for you to bear. However, when the Spirit of truth comes, he will guide you into all truth. He will not speak on his own authority, but will speak only what he hears; and he will reveal to you what is to come. He will glorify me because he will take what is mine and reveal it to you. All that the Father has is mine; that is why I said that the Spirit will take what is mine and reveal it to you.

"In a little while you will see me no more; and a little while later you will see me again. I tell you in all truth, you will weep and mourn, but the world will rejoice. You will be sad, but your sorrow will turn into joy. A woman in labor is in pain because her time has come; but when her baby is born, she forgets the anguish in her joy that a child has been brought into the world. So it is with you. At present you are sad; but I shall see you again, and then your hearts will fill with joy, and no one shall rob you of that joy.

"Until now I have been speaking to you in veiled language. But the time is coming when I shall no longer used veiled language, but tell you of the Father in plain words. When that day comes you will pray to him in my name; I do not say that I will pray on your behalf, because the Father loves you himself. The Father loves you for loving me and for believing that I came from God. I came from the Father and have come into the world; and now I am leaving the world and going to the Father." His disciples said: "Now you are speaking plainly, not in veiled language. We are certain now that you know everything, and do not need to be questioned. And so we believe that you have come from God."

FROM JOHN 16

PERFECT LOVE

Dear friends, let us love one another, since love comes from God. Everyone who loves is a child of God, and knows God. But those who do not love are ignorant of God, because God is love. God showed his love for us by sending his only Son into the world, that we might have life through him. This is what love is; not that we have loved God, but that he loved us and sent his Son to expiate our sins. If this is how God loves us, dear friends, we should love one another. No one has ever seen God, but if we love one another, he himself lives within us; his love is made perfect in us.

God is love: those who live in love live in God, and God lives in them. There is no fear in love; perfect love banishes all fear. Love has not been made perfect in anyone who is afraid, because fear implies punishment. We love because God first loved us. Christ has given us this command: those who love God must also love their fellow believers.

FROM 1 JOHN 4.

Clement of Rome

Clement, the bishop of the Christian community in Rome, was prompted to write to the Church in Corinth by news of internal divisions. Aware that the apostle Paul had tried a few decades earlier to heal these conflicts, Clement was robust and outspoken. But he tempered his criticisms with appeals to their spiritual feelings. He used the harmony of the actual order designed by God, as an image of the harmony that God wants to prevail among believers. Clement also showed how moral goodness is closely linked to a spiritual awareness of Christ's presence, with and among his followers.

Clement is thought to have been a slave in a wealthy Roman household. After his own conversion to Christianity, he converted his master and mistress; they in turn granted him freedom. Thus his education was poor, as the quality of his prose testifies. Yet he was a man of moral stature, with a clear vision of how the Christian faith should be put into practice. As the new religion faced increasing persecution, these qualities made him ideally suited to be a leader. He was appointed bishop around 90 C.E., and died about ten years later.

RIGHT *St. Clement, 100 C.E., taught that the natural harmony created by God should be reflected in the lives of his followers. A spiritual awareness of Christ would inevitably lead to moral goodness.*

SERENITY AND HARMONY

Let us turn our eyes to the Father and Creator of the universe. We can see in the universe his precious and priceless gifts of peace and order, so let us embrace these gifts for ourselves. Let us think deeply about God, observing with the eye of faith the patience and mercy he shows everywhere, and the complete lack of friction in the way in which he has designed the world.

The sky, as it revolves beneath God's heavenly kingdom, is totally obedient to him. The day and the night run the course that he has laid down for them, and neither interferes with the other. The sun, the moon, and the stars are like a heavenly choir, each with its appointed part to perform. Each season the busy earth, obedient to his will, brings forth great riches of food for humans, animals, and every other kind of living creature. The earth never objects to God's commands, and does not attempt to alter them in any way. God's commands are also heard in the fathomless depths of the sea and the untold regions of the underworld... spring, summer, autumn, and winter follow one another peacefully. The winds blow when God decrees, each wind from its own storehouse, causing no offense. The streams, created for our well-being and pleasure, continue to flow, giving us fresh water to sustain life. And even the tiny insects live together in tranquil friendship. The great Architect and Lord of the Universe urges all to live in serenity and harmony, for the good of all.

FROM THE EPISTLE TO THE CORINTHIANS, CHAPTERS 19 AND 20

A CANDLE IN THE DARK

Take care, my friends, to conduct yourselves in a manner worthy of God, only doing what is good and acceptable to him. Live in peace, lest his benevolence should turn to anger. Remember that God's spirit is a candle which lights up our hidden parts. So let us always bear in mind how near God is to us, and how he can observe all our thoughts and feelings. Do not try to run away from God and his commands. Rather than opposing God, it would be better to oppose the folly and stupidity of those who in their arrogance think they can do without him. Always look with reverence toward God, and toward the Lord Jesus Christ whose blood was given for us. So let us show respect toward those who have been set about us. Let us honor our elders, and train our young people to bow down to God. Let our women march on the road of goodness, becoming for us examples of the beauty of holiness by their sincere faith. Let them demonstrate the quiet virtue of self-control by speaking always with love, and let them show kindness in equal measure to all those who fear God. Let us ensure our children receive proper Christian instruction. They should learn that a humble spirit, a heart that is pure and loving, and a mind that wishes to learn his commands will bring great blessings from him. God knows all our thoughts and desires. He gives us the breath of life. And at his own good pleasure he will take the breath of life away.

FROM THE EPISTLE TO THE CORINTHIANS, CHAPTER 21

THE GIFTS OF GOD

How joyful and how marvelous are the gifts of God, my friends! Some of these gifts we already understand: the gift of life that knows no death; the shining splendor of God's justice; the fullness of God's truth; the faith that brings perfect assurance; the holiness that comes from obeying God's laws. But what of the things which God has prepared for us? Only the Creator and Father of eternity, the Most Holy One, knows the greatness and beauty of these. So let us strain every nerve to ensure that we are among those who will earn a share of these promised gifts. How can we do this, my friends? We do it by trusting God wholly with our minds; by finding out what is pleasing and acceptable to him; by doing whatever he wants us to do; and by following the path of truth. We must utterly renounce evil and wickedness of every kind—all greed, quarreling, malice, fraud, slander, back-biting, disrespect toward God, self-glorification, arrogance, conceit, and hostility toward strangers. Those who are guilty of these things, and also those who consent to them, are hated by God. By renouncing evil, and by conforming to God's will, dear friends, we shall find our salvation. We offer ourselves to Jesus Christ, our High Priest who helps us in our weakness. Through him we can look up to the highest heaven and see, as if through a window, the peerless perfection of the fact of God. Through him the eyes of our hearts are opened, and our dim and foolish minds unfold like flowers to the light.

FROM THE EPISTLE TO THE CORINTHIANS, CHAPTERS 35 AND 36

God knows all our thoughts and desires. He gives us the breath of life. And at his own good pleasure he will take the breath of life away.

Cyprian of Carthage

Cyprian was appointed bishop of Carthage in North Africa in 249, just before a terrible persecution broke out. When the persecution finished, the Church was bitterly divided over whether to welcome back apostates—those who had denied their faith in order to survive. Cyprian supported a more lenient view. But the bitterness of the conflict taught him the importance of Church unity. And he believed that this could only be fostered and maintained through prayer. He urged every Christian to recite each day the Lord's Prayer, meditating on each phrase. To assist this, he wrote a commentary on the Lord's Prayer, showing it to be the model for prayer.

He was born into a rich and cultured pagan family in the first decade of the century and became a celebrated orator. In 246, to the consternation of the entire city, he became a Christian, giving away most of his wealth to the poor. He was ordained priest; three years later, when the old bishop died, he was made his successor by popular acclaim. He was arrested and beheaded in 258 during a later persecution.

RIGHT *The family at daily prayer and grace before a meal. (By a German artist, 1909, in a German church in Stockholm, Sweden). St. Cyprian urged every Christian to recite the Lord's Prayer each day.*

PRAYING THE LORD'S PRAYER

When we pray, we should ensure that we understand the words we use. We should be humble, aware of our own weaknesses, and be eager to receive God's grace. Our bodily posture and our tone of voice should reflect the fact that through prayer we enter God's presence. To speak too loudly to God would be impudent; thus a quiet and modest manner is appropriate. The Lord has instructed us that we should usually pray in private, even in our own bedrooms. This reminds us that God is everywhere, that he hears and sees everything, and that he penetrates the deepest secrets of our hearts.

OUR FATHER

The one who teaches peace and fosters unity does not want us to pray as isolated and selfish individuals, concerned only about ourselves. Thus he does not tell us to say "My Father in heaven." Nor does he desire me to ask only for my own daily bread, nor for my sins to be forgiven, nor that I alone should not be led into temptation and delivered from evil. Christian

prayer is public, and is offered for all. We pray not as individuals, but as a community, speaking as one. And God will carry all of us to himself.

HALLOWED BE YOUR NAME

We do not imagine that God will be made holy by our prayers. Rather we are asking that his holiness should shine on us. God cannot be made more holy; it is he who makes others holy. We can become holy because he is holy. We started the process of becoming holy at our baptism. Our most earnest desire is that this process should continue day by day; and we pray for this day by day.

YOUR KINGDOM COME

When has God not reigned as king? God has reigned since before time began and will reign until after time has finished. Thus we pray that we may acknowledge God as king, and that he may rule our own hearts and minds. Yet we also ask that we may share his sovereignty. He sent his Son to proclaim his rule, and inherit his kingdom; and his Son has made us his fellow heirs.

YOUR WILL BE DONE

We are not praying that God may accomplish what he wants to do; nothing can prevent God from succeeding in whatever he intends. Rather we are praying that we may accomplish what God wants us to do. The devil constantly tries to direct our thoughts and actions away from obedience to God. Thus we pray that our wills may be perfectly aligned with God's will. This means that we are asking for God's help and protection in our battle with the devil. We are not strong enough by ourselves to resist the devil. We can only win with God's grace and mercy.

GIVE US TODAY OUR DAILY BREAD

We are asking God literally to ensure that our physical needs are met. But we are also making a spiritual request. We know that Christ is the bread of life. We pray that we may both receive this bread and also become part of it.

FORGIVE US OUR SINS

God is blunt in reminding us that we are sinners, and compelling us to pray for forgiveness. In the process of asking for forgiveness, we must look carefully at the state of our conscience. Moreover, since we are required to pray daily for forgiveness, we are prevented from imagining that even a day can pass in complete innocence. Indeed, spiritual pride, in which we delude ourselves that we are pure, is the surest route to perdition.

AS WE FORGIVE THOSE WHO SIN AGAINST US

God commands us to be in harmony and live in peace with one another. He urges those who have been born again through the waters of baptism to retain the character of this second birth. We who are children of God cannot just give lip service to the ideal of peace: we must make it a reality. Thus we must become one in heart and mind. God refuses to accept the worship offered by people who are at odds and have not forgiven one another. Thus we must first be reconciled with each other and only then can we turn to God. Indeed our mutual harmony as brothers and sisters is our greatest act of worship to God.

LEAD US NOT INTO TEMPTATION

These words reassure us that the devil can never win a final victory over us because God remains always in control. All power comes from God, so when we are assailed by temptation, we should turn to God in a spirit of fear and trust—fear of what would befall us if we gave way to temptation, and trust in God's strength to enable us to resist. When we pray these words, we are reminding ourselves of how weak and vulnerable we are, and hence how much we rely on God's help. If we were not weak, we would quickly become complacent and conceited, worshiping ourselves rather than God.

DELIVER US FROM EVIL

The last petition sums up the entire prayer, indeed it summarizes every prayer we offer. To be delivered from evil is to be saved from everything which the devil can devise against us. We pray these simple words in the conviction that God will always give help to those who ask for it—that we can utterly depend and rely on him. And when we have to be delivered from evil, there is nothing left to ask.

FROM ON THE LORD'S PRAYER, CHAPTERS 4 AND 28

Gregory of Nyassa

*L*iving in a period of furious doctrinal controversy, when theological differences were dividing the Church, Gregory of Nyassa taught that God can never be understood by intellectual speculation, and that divine truth can never be expressed in words. Instead, he believed that we should try to see the image of God in the order and beauty of his creation; and to do this we ourselves must truly reflect his image by cleansing our hearts of sin and becoming pure. Gregory was convinced that God has implanted in every human being an appreciation of beauty—and that all earthly beauty points to the infinite beauty of God. Thus the spiritual path consists in nurturing and developing this appreciation.

The child of an aristocratic Christian family that numbered several martyrs among its members, Gregory received an excellent education but achieved little success. He married a woman of strong faith who loved the arts, and she stimulated his esthetic sense. In 372, at the age of forty, he was invited to be bishop of Nyassa, near his hometown of Caesarea. He strongly supported the monasteries that his brother Basil had founded, believing that the monks had a particular role in the spiritual nurture of the common people.

He was inept at the administrative tasks of a bishop, but his sermons—which were later collected and circulated as books—enunciated his spiritual philosophy with great skill.

SEEING GOD IN CREATION

God in his essence, as he exists in himself, transcends all human knowledge. He cannot be approached or comprehended by intellectual speculation. Human beings do not possess a faculty to understand that which is beyond understanding; thus we are told that the ways of God are unsearchable and hence beyond human reason. Yet there is another way in which God can be apprehended; indeed, there are numerous ways. We can see him by inference through the wisdom reflected in the universe. Think of a human work of art: the mind can see the artist in his artistry. But note that the mind does not see the essence of the artist, merely the skill which he has revealed in his work.

Similarly, when we look at creation, we form an image not of the substance of the Creator, but of the wisdom he has revealed in his work. Consider, for example, human life itself. God created human beings not out of any necessity, but by the goodness of his own free will. Thus when we reflect on ourselves, we do not perceive God in himself, but we see his goodness. In the same way, we can see God's goodness in every object around us, and the contemplation of any object carries our minds upward to the supreme source of goodness.

FROM ON THE BEATITUDES. SERMON 6

LEFT *Detail from St. Gregory writing with scribes below. (Carolingian, Franco-German School, c.850-875). "As you look on God's beauty, he will continue to reveal himself to you ever more fully."*

BEAUTY HINTING AT GREATER BEAUTY

Fix your eyes on the infinite beauty of God. You will constantly discover the beauty anew. It will constantly seem strange, because it is different from what the mind normally conceives. As you look on God's beauty, he will continue to reveal himself to you ever more fully. And as he reveals himself, your desire to see him will increase. You will sense that the beauty you see now is merely a hint of the glorious beauty yet to be revealed.

You may try to communicate with God in words, but words can never encompass your relationship with him. Some will tell you that the object of your love is unattainable, that God can never be apprehended. At times, the frustration of not being able to see God in his fullness will be so great that you will feel spiritually beaten and wounded. But you will come to realize that the true satisfaction of your desire consists in the quest for God, in never ceasing to ascend toward him—and in desiring him ever more intensely.

FROM ON THE SONG OF SONGS, SERMON 12

ACQUIRING SPIRITUAL ENERGY WHILE EXPLAINING IT

There is nothing to break the impetus of the soul. The nature of goodness is that it always aspires to better. In the same way, the nature of the soul is that it always reaches upward, yearning for the supreme goodness of heaven. The soul never becomes weary of climbing new and higher summits; each summit gives the soul fresh energy to climb the next summit. This is because spiritual activity has the special and unique property of nurturing its own strength as it expands it. Thus as the soul climbs higher, it acquires the ability to climb higher still.

FROM LIFE OF MOSES, SECTIONS 225 AND 226

DARKNESS AS ENLIGHTENMENT

Religious knowledge comes first to people as light. Thus it is perceived to be contrary to darkness; indeed, religion is seen as escape from darkness. But as the mind progresses, and as it becomes more spiritually vibrant, it comes to realize how little of God it truly perceives; it recognizes that it remains in darkness.

Indeed, the darkness that comes from spiritual progress is far more profound than natural darkness. The mind leaves behind all natural light, because it becomes indifferent to the things of nature; and in this darkness, it becomes aware of its ignorance of God. It thus yearns for God. Eventually the yearning leads to an indirect knowledge of God. The mind becomes aware that seeing God consists in not seeing, because knowledge of God transcends all knowledge. The mind is thus surrounded on every side by darkness: yet the darkness is now a source of enlightenment.

FROM LIFE OF MOSES, SECTIONS 162 AND 163

INNER AND OUTER PEACE

We must not allow hostility to rise up in our hearts; it must be killed absolutely and permanently. We should never give way to anger or nurse grudges, because this would threaten our souls. And, above all, we must never act on these feelings, as this will only fan the feelings into an ever greater blaze. We bear the name of Christ, who is peace. For this reason we are called to put an end to all hostility. In every situation where people are divided, Christ can break down the wall which separates them, and make peace. Thus when people attack us, we should, through prayer, invite Christ to reconcile us with our attacker. But we can only do this if we ourselves are free from all hostile feelings. So our spirit and our flesh are not in conflict. When we are at peace within ourselves, then Christ can work through us to make peace with others.

FROM A TREATISE ON PERFECTION

John Climacus

*I**n the Orthodox churches of Eastern Europe and
Russia no book—apart from the Bible itself—has
been more studied and copied than The Ladder of
Divine Ascent by John Climacus. Even today in Orthodox
monasteries it is read aloud at mealtimes through the season of
Lent. It is regarded as the summary of the wisdom that first
blossomed in the Egyptian desert, and spread rapidly across
the Christian world.*

*He was born around 580, and at the age of sixteen went
to live at the foot of Mount Sinai. For forty years he lived as a
hermit. But when he was an old man a group of monks
arrived from a nearby monastery and begged him to be their
abbot. He was horrified, but felt that they were expressing
God's call. He wrote his book at the monks' request, using as
his central image Jacob's ladder to heaven.*

BELOW *St. John Climaco and hermits on
Mount Sinai. (From a 13th-century Greek
manuscript, Biblioteca Marciana, Venice).
"Humility is a gift from God of indescribable
beauty and immeasurable value."*

THE SALVATION OF ALL

God is the life of all free beings. He is
the salvation of all: of believers and
unbelievers; of the just and the unjust; of the
devout and those who ignore religion; of those
free from evil passions and those enslaved by
them; of monks and those living in the world;
of the educated and the illiterate; of the healthy
and the sick; of the young and the old. He is like
the light and the heat of the sun, and the
changes in the water, which are the same for
everyone, without exception.

FROM STEP 1

COMMUNION WITH CREATION

Friends of God are those who live in
communion with his creation, and who are
thus free from sin. They take every opportunity
to do good. They are self-controlled, holding
fast to God amid the trials, snares, and noise of
the world. They rise above all difficulties.

FROM STEP 1

PERFECTION IN THE WORLD

Those who are married can attain the same
state of perfection as monks. They should
be generous. They should speak evil of no one,
rob no one, and tell no lies. They should despise
no one, and never carry hatred. They should
not imagine themselves spiritually superior to
anyone. They should show compassion to the
needy. They should not intentionally cause
offense to anyone. They should be satisfied
with their lot.

FROM STEP 1

CULTIVATING VIRTUE

To cultivate virtue is hard, and we can often
feel burdened by the demands that virtue
makes of us. But a moment comes when the
sense of burden lifts, and a flame of joy lights
in our hearts.

FROM STEP 1

RENEWING OUR CONTRACT

Repentance is the renewal of our contract with God, giving us a fresh start. Repentance goes into the spiritual marketplace and tries to purchase humility. Repentance distrusts excessive bodily comfort. Repentance means standing in a watchtower, keeping guard over oneself. Repentance is the daughter of hope, and the son of refusal to despair. Repentance means acknowledging guilt, and yet not being disgraced.

FROM STEP 5

SPIRITUAL SUICIDE

Those who take pride in their repentance and congratulate themselves in their tears of remorse are like a man who asks a king for a weapon against the enemy—and then uses it to commit suicide.

FROM STEP 7

SINCERE REPENTANCE

When people sincerely repent, God does not want them to continue weeping with remorse. He wants them to rejoice that they are reunited with him. He wants their souls to rejoice. After all, if the sin has been taken away, tears are superfluous. Why look for a bandage when the wound has already healed?

FROM STEP 7

FINAL JUDGMENT

When we die, we shall not be criticized for having failed to work miracles. We shall not be accused of having failed to understand theology or to attain mystical visions. But we shall certainly be rebuked if we have not frequently repented.

FROM STEP 7

BODY AND VOICE IN PRAYER

In the early stages of prayer, bodily movements and postures can be very helpful. These include stretching out the hands, beating the breast, raising the eyes toward heaven, deep sighs, and even lying down face downward. But this is not always feasible when other people are present.... So, if you can, go somewhere private in order to pray. Try to raise the eyes of your soul, and to assist your spiritual eyes, lift your arms over your body in the shape of a cross. Then cry out to God, who has the power to serve you. Do not bother with elegant and clever words. Just say repeatedly: "Have mercy on me, for I am a sinner."

FROM STEP 15

ENJOYING HUMILITY

Do you imagine that words can precisely, or truly, or appropriately, or clearly, or honestly describe the divine joy that humility brings—the purity, the enlightenment, the wonder, the serenity that comes from a humble heart? Do you think that you could ever describe these things to someone who has not experienced them? It would be like using words and metaphors to convey the sweetness of honey to people who had never tasted it.

FROM STEP 25

DEFINING HUMILITY

One person says: "Humility is forgetting your own achievements." Another says: "Humility is regarding oneself as the least important person in the world and the greatest sinner." A third person says: "Humility is awareness of one's own weakness and vulnerability." A fourth says: "Humility is being quick to end a quarrel by offering words of contrition." A fifth says: "Humility is the acknowledgement of divine grace and mercy." A sixth says: "Humility is an attitude of obedience in which one submits to God." I have thought about all these statements carefully and quietly. All seem correct, but none seems complete. Like a dog gathering crumbs from the table I put these wise words together and say: "Humility is a gift from God, of indescribable beauty and immeasurable value. Its name is known only to those who have experienced it."

FROM STEP 25

Isaac the Syrian

*I*saac taught that the purpose of prayer is to carry the soul into a spiritual realm where prayer ceases, and that in this realm, spiritual knowledge melts away, leaving the soul in a state of unknowing. His homilies are directed at monks, but he constantly stressed that everyone is capable of the same spiritual progress. He urged his hearers to be highly disciplined in their prayer, especially when prayer is dry and unrewarding. Then suddenly they will be given a sense of great spiritual sweetness, followed by a spiritual fire burning within them.

This is the prelude to receiving the divine vision. Yet this vision itself is only an image of the ultimate truth. The final stage comes when the soul encounters the truth directly. Isaac calls this stage "pure prayer," but adds that pure prayer marks the end of prayer. Isaac lived in the seventh century, and was appointed bishop of Nineveh. But he hated high office, and five months later disappeared in the Syrian desert. He lived in solitude for some years, but when his whereabouts were discovered, others came to join him. His homilies were written down and widely circulated in the Eastern Orthodox churches.

RIGHT *Hands of an apostle (Albrecht Dürer, 1471–1528, Graphische Sammlung Alberti-na, Vienna). St. Isaac stressed the need for regular prayer if the soul is to reach "motionless communion with God."*

STARTING TO PRAY

When you start to pray, come before God like a baby who has not yet learned to talk. Do not try to speak to God at first; and do not show off any theological knowledge you may have. All the thoughts in your mind should be those of a child. Look upon him as a child looks upon its father or mother, in a spirit of total trust.

FROM HOMILY 117

TEARS OF SORROW AND RELIEF

A central part of starting to pray is repentance. Allow yourself to weep over your sins. Only when you reach the plane of tears does your soul begin to emerge from the prison of this world, and set foot on the path to freedom—the freedom of "pure prayer." As you breathe the air outside the prison, your tears of sorrow become tears of joyful relief. You are like a baby emerging from the womb at birth; the process of birth is an intense struggle, and the relief when the birth is complete is equally intense. Your mother is divine grace, who wants to bring every soul on earth to spiritual birth. Just as a baby suddenly starts breathing air, and can sense all the smells which the air carries, so, as you come to spiritual birth, you can smell a sweet fragrance—a spiritual fragrance that suggests the ecstatic bliss that is waiting for you.

FROM HOMILY 117

THE SPIRITUAL FIRE

When you practice self-discipline, when you mount the steps of repentance, a gift comes down upon you from heaven: you taste the sweetness of spiritual knowledge. You become certain that God loves and provides for every person and every creature on earth. You are filled with wonder at the gracious way in which he governs the world. Gradually the sweetness that you can taste turns into a spiritual fire that burns within your heart and spreads throughout your soul and body. You feel a passionate love for every person and every creature you encounter. You become drunk with love, as if you had been imbibing the finest wine.

Your limbs grow limp, and your mind stands still in awestruck wonder. Your heart is captivated by God. Your inner senses grow strong, and you can begin to see God himself, as he is.

This experience is open to all those who struggle to lead righteous lives, who are vigilant in their care for others, and who devote much time to spiritual reading and to prayer. Gradually God's power takes hold of the soul. And when this experience occurs, you forget yourself; although you remain within the body, you become utterly unaware of yourself as a distinct individual.

From Homily 49

THE SEED OF TRUTH

Once this spiritual fire has consumed you, then the soul begins to grow and deepen in its understanding of the hidden mysteries of God. The soul transcends the body, and is no longer constrained by bodily needs and feelings. It is thus free to receive every kind of revelation that the Spirit of God can give. It is as if a seed has been planted in the soul; and the warmth of the spiritual fire has caused the seed to rise up and thrive, bearing spiritual fruit in the form of heavenly knowledge. Indeed, this seed is present in every soul from the moment of birth. But most people are so distracted by vain concerns, by transient and fleeting pleasures, that they are never aware of it; so it remains dormant. Blessed are those who recognize the seed within their souls and nurture it.

From Homily 49

THE DIVINE VISION

The sweetness of prayer is one thing; and the divine vision that is the ultimate fruit of prayer another thing. Just as an immature child turns into a mature adult, so the sweetness of prayer is the prelude to the divine vision. Sometimes a verse from the Scriptures or a hymn becomes sweet in your mouth. You find yourself repeating it over and over again, not tiring of it, so that you are unable to move on to the next verse. But this repetitive prayer may lead to a divine vision—and then the repetition is suddenly cut short. You feel as though the breath is leaving your body, so you are unable to speak. This divine vision is not some image or form; it is not a picture in the mind. But this vision still has distinctive features. This is because you are still praying; you are still active. You have not transcended prayer; you have not yet risen to the spiritual place where there is no prayer. Your heart is still moving; you are not yet in the secret chamber when the heart becomes utterly still.

From Homily 23

PURE PRAYER

Just as the laws and commandments ordained by God are aimed at purifying the heart, so every form and mode of prayer is aimed at purifying the soul—and hence leads to pure prayer. Sighs, protestations, heartfelt supplications, cries of repentance, and every other expression to God help to prepare the soul for pure prayer. But a moment comes when the soul crosses the boundary from these active forms of prayer into the realm of pure prayer. At that moment, active prayer ceases; so does activity of every kind—and so does material and spiritual desire. When the soul enters pure prayer it ceases to pray. Before entering this realm, prayer is a constant struggle, in which the soul struggles to gain authority over wayward thoughts and feelings. Beyond this boundary, prayer is replaced by awestruck wonder in which the soul marvels at the beauty of God.

From Homily 23

THE STATE OF UNKNOWING

You may ask why this motionless communion with God is called prayer if it is not prayer. The reason is that prayer is the means by which the soul attains such a state. There is no other way of reaching it except through prayer. The soul is led by prayer toward it; prayer prepares the soul to receive it, and it occurs during prayer. There are countless testimonies from the saints that this is so… while we pray, we are concentrating on God; in every moment of prayer the soul is reaching out to God; in prayer the soul is opening itself to God with eager longing.

From Homily 23

Symeon of Galatia

ithin Eastern Orthodoxy in the first millennium, there were two distinct spiritual approaches: the esthetic approach, exemplified by Gregory of Nyassa, in which God is sought in the material world; and the approach of such teachers as John Climacus, in which the seeker is required to withdraw from all material concerns. Symeon tried to synthesize them. His central image was God as light—a supernatural brightness that draws individuals toward it. Yet he stressed that the body, as well as the soul, must be involved in this movement; unless people learn to practice virtue in their outward actions, they will be blind to the light.

Symeon used his own experiences to illustrate his teaching, so we learn about his life from his own pen. He was born into one of the leading families in Galatia in 949; his brilliance was such that he was sent to the royal Byzantine court for his education. But as a teenager he met a venerable monk, also called Symeon, and under his influence took monastic vows himself. At the age of thirty-one he became abbot of a monastery, and his discourses, which form the main body of his writings, were addressed to the monks. In 1009 he was forced into exile by the local bishops, who were jealous of his reputation as a spiritual teacher. But the Patriarch later withdrew the sentence, offering Symeon an archbishopric in reparation—which Symeon refused.

GOD IS LIGHT

Let no one deceive you. God is light; and those who have entered into union with him experience great inward brightness. The mind, which is the lamp of the soul, is lit by the divine fire, and bursts into flame. It is a miracle. By this means your body too is heated. Thus the body, mind, and soul together are united to God. Just as the mind cannot be separated from the soul, neither can the body; the whole person becomes joined to God, sharing his eternal life.

THE DISCOURSES 15

THE PATH TO GOD'S LIGHT

How then do we attain God's light? How can we run toward his brightness? The path to his light leads by way of repentance. Do not be frightened of repenting your sins. His light is so strong that it illuminates your footsteps as you tread this path. But you must hurry; you must run while there is still time. You must repent before the darkness of death overtakes you.... When you have reached the place of repentance, allow yourself to weep; your tears are an acknowledgment of your sin. And as you weep, the Lord will fulfill his promise of mercy. He will forgive you.

God wants us to run the path to his kingdom, and to knock on the door of heaven, while we are still on earth.

If we refuse to go to his kingdom while we are alive, why should he let us in when we are dead?

THE DISCOURSES 15

FILLED WITH JOY

One night, when I was still a young man, I went to the place where I usually prayed. As usual, I opened my heart to God. But on this occasion I was suddenly moved to tears, and my whole body and soul were seized with desire for God. At first I thought that my tears were from sadness; then I realized that I was filled with joy and pleasure. I fell prostrate on the ground, and at once I saw a huge light. It was not a material light, but a spiritual light. It shone upon me, penetrating my mind and soul. I was utterly amazed and overcome with ecstasy. I became quite oblivious of where I was, or even who I was. I could only cry out, "Lord, have mercy."

Eventually I returned to my normal state, and found myself still reciting, "Lord, have mercy." I began to reflect on my experience and ask questions. Who was moving my tongue? Was I inside or outside my body when I saw the light? God alone knows the answers. But I knew that the experience had changed me. It had scattered the mist of my soul, and cast out every earthly care. It had made my body light, so that my limbs no longer felt sluggish and heavy. My muscles were strengthened and invigorated. My mind was stripped of its garment of corruption. And my soul had a sensation of sweetness, greater than that of the sweetest food. My thoughts were directed entirely toward the things of heaven, and I no longer felt any fear of death. My mind and my soul were wholly absorbed in the affable joy of that light.

THE DISCOURSES 16

SYMBOLS OF HEAVEN

After a time the light which I had seen faded, and disappeared completely. I felt utterly alone, and I was gripped by a pain and grief so great that I cannot describe it. It was like a fire consuming my heart. It seemed to me that the light had represented the infinite love of God, which had wholly captivated my emotions; and now I was separated from this love. So I went to seek advice from the old man who was my spiritual guide.

He said to me: "The light, and the experiences which accompany it, are only symbols of heaven, not heaven itself; they are a foretaste of the bliss of heaven. You will not taste heaven itself while you are still alive on this earth. What matters is that you do nothing that can hinder you from eventually entering heaven. Undoubtedly you will fall from time to time, committing some sin. Do not despair; those occasional lapses ensure that you remain humble. So continue to cultivate a spirit of repentance, knowing that God alone can blot out past and present failures."

When I heard these words I felt a wonderful sense of relief. I recognized that this old man

ABOVE *The Resurrection (Mattias Grunewald, 1455–1528, Musée d'Unterlinden, Colmar, France). "God is light; and those who have entered into union with him experience great inward brightness."*

spoke from a great height of spiritual knowledge; and he had acquired that knowledge because he trusted God without reserve.

THE DISCOURSES 16

THE POWER OF LOVE

Once I had started on the path, I became obsessed with fear; I felt that evil forces were trying to attack and destroy me. Yet in fact the warfare was provoked not by evil, but by love; the power of love had entered my soul, and was attacking the evil that had always lurked there. Sinful habits were deeply rooted within me, so the battle between love and evil was fierce and long. But when I recognized the true nature of the battle, I joined forces with love by imposing on myself a strict discipline of prayer and constant meditation on the Scriptures.

THE DISCOURSES 17

Hildegard of Bingen

One of the towering geniuses of the medieval period, Hildegard was a composer whose music still grows in popularity; a forceful monastic leader, who asserted the rights of women; and toward the end of her life a popular preacher. She was also a visionary, who taught people to find God both in themselves and in all living creatures. In contrast to most mystics of the time, she believed the material, as well as the spiritual, aspects of the creation are holy and should be cherished for their own sake.

Born in 1098, she was the youngest child of a wealthy family. She started having religious visions as a child; her parents responded by sending her at the age of eight to live with an anchoress attached to a monastery. As she reached adulthood, Hildegard's reputation gradually spread, and other women asked to live with her. These women, and also visitors seeking Hildegard's counsel, brought considerable income to the monastery, which the monks appropriated. Hildegard eventually took the women away and formed a new convent at Bingen on the banks of the Rhine.

BELOW *"God is known through all the various species of plants and animals in the world… And the Holy Spirit is God's breathing, by which he enters all people."*

APPRECIATING GOODNESS

Use all your faculties to appreciate God's creation. Use your soul to understand other souls. Use your body to sympathize with other people's bodily experiences. Use your emotions of anger and revenge to understand war. Appreciate goodness through distinguishing it from evil. Appreciate beauty through distinguishing it from ugliness and deformity. Define poverty by contrasting it with wealth. Rejoice in good health by comparing it with sickness. Distinguish the various opposites: length and shortness; hardness and softness; depth and shallowness; light and darkness. Enjoy every moment of life by constantly reminding yourself of the imminence of death. Look forward to paradise by reminding yourself of eternal punishment. You understand so little of what is around you because you do not use what is within you.

Scivias, Part 1

KNOWING GOD'S POWER

The power of God is known through all the various species of plants and animals in the world, which have been created by the Word of God. As the power and honor of a person is known through the value of that person's word, so the holiness and goodness of the Creator is known through the value of the Creator's Word. And that value is made manifest through the creation.

Scivias, Part 2

DIVINE ELEMENTS

A word which is spoken has three elements: sound, goodness, and breathing. A word has sound in order to be heard; goodness in order to be understood; and breathing in order that it may be completed. So too with God. The creation is God's sound, by which he enables all to perceive his power and glory. The coming of Christ is God's goodness, which prompts him to become a human being. And the Holy Spirit is God's breathing, by which he enters all people.

Scivias, Part 2

THE WORD IN CREATION

God is shown through the Word; the Word is shown through the creation of the world and all the species which inhabit it; and the Holy Spirit is shown through the Word being made flesh. What does this mean? God is the one who brought the Word into being before the beginning of time. The Word is the one through whom all creatures are made. The Holy Spirit is the one who enters creation at particular moments.

SCIVIAS, PART 2

THE BEAUTY OF CREATION

The Word of God showed the power of God by creating the world. The Word called into being from nothing all the different species which inhabit the world. These species all shine with beauty, reflecting the beauty of their origins. They sparkle in the beauty of their perfection, as if they have all been made of burnished copper. Their light shines in every direction, so the whole earth glows with beauty.

SCIVIAS, PART 2

SEEING WITH THE SOUL

When you see God's beauty, you are not looking with mortal eyes, but with the eyes of the soul. When you hear his Word, you are not using mortal ears, but listening with the ears of your soul to the wisdom he has implanted within you.

SCIVIAS, PART 2

GOD'S WORD IN PEOPLE

The Word of God is burning love. The Word brings life to those who are dead in soul. The Word is a light which exposes sin, and a flame which burns the ropes that bind sin to the soul. The Word exists in every person before the person is aware of the Word. The Word is the source of holiness in each person, and makes people desire to become holy. The Word is magnificent and glorious, and can never be comprehended by the human intellect.

SCIVIAS, PART 3

THE GREATNESS OF GOD

Imagine the highest and widest mountain in the world. Its size reflects the grandeur of God, and thus honors God. It is not greater than God; nothing on earth is greater than its Creator. God is higher and wider than the human mind can comprehend. He is holier than we could possibly understand. No creatures can attain the holiness of God, because the holiness of God is above all creatures. Yet human beings, alone among the creatures on earth, are reluctant to honor God. They claim that it is difficult and tedious to worship God; they feel too weak to praise him. Every human being is a rebel against God.

SCIVIAS, PART 3

BEING OPEN TO GOD

Those who love God open themselves entirely to him. They ask him to enter their senses, their souls, and their minds. They receive him with joy; they embrace him with every thought and feeling; they want to perceive him with all their senses. And God rejoices in them, regarding them more fragrant than the most fragrant flower in creation, as brighter than the brightest jewel, as nobler than the noblest mountain. And he wants to make them sweeter in smell, even more sparkling, and yet more handsome.

He feasts their minds with delicious thoughts, and he presses his justice into their hearts. He gives them the sweetest spiritual water to refresh their souls. Yet sometimes he seems to abandon them, so that they find themselves without his help. He does this so that they do not become puffed up with spiritual pride. They weep and moan, and may even become angry with God. In this way their faith is tested.

SCIVIAS, PART 3

Hadewijch of Brabant

Hadewijch was one of the first members of the Beguine movement of the thirteenth century, and its greatest writer. The movement consisted of small groups of widows and unmarried women living together in ordinary houses, and devoting themselves to prayer and acts of charity. This way of life proved hugely popular, so that by 1300 almost 10 percent of the female population of northern Europe lived in Beguine communities.

Little is known about Hadewijch herself. She was probably born in the late twelfth century, and became mistress of a Beguine house somewhere in the Brabant region between Brussels and Antwerp. In her letters to Beguine women she described their vocation as sharing the humanity of Christ. She also encouraged them to pursue mystical union with Christ, in which they would feel his touch and be permeated with his love. She often wrote of Christ simply as Love, and the sexual imagery seems deliberate.

THE HUMANITY OF GOD

All of us want to live with God in comfort, enjoying his spiritual treasures and sharing in the pleasure of his glory. We all want to be gods with God. But God alone knows how few of us want to live as humans with his humanity, to carry his cross with him, and to be crucified with him in order to pay the price for the world's sins....

When we live on earth with the humanity of God, we simultaneously experience suffering and distress, while rejoicing inwardly in the sweet love of the almighty and eternal Godhead. These are two sides of a single experience. And just as Jesus Christ on earth submitted to the will of the majestic Father, so we too should submit lovingly to the Father and the Son. We should serve them in humility, following their commands in every aspect of our lives. Let them do with us whatever they want.

We should not hold back anything from God. We should work for God with ready and faithful hands, practicing every kind of virtue. And we should not love the Godhead with devotion alone, but with desires so deep that they cannot be expressed or described....

God's love will then explode into our lives, lifting us out of ourselves so that we are brought

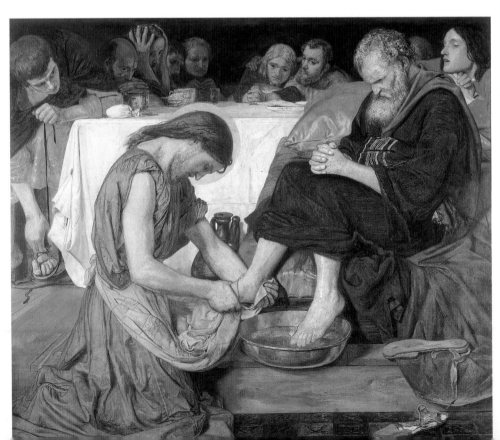

RIGHT *Jesus washing Peter's feet (Ford Maddox Brown, 1853). "The measure of love lies not in our feelings but in the degree to which we serve others."*

into spiritual unity with God. It shall no longer be an obligation and duty to serve God, but a joy and privilege, undertaken with inexhaustible vigor. Our goal will be to ensure that God's love takes her rightful place in the lives of all people and all creatures—to ensure that the whole world dies with Christ on the cross, and rises with him to new life.

LETTERS 6

THOSE WHO LOVE

Those who love are bound to renounce all worldly ambitions, and to renounce too all pride in their own abilities and achievements; their only desire will be to know Love in their lives. Those who love rejoice in being corrected by others; they do not try to excuse their own mistakes, and eagerly learn how to follow God more closely. Those who love are willing to endure anything for the sake of love. Those who love happily accept insults and blows in the pursuit of love. Those who love are happy to be in company or to be alone, as love requires.

LETTERS 8

PERMEATED BY GOD

May God make known to you who he is, and how he treats his servants—how he draws them into himself. From the depths of his wisdom he will teach you about his love. He will live in you, and you will live in him, so that you taste his wonderful sweetness. You will be like two lovers, who do not know themselves from each other. You will possess one another in mutual delight, mouth in mouth, heart in heart, body in body, soul in soul. The divine nature will flow into you, permeating you. You will find yourself by finding him.

LETTERS 9

THE MEASURE OF LOVE

Those who love God also love his works. The works of God are expressions of supreme virtue. Therefore those who love God also love virtue. The love of virtue brings great joy and strength. Acting virtuously is the clearest demonstration of love. Indeed virtuous action is a better proof of love than religious observance or the sweetness which often accompanies religious observance. A person may be devout in their religion, and gain great pleasure from it, yet be empty of love. The measure of love lies not in our feelings but in the degree to which we serve others.

LETTERS 10

SELF-KNOWLEDGE

If you want to be perfect, you must first know yourself. You must understand what you are able to do and what you are willing to do; what you love and what you hate; what you trust and what you distrust; and how you react emotionally to events. You have to reflect on how you respond to people opposing you, and how you cope in unfamiliar surroundings.

You have to ask yourself how you endure the loss of things you like. And you have to examine whether you rise quickly and eagerly to opportunities for good. As you understand yourself, so you will be able to control yourself, remaining serene and tranquil in all circumstances. Thus you will be able to remain constantly close to God—and perfection.

LETTERS 14

THE ESSENCE OF THE SOUL

Now we must inquire into the deepest essence of the soul—what the soul is. The soul is an essence which is transparent to God, and to which God is transparent. Indeed, the soul is more than this; it is an essence which wants to give delight to God. The soul is a divine essence, which retains its divine qualities so long as it does not become enmeshed in things which are alien to it.

If the soul remains true to itself, it becomes a receptacle of infinite dimensions into which God can enter, and in which God can receive and bestow great joy. The soul is the path by which God enters human beings; the soul is God's home on earth. So long as God is not completely filling the soul, then the soul is not satisfied.

LETTERS 18

Jan van Ruusbroec

ften regarded as the most profound of the medieval mystics, Ruusbroec emphasized the importance of pure intentions in all actions, urging people constantly to examine their inner motives. He taught that the process of introspection is the first stage in reaching downward into the soul; eventually the soul will find within itself the radiance of God himself. He believed that all people are capable of a direct encounter with God through interior contemplation, without any kind of intermediary.

He was born in 1295 in a small village near Brussels, from which he acquired his name; and at the age of eleven went to live with relatives in the city to be educated. He was ordained priest in 1317, and spent the following twenty-six years as a chaplain in the cathedral. He barely went out of the cathedral precincts, devoting himself to prayer and to spiritual counsel. He wrote The Spiritual Espousals for the growing numbers who sought his advice. Eventually he found even the cathedral too distracting, and retired to be a hermit in the valley of Groenendaal, a few miles away. He remained there for thirty-two years, until his death in 1381.

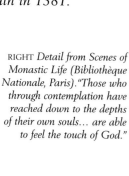

RIGHT *Detail from Scenes of Monastic Life (Bibliothèque Nationale, Paris)."Those who through contemplation have reached down to the depths of their own souls... are able to feel the touch of God."*

OBEDIENCE AS THE ANTIDOTE TO PRIDE

To be obedient is to deny your own will in deference to God's will. It is quite possible to act in a good and virtuous manner, and yet still to be self-willed.... Obedience means no longer deciding what actions should be performed and what actions should be avoided; it means no longer deciding what hardships should be endured and what may be escaped. In this way, pride is banished and humility is nurtured and made perfect. God becomes master of the will; and the will becomes so united to God that the individual desires nothing else apart from this unity.

THE SPIRITUAL ESPOUSALS, 125

THE INTIMACY OF GOD

The grace of God, which flows from God, is an interior impulse or prompting. It comes through the Holy Spirit, and directs our spirit from within, guiding our outward actions in the way of virtue. This grace is inside, not outside us, for God is more interior to us than we are to ourselves; and his interior prompting is closer to us and more intimate than our own thoughts and feelings. Thus God starts inside us, and works outward; whereas all other influences start outside us, and work inward.

THE SPIRITUAL ESPOUSALS, 147

THE TOUCH OF GOD

The touch of God occurs when the grace of God floods into the soul like a mighty river; or when it burns into the soul like a blazing fire; or when it bubbles up from within the soul like a spring; or when it appears like a plant, with its roots embedded firmly within the soul. You receive the touch of God passively; and it brings all the disparate powers of the soul into unity.

God alone is active; he alone is the cause of this blessing. We cannot explain what is happening; we cannot describe the divine love which we feel; we cannot understand the manner of God's touch, or what it comprises. This touch is the source of all graces and all gifts; and it is the last intermediary between God and the soul.

THE SPIRITUAL ESPOUSALS, 196

PENETRATING THE DOOR

Those who through contemplation have reached down to the depths of their own souls, and thence come to the door of eternal life, are able to feel the touch of God. The radiance is so great that all the intellectual powers of the mind fail, and cannot go onward; the mind must remain outside the door. Only love can penetrate further, and go through the door, because love has no wish to understand God; it wants only to enjoy him. Love desires to taste and savor God, not to analyze him. That is why love can go in, while the mind stops outside.

THE SPIRITUAL ESPOUSALS, 198

PURE INTENTIONS

We can meet God in all our activities, becoming more like him, and growing closer to him in blissful love. Every good work, however small it may be, which is undertaken out of love for God, with a pure and righteous intention, renews us in his image and prepares us for eternal life in him. A pure intention unites the diverse powers of the soul in harmony, and directs the soul toward God.

A pure intention is the source and purpose of virtue, and is a thing of beauty. A pure intention is an act of praise to God, honoring his name. A pure intention transcends itself, carrying the soul upward to heaven. An intention is pure of God in its origin, and it sees all things in relation to God.

THE SPIRITUAL ESPOUSALS, 209

THE SOUL IN HARMONY

When our intentions are pure, the powers of the soul are brought into harmony. We offer our whole lives to God, and we encounter him in every virtuous act. Indeed our actions become his actions. Thus, on the foundation of pure intention, we transcend ourselves, and we meet God without any intermediary. We rest in his presence, and there take possession of the inheritance which has been preserved for us from all eternity.

THE SPIRITUAL ESPOUSALS, 210

MYSTICAL UNION

Sometimes those who live the interior life are drawn into themselves. They disengage themselves from outward virtues and activities, and find within their own soul the source of love. They meet God without any intermediary; and as they gaze on him, they experience perfect bliss. They perceive a light which comes from the depths of God's unity; and beyond this light they see only darkness, emptiness, nothingness.

To outward appearances, these people seem to be enveloped in darkness; they are dead to the world. But inwardly they are basking in God's radiance. Outwardly all life seems to have drained away from them; inwardly they are overwhelmed by the vibrant love of God, which lasts forever. The divine essence permeates their souls; and in union with God, they are in ecstasy.

THE SPIRITUAL ESPOUSALS, 223

CAUGHT UP BY GOD

Sometimes we who are seeking God suddenly find ourselves caught up by God. Our desire for God begins to burn furiously. We can give God all glory and honor. We can offer ourselves and all our efforts to God....

Deep within our souls we can perceive and sense the presence of God. And as we perceive God's presence, we recognize him as the source of all virtues, and also the end to which all virtues are directed. We recognize him as the dwelling-place of love. As a result we ourselves aspire to acquire every virtue, and our sole desire is to live in union with him.

THE SPIRITUAL ESPOUSALS, 225

Johannes Tauler

*T*auler *taught that the seed of God exists in all human beings; and that, if this seed is allowed to grow and flourish, they can become a true incarnation of God—like Christ himself. This requires people to lose all sense of self, since selfhood occupies the soul and smothers the seed. The most difficult part of this self-denial, Tauler recognized, is to regard all suffering, both bodily and mental, as sent by God—since the desire for pleasure and even peace are assertions of the self. Thus the soul must become totally passive. Tauler described the change from selfhood to self-denial as the Christian act of conversion.*

At the age of fifteen, in about the year 1315, Johannes Tauler joined the Dominican friars in his native town of Strasbourg. As an order of preachers, the Dominicans put a strong emphasis on theological expertise; but Tauler was an inept scholar, failing even to master Latin, the language in which all theology was written. This disappointment turned him inward and set him on the mystical path. And as he progressed, he became a brilliant speaker on spiritual matters, with a gift for expressing profound truths simply and clearly. He never wrote anything down, and his so-called Sermons were transcriptions of his informal addresses, probably given to groups of devout lay people.

THE ACT OF CONVERSION

Our purpose is that God should be born within the soul. This requires a decisive act of conversion, in which all our powers and faculties, from the lowest to the highest, are directed toward God. It requires a gathering of the whole self, taking away every aspect of the self from worldly distractions, and placing the self in the arms of God. In this way, the different aspects of the self no longer conflict with one another, but are brought into harmony.

The act of conversion may be compared with an archer who wants to hit the middle of the target, and closes one eye in order that the other eye can see clearly. In the same way, conversion requires total and accurate attention onto the soul, which is the location of divine truth; and this means becoming blind to all else. The act of conversion may also be compared with a tree, in which the sap ceases to flow from the trunk to the branches, but flows back into the trunk. In the same way conversion requires all energy and all life to flow back into the soul, which is the source of life.

Through the act of conversion we are raised above and beyond ourselves. We remove all selfish intention, desires, and actions, and strive for God alone. We cease to exist as individuals within ourselves; we are in a constant process of becoming—of becoming like God. We belong to him; he is so close to us that we no longer distinguish between ourselves and him. This is what is meant by God being born within the soul: the seed of God was always there, but now we no longer hinder the seed's growth—so God flourishes within the soul.

SERMON 1

PEACE IN THE ABSENCE OF PEACE

There are many people who wish to be witnesses of God when their souls feel peaceful, and when their religious observance is giving pleasure. These people want to be holy, so long as their religious efforts do not become burdensome. But when darkness comes, when God seems remote and distant, when they feel lonely and abandoned, when their minds or bodies become sick—then they turn away from God, and show themselves not to be his true witnesses.

It is natural for all of us to seek peace, both in what we do and in what we are. The true witnesses of God learn to find peace where peace is absent. This is because they are not concerned for peace in itself, but want to discover the source of peace—which is God. They learn to find joy in grief, serenity in disturbance, consolation in bitterness.

SERMON 21

THE HIDDEN CHAMBER OF THE SOUL

Within the soul there exists a hidden chamber which is outside time and space, and which transcends that part of the soul giving life and movement to the body. It is within this hidden chamber that we encounter divinity; it is there that we become utterly still, totally true to ourselves, completely detached from all material concerns.

The atmosphere within that chamber is pure; within that chamber we are free from all bonds. God dwells, acts, and rules within that chamber. Entering the hidden chamber cannot be compared with any other aspect of our lives, even our most devout religious observance. There we are united with God; there the fire of his love burns, and we are consumed by it.

SERMON 24

BECOMING PERFECT

If you want to become perfect and to fulfill your spiritual potential, you must bear two points in mind. Firstly you should free your heart from all material and worldly things; you must even free your heart from any concerns about yourself. In this way, you will not obstruct the work of the Holy Spirit within you.

ABOVE *St. Johannes Tauler preached that in finding God, "We cease to exist as individuals within ourselves; we are in a constant process of becoming – of becoming like God."*

Secondly you must accept all difficulties—whatever their cause, whether they are material or spiritual—as coming from God. In this way, you will learn to submit yourself to God, giving yourself totally to him; and he in turn will be able to bestow the full riches of his spiritual gifts upon you.

SERMON 25

THE BIRTH OF GOD IN THE SOUL

Two beings, two entities, cannot occupy the same space. If warmth enters a space, then cold must leave. In the same way, God and the self cannot both occupy your soul. If God is to enter your soul, then the self must leave. This means if God is to be born within your soul, you must cease to assert yourself and become totally passive. All your faculties must be stripped of their power of action; you must suppress your will; your pride must evaporate into the air. The more you become nothing, the more God will grow in your soul.

SERMON 31

Two beings, two entities, cannot occupy the same space. If warmth enters a space, then cold must leave. In the same way, God and the self cannot both occupy your soul. If God is to enter your soul, then the self must leave. This means if God is to be born within your soul, you must cease to assert yourself and become totally passive.

SERMON 31

Richard Rolle

*I*n the fourteenth century, England became renowned for the number of its recluses and hermits, living either in cells connected to churches or in huts in the forest. And some of these men and women were great writers, producing mystical literature that had popular appeal. The first of these hermitical writers was the brilliant and rebellious son of a peasant family from Yorkshire.

Richard Rolle composed Christian songs that expressed in the simplest terms deep spiritual ardor; and from time to time he left the hermitage, touring local villages to sing to the common people. He also wrote several works of mystical guidance; in the greatest of these, The Fire of Love, he described the physical and emotional feelings that frequently accompany profound prayer. He also related how prayer turns from a matter of religious observance to the central focus of daily life.

ABOVE *"I cannot describe to you how astonished I was the first time I felt my heart begin to warm. The warmth was real, not imaginary… and this sensation gave me great pleasure and comfort."*

He initially inhabited a shack in a churchyard. But he became unpopular among local clergy by accusing them of corruption and hypocrisy and was forced to retreat into remote woodland. Near the end of his life he attached himself to a convent at Hampole and during the Black Death he was tireless in ministering to the sick and dying; he succumbed to the disease himself in about 1350.

THE MOMENT OF CHANGE

From the time when I changed my way of life and attitude of mind, to the time when the door of heaven swung open, three years passed, less three or four months. Only then was the face of my beloved revealed, and I was able to embrace him and to contemplate the things of heaven.

I was sitting in the church, trying to find pleasure in prayer and meditation, when suddenly I felt within me a strange and pleasant heat. At first I wondered where it came from, but gradually I realized that it did not have a natural cause: it came from the Creator himself. The warmth was extremely intense and gave me great joy.

Nine months later a wonderful sensation of sweetness was added to the sensation of heat. And I also began to hear spiritual sounds, which seemed to fill the church. These sounds were hymns of eternal praise, sung to a heavenly melody which I had never heard on earth. Indeed they cannot be heard except by those who have received it from above, and who have purified themselves from the things of this world.

That night, as I sat in the church before supper, reciting psalms, I heard above me again the sound of holy words being sung. With all my heart I was reaching out to heaven: and this symphony seemed to me, in a manner I cannot explain, to be heaven's response to me. And in my mind I felt myself to be in perfect and delightful harmony with the music.

Then and there my thoughts turned themselves into a heavenly melody, and my meditation became a poem: every prayer I uttered, and every psalm I recited, swelled this wonderful chorus. Through this inner sweetness my whole being began to sing: but I sang without any outward sound, so that only my Creator could hear.

THE FIRE OF LOVE, CHAPTER 215

WARMTH, SWEETNESS, AND SONG

I have found that to love Christ above all also has three effects: warmth, melody, and sweetness. And I know from my own experience that these cannot persist for long without bringing great inner stillness and silence.

These three things are signs of pure love: they are tokens of the spiritual perfection which is found in the Christian religion. To the limits of my meager nature I have received them, as a gift from Jesus.

Yet I dare not compare myself with the saints who experience these things, because they had received them far more fully. But I shall continue trying to grow in virtue, so that my love burns more fervently, my song becomes sweeter, and I taste the sweetness of love more fully.

I call it fervor when the mind is truly ablaze with eternal love, and the heart burns with love that is real, not imaginary. A heart in which fire is kindled radiates love.

I call it song when the heart overflows with a joyful sensation of heavenly praise; when thought turns into melody; when the mind is overwhelmed by perfect harmony. Fervor and song are not achieved by doing nothing; they require the utmost devotion. And from them comes indescribable sweetness.

THE FIRE OF LOVE, CHAPTER 14

HOLY AND CARNAL FLAMES

I cannot describe to you how astonished I was the first time I felt my heart begin to warm. The warmth was real, not imaginary; it seemed as if I were actually on fire. I was amazed at the way the heat surged through me; and this sensation gave me great pleasure and comfort—which surprised me also. I kept feeling my chest to convince myself that there was no physical cause.

Once I was sure that this fire of love was not the result of some illness, bodily or mental, but was a gift from my Maker, I was utterly delighted, and I wished the fire to burn ever brighter. And the desire was enhanced by the wonderful inner sweetness I could taste as the fire blazed. I had never imagined that sinful human beings could enjoy such spiritual warmth and sweetness....

No one could survive this fire if it continued to burn fiercely; the body and the soul would wilt in the face of such intense heat. Yet once you have experienced the heat, and the sweetness which accompanies it, you desire nothing else; with every breath you long for the heat and the sweetness to recur. Indeed, you want to quit this world, in order to enjoy permanently this honeyed flame in heaven.

Yet while you remain in this world, feelings often rise up in the heart which compete with this flame. Carnal desires and affections continue to blaze from time to time. This sinful fire cannot take away the holy fire; once the holy fire has started to burn, it can never be removed. But the carnal fire can seduce you into ignoring it, and the holy flames die down, so that you become spiritually frozen. So it is vital that you continually remind yourself about the holy fire, and rekindle it.

THE FIRE OF LOVE, PROLOGUE

KNOWLEDGE AND LOVE

Many things clamor for our attention. But let us make loving God our prime concern. This is far more important than acquiring knowledge or engaging in theological discussion. It is love which delights the soul and sweetness the conscience, drawing us away from lesser pleasures and diverting us from the pursuit of our own glory.

THE FIRE OF LOVE, CHAPTER 5

Julian of Norwich

In her lifetime, people came great distances to hear the wise and gentle counsel of the Norwich anchoress. And through her writings, Julian's popularity has continued to grow over the centuries. She constantly stressed God's love, declaring that he can even use human sin as a means of blessing. And most famously she emphasized the feminine qualities of God, speaking of him as a mother.

On May 8, 1373, when she was aged 30 and lying seriously ill, she had a series of visions that she called "divine showings." When she recovered, she decided that God wanted to her to dedicate herself entirely to him; and she went to live in a small cell, attached to the Church of St. Julian—from which she acquired her religious name.

She continued to reflect on her visions, trying to discern their spiritual meaning; and she finally wrote down her reflections. She confessed that at times she could not reconcile her ideas with doctrinal orthodoxy, particularly on the subject of sin. But she believed that divine truth transcends human doctrine, and can only be attained through direct revelation.

ABOVE RIGHT *Julian of Norwich (detail from the Benedictine window in Norwich Cathedral, Moira Forsyth, 1964). "We should despise nothing that God has created and delight in everything."*

CREATION IN A HAZELNUT

Our Lord showed me something small, no bigger than a hazelnut. It seemed to lie in the palm of my hand, and was as round as a ball. I gazed on it with the eye of understanding and thought: "What can this be?"

I received the answer: "It is all that is made."

I marveled that it could last; it was so small that I thought it would quickly disappear. And in my understanding I received a further answer: "It lasts, and will last forever, because God loves it; all things exist through the love of God."

In this little thing I saw three properties. The first is that God made it; the second is that God loves it; the third is that God preserves it. I saw in it that God is creator, lover, and preserver. And until I am wholly united to him, I can never enjoy perfect rest or true happiness. I must become attached to him in such a way that nothing stands between me and him.

The little thing seemed to me so small that it could have faded into nothing. We should despise nothing that God has created, and delight in everything. By this means we love and understand the uncreated God.

FROM DIVINE SHOWINGS, CHAPTER 5

THE NECESSITY OF SIN

I saw nothing hindered me except sin. This is true for all of us. And it seemed to me that if there had been no sin, we should all have been pure, just as the Lord created us. Indeed, prior to this time, I often used to wonder, in my folly, why God in his great and prophetic wisdom had not prevented sin from ever existing. If sin did not exist, it seemed to me all would be well.

These thoughts should have been suppressed. But lacking insight, I felt deeply sad and sorrowful at the existence of sin. Jesus in a vision told me what I needed to know about this. He said: "Sin is necessary. But all will be well; and all will be well; and every kind of thing will be well...."

It is true that sin is the cause of pain. But all will be well and every kind of thing will be well. These words were spoken most tenderly, showing that no blame attached to me or to anyone who will be saved. Thus it would be quite wrong of me to blame God for sin, or to criticize him for letting me sin, since he does not blame me.

FROM DIVINE SHOWINGS, CHAPTER 27

THE NECESSITY OF PAIN

I saw that the Lord rejoices, with pity and compassion, over the tribulations of his servants. And on every person whom he loves he imposes some burden. This burden is not a defect in his sight, but is an aid to the attainment of eternal bliss. It may cause a person to be humiliated and despised in this world, to be scorned, mocked, and rejected. The Lord does this to prevent the damage which comes from hubris, pride and self-importance in this wretched life, and thus to prepare the path to the eternal, everlasting bliss of heaven. The Lord says: "I shall completely break down within you empty ambition and vanity. As I shall gather you in my arms to make you meek and mild, pure and holy."

FROM DIVINE SHOWINGS, CHAPTER 28

GOD AS MOTHER

Just as God is truly our Father so is God truly our Mother. God reveals this in everything, and especially in these sweet words which I heard: "I am the power and goodness of fatherhood. And I am she: I am the wisdom and love of motherhood."

FROM DIVINE SHOWINGS, CHAPTER 59

THE PRACTICE OF DIVINE MOTHERHOOD

The natural mother can give her child milk from her breasts. Our spiritual mother Jesus can feed us with himself with great dignity and tenderness. He feeds us through his sacrament, which is the precious food of eternal life; and he feeds us through his most merciful actions and gracious words. This is what he meant when he said to me: "I am the one who preaches to you and teaches you the truth. Through me your spiritual health is restored."...

This beautiful and enchanting word "mother" is so sweet and alluring that it cannot be truly applied to anyone except the one who is the mother of all creation. To motherhood belongs life, love, wisdom, and knowledge; and these are properties of God. Certainly our physical birth is a simple and insignificant event compared with our spiritual birth. But the natural mother who brings a child physically to birth is guided and strengthened by the spiritual mother of all births.

The kind and loving natural mother knows and understands her infant well, and out of natural instinct she protects and provides for her infant. As the infant grows and develops, she acts differently, but her love does not change. She rebukes her child to deter misbehavior and to encourage virtue and grace. Everything which the natural mother does is lovely and good. And the way our Lord treats us, his children, is the same. Everything which our Lord does is lovely and good; and for this reason we can call our Lord "Mother."

FROM DIVINE SHOWINGS, CHAPTER 60

Walter Hilton

In late medieval times one of the most popular spiritual books was the guidance offered by an obscure English monk to an unknown female recluse. The Ladder of Perfection circulated in numerous handwritten works throughout the fifteenth century; and then, in 1494, it was one of the first spiritual books to be printed, becoming standard reading in devout households.

The author, Walter Hilton, employed the conventional image of a ladder to describe the soul's ascent toward God. But the most popular passage changes the metaphor to that of a pilgrimage to Jerusalem. He compared the various temptations that the soul faces with attacks by thieves. And he described vividly the spiritual darkness that the soul enters after warding off these attacks. Jerusalem itself represents the mystical vision of God. The immense popularity of this book indicates how popular mystical prayer has become in this period.

Hilton was born in the county of Nottinghamshire in central England. For a time he lived as a hermit, but in 1375 he entered a monastery at Thurgarton, near Southwell. Thereafter he appears to have passed an uneventful life, devoting himself to writing and to giving spiritual counsel to visitors.

STARTING THE PILGRIMAGE

A real pilgrim going to Jerusalem leaves his house and land, his wife and children: he strips himself of all he possesses in order to travel light without any hindrances. Similarly if you wish to be a spiritual pilgrim, you must strip yourself of all you possess. You must leave behind your bad deeds, and you must even leave behind your good deeds.

You must regard yourself as spiritually poor, so that you have no confidence in your own actions. Instead you should always desire the spiritual presence of Jesus, and his profound love. If you do this, your heart will be wholly set on reaching the spiritual Jerusalem—on obtaining the love of Jesus and such vision of him as he sees fit to give you.

BOOK 2, CHAPTER 21

ENEMIES' ATTACKS

You are now on the road, and you know the way. But beware of enemies who will try to obstruct you if they can. They hate your desire and your yearning for the love of Jesus, so they want to uproot this desire and yearning from your heart, and turn your heart back to worldly things. Your chief enemies are bodily desires and foolish fears which can rise up in your heart, and which can stifle your love of God, taking full possession of you. These are your deadliest foes.

There are other enemies also, who will use every trick to deceive you. But you have one sure means of resisting them. Whatever they say, do not believe them, but stride firmly onward, thinking only of the love of Jesus. When they persist, say: "I am nothing, I have nothing, I desire nothing but the love of Jesus."

Your enemies may begin by assailing your mind with doubts, hinting that your confessions have been invalid, because you forgot to confess particular sins—so you must give up your journey, go back to the beginning, and make a full confession. But do not believe their lies; your confession has been complete. Rest assured that you are on the right road, and that there is no need to search your conscience about the past. Look steadily forward with your eyes directed to Jerusalem.

They may say: "You are not fit to enjoy God's love, so why yearn for something you cannot possess and do not deserve?" Do not be put off, but reply: "I desire the love of God not because I am worthy but because I am unworthy—and I want it in order to become worthy. God created me to enjoy his love; and though I may never fully attain it, I will still desire it, pray for it, and hope for it."

BOOK 2, CHAPTER 22

ENTERING THE DARKNESS

Those who love God live in his light. When people realize that the pleasures of this world are false and transitory they want to abandon the world, and seek God's love. But they cannot experience God's love immediately; they must stay for some time in darkness. They cannot move instantly from one light to another, from the pleasures of the world to the perfect love of God.

This darkness is the complete withdrawal of the soul from worldly pleasures, motivated by an intense desire to love, see, and know Jesus and the things of the spirit. It is a real night. Just as the darkness of the natural night hides material objects and brings bodily activity to a halt; so those who set their hearts on Jesus and his love must hide all material desires from themselves.

BOOK 2, CHAPTER 24

ABOVE *The Ladder of Virtue (16th-century fresco, Sucevita Monastery). "Rest assured that you are on the right road… Look steadily forward with your eyes directed to Jerusalem."*

THE LIGHT OF THE HEAVENLY CITY

You are now fast approaching Jerusalem. You have not yet arrived, but you can see the city in the distance because of the gleaming rays of light shining from it. Remember that, although your soul dwells in peaceful darkness and is untroubled by thoughts of the world, it is not yet at the end of its journey. The soul has not yet been clothed in light, nor has it caught fire with divine love. The soul is still aware that the object of its ardent desire is beyond its reach. This object is nothing other than the vision of Jerusalem.

BOOK 2, CHAPTER 25

What, then, is the nature of this darkness? It comes solely from the desire to enjoy the love of Jesus—a desire which is instilled by divine grace. As you yearn to see God, and to possess his love, all worldly thoughts and interests are driven from your mind. The soul begins to reflect, wondering how it may attain its goal; and in this way it enters a dark void.

But the soul does not experience complete darkness and emptiness during this time; it is hidden from the last light of the world, and as a result there is a glimmer of the true light.

Catherine of Siena

Catherine of Siena yearned for, and enjoyed, the highest state of mystical ecstasy. But, far from seeking solitude as the context for mysticism, she devoted herself to acts of charity among the poor and sick of her city. Her book, The Dialogue, records her brief utterances to God and his very lengthy replies. The spiritual way that is described within The Dialogue is extremely intense, involving total emotional commitment.

The twenty-fourth child of a prosperous wool merchant, she vowed her virginity to Christ at the age of seven; at the age of fifteen she cut off her hair, to thwart her parents' efforts to find her a husband. Three years later she joined a branch of the Dominican order for single women living in the world. In addition to her charitable work she also became involved in ecclesiastical politics, striving to heal the schism in the papacy which occurred in 1378. She wrote letters to the rival popes in Rome and Avignon, and to various European rulers, urging them to put aside the lust of power. Her tireless activity and her persistent fasting undermined her health and in 1380, at the age of thirty-three, she suffered a fatal stroke.

RIGHT *St. Catherine of Siena (Bartolommeo, 1472, Museo Di San Marco Dell'Angelico, Florence). "Though she is mortal, she tastes the joy which immortals know."*

THE BRIDGE

I want to describe a bridge for you. It stretches from heaven to earth, since I have joined myself with your humanity, which I formed from the earth's clay.

This bridge is my only-begotten Son. It has three stairs. Two of them he built with the wood from his most holy cross; and the third was made from bitter gall and vinegar they gave him to drink. You will recognize in these three stairs three spiritual stages.

The first stair is the feet, which symbolize the emotions. Just as the feet carry the body, the emotions carry the soul. My Son's soiled feet are the stair by which you climb to his side, where you will see his inmost heart. When the soul has climbed up on the feet of emotion, and looked with her spiritual eye into my Son's open heart, she begins to feel within herself his self-giving love, which is beyond words. (I say self-giving, because it is not for his own good that he loves you; you cannot do good to him, since he is united with me.) Then the soul, seeing how wonderfully she is loved, is herself filled to the brim with love. Thus, having climbed the second stair, she reaches the third. This is the mouth, where she finds peace from the terrible war she has been waging against her own sin.

At the first stair, lifting the feet of her emotions from the earth, she stripped herself of sin. At the second she dressed herself in love, to become virtuous. And at the third she tasted peace.

THE DIALOGUE, CHAPTER 26

THE UNIFIED SOUL AND THE WEIGHTLESS BODY

Once souls have risen up in eager longing, they run in virtue along the bridge of the teaching of the crucified Christ, and arrive at the gate to offer themselves up to me. As they cross over, they are drunk with the blood of my Son, and aflame with the fire of love. And they taste in me the eternal Godhead, and I become to them a peaceful sea with which the soul becomes so united that she only moves within me.

Though she is mortal, she tastes the joy which immortals know, and though she is still weighted down with the body, she feels wonderfully light. Indeed the body itself is often lifted off the ground because of the soul's union with me, as if the body itself had become weightless....

So I want you to know that it is a greater marvel to see the soul unified with me, and yet not leaving the body, than to see a host of dead bodies resurrected.

From time to time I break that union for a while, and make the soul again become imprisoned within the body. Thus bodily feelings, which had been completely lost, return. I do not mean that the soul ever left the body, because this happens only at death; neither that her powers and emotions had become united with me in love. When the soul is locked in the body again, the memory of the earlier union with me overwhelms her. She constantly gazes up at my truth. She yearns to be reunited.... Then I allow the sound to come back to me—and she now has an even greater appreciation of me.

THE DIALOGUE, CHAPTER 79

THE REASONS AND
THE FRUITS OF TEARS

Dearest daughter, whom I love so deeply, you have asked me to tell you the reasons for tears, and to explain the fruits of tears. I do not reject your request. Open wide the eyes of your soul, and I shall show you the different stages of tears.

Firstly there are tears of damnation. These are the tears shed by those who are evil.

Secondly there are tears of fear, shed by those who are frightened of the punishment they will suffer for their sins.

Thirdly there are the tears of those who have risen above sin, and are beginning to taste me. They weep out of attraction toward me, and they begin to serve me. But since their love is imperfect, so is their weeping.

Fourthly there are the tears of those who love their neighbors perfectly, and who love me without any self-interest. Their weeping is perfect.

Fifthly there are sweet tears shed with great tenderness.

Sixthly there are tears of fire, shed without physical weeping, which may satisfy those who want to weep, but cannot.

I want you to know that the soul can experience all these stages of weeping as she rises out of fear, through imperfect love, to attain the perfect love of union with me. I want you to know that all tears come from the heart, and that no other part of the body can satisfy the heart as the eyes can.

There is a seventh and final stage of tears which may be called unitive tears. These are shed by those who fully understand the suffering of Christ crucified and who long to share this suffering.

Strangely, when these tears are shed, the soul feels wonderfully calm. She is like an infant sucking at the breast, enjoying the perfection of maternal milk. The soul is drinking directly the spiritual milk of Christ, sucking at the breast of divine charity; she is taking into herself the flesh of the crucified Christ.

In other words, the soul is following the teaching and the footsteps of Christ without deviation. Yet although God the Father can experience no pain, God the Son, the gentle, loving Lord, takes upon himself all the pain and suffering of the world. So when the soul walks in the footsteps of Christ, she too feels great pain; and through the pain the soul acquires virtue.

The soul is resting on the breast of the crucified Christ, and drinking the milk of virtue. And in this virtue the soul receives the life of grace, tasting the beautiful sweetness of the divine nature. Indeed, whereas previously the soul gained no pleasure from virtue, now through sharing the suffering of Christ, the soul is delighted by virtue.

THE DIALOGUE, CHAPTERS 88, 89, AND 96

Thomas à Kempis

The Imitation of Christ is probably second only to the New Testament as a source of inspiration among Christians; people from all social backgrounds and traditions have testified to its spiritual influence. Thomas à Kempis rejected theological scholarship as a means of spiritual attainment, and spurned all notions of a religious elite. Instead he said that everyone can learn to imitate Jesus in attitude and behavior, and hence attain the highest spiritual level. The way to do this is to turn away from worldly ambitions, and to direct all one's emotions to the person of Jesus, as depicted in the Bible.

Born in 1380 in the small town of Kempen, near Cologne, he went at the age of thirteen to live in the Netherlands, in an informal religious community called the Brethren of the Common Life. He was captivated by the warmth and simplicity of their devotion. At nineteen he joined a conventional monastery at Zwolle, remaining there in quiet seclusion. His famous book consists of four separate treatises, written over a fifteen-year period. Although it reveals a mind trained in theology, it reflects the spirituality of the Brethren with whom he spent his youth.

ABOVE *"Even if I were to know everything in the world, yet lacked love, I would be worthless in the eyes of God." (The Imitation of Christ).*

IMITATING CHRIST

Christ urges us to mold our lives and our characters in the image of his, if we wish the light of truth to shine in our hearts. So above all else, we should devote ourselves to meditating on the life of Jesus Christ.

The teaching of Christ is better than all the teaching of holy and wise people; and anyone guided by the Spirit will find hidden nourishment there. Many people hear the gospel frequently and yet feel little desire to imitate Christ. This is because they do not possess the Spirit of Christ. Those who wish to understand and savor the words of Christ to the full must ensure that their whole lives conform to the pattern of Christ's life.

People may discuss the doctrine of the Trinity with great theological skill; but if they lack humility, they will displease God. Intellectual arguments do not make people holy and righteous; God wants us to lead good lives. I would rather feel repentance in my heart, than define it with my mind. You could know the entire Bible word for word, and be familiar with every exposition written by scholars; but if you lack the grace and love of God, the knowledge is useless.

We live in a world of shadows. The only reality consists in loving God and serving him alone. The highest wisdom is to seek the kingdom of heaven, rejecting the things of this world. If you pursue riches, and believe they will make you happy, you are pursuing an empty fantasy. It is equally foolish to seek social status and honor, to become a slave to your natural appetites, to prefer a long life over a good life—to set your heart on anything in the world, which will soon pass away. Instead look only toward that place where lasting joy is to be found.

THE IMITATION OF CHRIST, BOOK 1, CHAPTER 1

THE USELESSNESS OF KNOWLEDGE

Human beings have a natural desire for knowledge. But what good is knowledge without love and fear for God? Those who are humble and ignorant, and yet serve God with all their hearts, are better than proud scholars who observe the movements of the stars in heaven, yet never give a thought to their souls.

Those who really know themselves set no value on themselves, and take no pleasure in being praised by others. Even if I were to know everything in the world, yet lacked love, I would be worthless in the eyes of God.

So give up the passion for knowledge, which distracts you and leads you astray. Scholarly people like to be admired and to acquire a reputation for wisdom.

But most knowledge does little or no good to the soul; and the person who gives his mind to things which do not contribute to salvation, instead of those that do, is a fool. The soul can never be satisfied by words, even in their thousands, whereas a good life sets the mind at peace, and a pure conscience brings friendship with God.

THE IMITATION OF CHRIST, BOOK 1, CHAPTER 2

THE USELESSNESS OF EMOTIONS

We are too concerned with our own emotions, and too concerned with the transitory objects of our emotions. We rarely try to overcome our emotional faults, but merely offset their worst effects. Thus we are not on fire to make progress. Yet if we had true control of our emotions so that they were stripped of all transitory attachments, then we would be free to gain a glimpse of God, and to experience a taste of the joys of heavenly contemplation.

Thus our emotional desires are our main and our most intractable stumbling-block, preventing us from fully imitating Christ. And it is not merely desire and attachments which hinder our progress; it is also the tendency for our emotions to be cast into a pit of gloom at the least adversity….

Let us learn to be firm with our emotions; and if we succeed in this, we shall find the path of Christ easy and delightful.

THE IMITATION OF CHRIST, BOOK 1, CHAPTER 11

ABOVE *This still life painting by Simon Renard de Saint-André, 1613–1677, includes the influential Imitation of Christ, which teaches that spiritual growth requires the rejection of worldly ambitions.*

JESUS AS LOVER

If we disregard ourselves for the sake of Jesus, then we are truly blessed. If we abandon all other facets of love, and love Jesus above everything, then we are truly blessed. The love of other people is fickle and changeable, but the love of Jesus is consistent and enduring. Those who love material objects will decay and crumble as those objects decay and crumble. But those who embrace Jesus will be upheld forever.

When all else fades away, Jesus will still be present. Jesus never leaves us; he never lets us perish. Inevitably at some point in the future we will each die, and will have to leave all our possessions and all our earthly friends behind. But Jesus is with us in death, as in life. So keep close to Jesus not only when you are healthy, but when death approaches also. Place all your trust in him, because he can help you when all else fails.

Jesus is a lover who tolerates no rivals. He wants to have your heart entirely to himself, and to rule there like a king. Thus you must strip your heart of all the attachments, so Jesus can possess your heart completely.

THE IMITATION OF CHRIST, BOOK 2, CHAPTER 7

Ignatius of Loyola

The most influential religious order founded during the Catholic revival was the Society of Jesus, whose members came to be known as Jesuits. Its founder, Ignatius of Loyola, envisaged it as an army in the direct service of the pope, to do spiritual battle in every part of the world. And within a generation, there were Jesuits in China, India, Africa, and North and South America.

New Jesuits were required to study philosophy and theology to the highest level. But at the core of their training were The Spiritual Exercises, a detailed program of contemplation and reflection on the human condition and the life of Christ. The first exercise, on the subject of sin, sets the pattern, which over four weeks is applied to other topics.

The son of a noble family in the Basque region of Spain, he started to follow the family tradition of a military career. But in 1521, at the age of thirty, he was seriously wounded, and during a long convalescence he decided to devote his life to the Church. Ignatius spent a year in prayer and penance, and his experiences in this time were to form the basis of The Spiritual Exercises.

After a pilgrimage on foot to Jerusalem, he studied theology in Paris, where he formed the group that became the basis of the Jesuits. The group moved to Rome, where at first the members ministered to the sick and the dying. The pope recognized their potential, and began sending them on more adventurous missions. By the time Ignatius died, barely two decades later, there were thousands of Jesuits, and Jesuit schools and colleges were springing up across the world.

STRENGTH THROUGH INDIFFERENCE

Human beings were created to praise, worship, and serve the Lord God, and by this means their souls. The other things on this earth were created for his sake, to help achieve the purpose for which they were created. It follows that human beings should make use of these things insofar as they promote salvation, and avoid them insofar as they hinder salvation.

Therefore it is necessary that we should make ourselves indifferent to all created things, as far as our free will allows. We should not wish for health rather than sickness, for wealth rather than poverty, for honor rather than dishonor, for a long life rather than a short one; and in all other matters, we should desire only those things which help us to praise, worship, and serve God.

THE SPIRITUAL EXERCISES, SECTION 23

THE FIRST EXERCISE

The first exercise, using the three faculties, is a meditation on the first, second, and third sin. It contains a preparatory prayer, two preludes, three principal points, and a colloquy.

The preparatory prayer is to ask our Lord God for the grace to direct all my thoughts, intentions, and actions to the service and praise of his divine majesty.

The first prelude is an imaginative representation of the place. By this I mean a picture in the mind of the physical place where the event to be contemplated occurs. This could, for example, mean a temple or a mountain where Jesus is present. Where the subject matter is not visible—as in the present case of sin—the picture will be the idea, produced by an effort of the imagination, of the soul as a prisoner in this corruptible body; and of the whole self, body and soul, as condemned to live on earth as a stranger in a foreign land.

The second prelude is to ask our Lord God for what I want. This prayer must be appropriate to the subject matter. If, for example, I am contemplating the resurrection, I shall pray for a share in Christ's joy; if it is the passion, I shall ask for suffering, grief, and agony, to share in Christ's agony. Now, when the subject is sin, I shall pray to feel wholly ashamed of myself, thinking how often I have deserved eternal damnation for my sins, and how many have been lost for a single sin.

Note that each contemplation in these exercises should be preceded by the preparatory prayer, which never changes, and the two preludes just mentioned, which vary with the subject matter.

THE SPIRITUAL EXERCISES, SECTIONS 45–54

MAKING DECISIONS

To ensure that I make a sound decision about anything, my intention must be as single-minded as possible. I must reflect, in relation to every decision, on the purpose of my creation, which is to praise God and to save my soul. It follows that, whatever choice I make, the purpose should be to further this end. The end should not be forced to suit the means, but the means should be directed toward the end.

For instance, many decide to get married, and only later reflect how they may serve God in this state; but they should have asked themselves whether marriage would help them serve God, since marriage is a means, not an end. Similarly, some priests are ambitious to obtain high position in the Church, and only later ask how they can use their position to serve God. They too are confusing the end with the means.

In every decision the desire to serve God should be the primary objective, since this is our end. The acceptance of an ecclesiastical position, or marrying a wife, or any other decision, should be judged as to whether it promotes this end. I should choose anything to enable me to praise and serve God better, and reject anything that hinders me in this.

THE SPIRITUAL EXERCISES, SECTION 169

ABOVE *The teachings of St. Ignatius have stood the test of time, with Jesuit priests across the world continuing to practice The Spiritual Exercises of contemplation and reflection.*

John of the Cross

In his most famous book, whose title The Dark Night of the Soul has passed into common speech, John of the Cross described with stark clarity the suffering involved in the mystical way. He showed how the aspiring mystic must be cut off not only from sensory pleasures, but from spiritual ones also, in order to enter true unity with God. John, like his older mystical contemporary Teresa of Avila, was also a dynamic organizer, founding a reformed Carmelite order for men. And this provoked such hostility among those who preferred a more lax form of monastic life, that John was at one point kidnapped and imprisoned.

Born only a a few miles from Avila in Spain, John entered a Carmelite monastery in 1562 at the age of twenty, and went on to train for the priesthood. With the support of Teresa of Avila, he founded the first reformed Carmelite monastery. After his imprisonment in 1578 he resumed the leadership of the reformed Carmelite movement, but soon afterward was forced out of office. He retired into obscurity, and during the last fourteen years of his life devoted himself to writing.

THE PURPOSE OF THE DARK NIGHT

God cures our imperfections by putting the soul into a dark night. Through pure dryness and interior darkness he weans us away from the breast of earthly gratification and delight, draws us away from all trivial and childish concerns, and leads us into the quite different path of virtue. Even if we practice with great passion and zeal every kind of self-mortification, we achieve nothing until God purges us by means of the dark night—and we passively submit.

THE DARK NIGHT OF THE SOUL, BOOK 1, CHAPTER 7

THE KINDS OF DARKNESS

This night, which is experienced through contemplation, causes two kind of darkness, according to the two parts of the soul: sensory and spiritual. In the sensory night the senses are purged and harmonized with the spirit. In the spiritual night the spirit is purged and denuded, and thence prepared for loving union with God.

The sensory night is common and happens to many; those begining in the way of prayer experience it. The spiritual night is reserved for a few—those who are becoming proficient. The sensory night is bitter and terrible; but it is nothing compared with the spiritual night.

THE DARK NIGHT OF THE SOUL, BOOK 1, CHAPTER 8

B.IOANES A CRVCE EXTATICVS, AT QVE SVBLIMIS DOCTOR MISTYCVS

LEFT *St. John of the Cross (18th-century engraving). "We achieve nothing until God purges us by means of the dark night – and we passively submit."*

THE SIGNS OF THE DARK NIGHT

It is easy to confuse the dark night of the soul with the mental disturbance that can be caused by sin, weakness, luke-warmness of spirit, melancholy, or some bodily illness. There are three principal ways of discerning whether dryness and darkness are caused by these problems, or whether they are truly the means of spiritual cleansing.

The first is that during the dark night, the soul derives no satisfaction or consolation from worship, nor from material blessings. God puts the soul into the dark night because he wants the sensory appetites to wither away; so he does not allow the soul to find sweetness or delight in anything....

The second sign is that during the dark night, the soul feels it is no longer serving God, but turning away from him. Normally in times of difficulty the soul turns to God for help; but the soul feels such distaste for God during the dark night, that it cannot ask his aid. It is obvious that this aversion to God is not the result of laxity, but is caused by God himself, taking his strength away from the senses....

The third sign is that during the dark night, the soul feels utterly powerless. Its efforts to meditate and to use its imagination to sense God's presence which had previously been effective—now prove useless. God no longer communicates through the senses, as he did before, nor through reflection on the doctrines of the faith. Instead he begins to communicate in a purely spiritual manner, directly with the soul; and the form of communication involves neither the heart nor the mind—neither feelings nor thoughts.

THE DARK NIGHT OF THE SOUL, BOOK 1, CHAPTER 10

RESPONSE TO THE DARK NIGHT

During the dark night people should not try to meditate on theological and doctrinal matters, since this is not the appropriate time. They should allow their souls to be quiet and tranquil. They may feel that they are wasting their time, and they may be inclined to rebuke themselves for laxity. But if they remain patient and relaxed, their lack of activity will itself accomplish a great deal.

All that is required is freedom of soul, in which they liberate themselves from the hindrance and weariness of rational thought. They should content themselves with a loving and peaceful attentiveness to God, and be utterly unconcerned that they cannot taste or feel God—nor have any desire to taste or feel him. They should remember their desires and feelings disturb and distract the soul; so idleness is the appropriate response to the dark night.

THE DARK NIGHT OF THE SOUL, BOOK 1, CHAPTER 10

FROM DARKNESS TO LIGHT

Even though the night darkens the spirit, its purpose is to impart light.

Even though it humbles those who experience it, and reveals the depths of their wretchedness, its purpose is to exalt and uplift them.

Even though it empties them of all feeling, and detaches them from all natural pleasures, its purpose is to fill them with spiritual joy, and attach them to the source of that joy.

THE DARK NIGHT OF THE SOUL, BOOK 2, CHAPTER 9

Francis de Sales

*F*rancis de Sales was the master of the apt metaphor, which made profound spiritual truths clear and accessible. At a time when the Roman Catholic Church was undergoing a spiritual renewal—the so-called Counter-Reformation—Francis de Sales' purpose was to carry the insights of the monasteries and convents into the lives of men and women in the world. As a bishop, his serene and gentle personality drew people to seek his counsel. And he summarized his advice in two books, the second of which, On the Love of God, shows how a lay person can aspire to the heights of mystical union.*

The eldest of thirteen children, he was born in the castle of Sales in Savoy, and received a largely secular education in Paris and Padua. But although he seemed destined for a brilliant career in law or politics, he had from childhood yearned to be a priest. He was ordained in 1593 at the age of twenty-six, and asked to be sent to Geneva, which had become a Protestant stronghold; he became the Catholic bishop of the city in 1602.

ABOVE *"God accepts both service to the rich and service to the poor; but since God prefers service to the poor, the devout heart chooses it."*

Although he avoided direct confrontation, he regarded Protestantism as spiritually cold and empty. By the time of his death, the Catholic church in Geneva was about as strong as its Protestant rival.

IVY ON A TREE

There are particular acts and movements that a soul can make in prayer in order to be more closely united and joined to God's goodness. There is a distinction between uniting and joining. Think of ivy on a tree. The ivy does not simply stand in unity with the tree; it clings to the tree, penetrating the bark, so that it actually joins itself to the trunk. In prayer we can not only stand in unity with God, but also cling to him and penetrate him in love, so we are joined to him....

This happens through small but frequent advances of the soul toward God. If you watch a little infant united and joined to its mother's breast, you will see that from time to time it presses the breast with its face and clasps her close. These movements are stimulated by the pleasure it takes in drinking her milk. So too the soul in prayer can press herself more closely to God, and cling more tightly, stimulated by the pleasure of the divine sweetness.

At other times the soul grows closer to God, not through repeated movements, but by continual pressure. Observe a large lump of lead or brass, or a large stone, sitting on the ground. It does not force its way down; it is gradually pulled by its own weight downward into the earth. Similarly, when the soul rests on God in prayer, its own dependence on God pulls it further and further into God's love.

ON THE LOVE OF GOD, BOOK 7, CHAPTER 1

BEES IN A HIVE

Sometimes the soul is drawn closer to God without any effort on its part. The soul is like a little child who yearns for its mother's breast, yet it is so feeble that by itself it cannot get to it or cling to it. The child is only happy when the mother takes it up in her arms, and presses it to her breast....

In the same way, when the soul is waiting quietly before God, it can find itself yearning to be closer to God. Then, without thought or effort in the soul's part, it finds itself being gently and almost imperceptibly lifted upward to God....

When this happens, the Lord infuses the soul with a feeling of sweetness and serenity, that assures the soul of his presence. The powers of the soul, and even the senses, turn inward, to the place where this most beautiful spouse has entered. Think of a swarm of bees about to take flight.

The beekeeper can call it back by softly striking a metal basin, and by filling the air with the aroma of wine mixed with honey; the swarm is stopped and drawn into the hive. So too, the Savior softly utters words of love, and pours the most delicious spiritual wine into our hearts; so we are drawn into the depths of the soul, to enjoy his sweetness.

On the Love of God, Book 7, Chapter 2

HONEYED WINE

Wine sweetened with honey is used to call bees out of their hive and call them back, and also to pacify them. When bees start to attack and destroy one another, the best remedy is for the beekeeper to pour honeyed wine among the enraged populace. When the bees smell this pungent and pleasant odor, they become peaceful; they sit quietly, relishing the fragrance.

Similarly, when our hearts are in turmoil, the eternal God pours a spiritual wine into us, that is sweeter than honey and more delicious then wine. All the warring powers of our soul fall into a delightful repose. We feel and sense nothing except the pleasure of the spiritual fragrance. We do not even have religious thoughts; we simply enjoy God.

On the Love of God, Book 7, Chapter 2

A BALL OF WAX

The devout heart is like a ball of wax in the hands of God, receiving with equal readiness all the impressions which God wishes to make. The devout heart does not want to assert itself, but is entirely passive in the face of God's will; it wants whatever God wants.

In God's eyes, various options may be acceptable; the devout heart chooses the best, regardless of cost. God accepts both marriage and celibacy; but since God prefers celibacy, the devout heart chooses it. God accepts both service to the rich and service to the poor; but since God prefers service to the poor, the devout heart chooses it. God accepts both moderation in pleasure, and patience amid tribulation; but since God prefers the latter, the devout heart prefers it also.

In short, the devout heart regards God's will as its king.

On the Love of God, Book 9, Chapter 6

THE CHILD AT THE BREAST

Consider a little child holding fast to the breast and neck of its mother. If you want to put the child in its cradle, it resists as best it can, because it prefers the comfort of its mother's bosom. If you make it let go with one hand, the child grabs with the other. If you lift the child up, it bursts out crying, and looks down with longing eyes to its mother; it does not stop crying until its mother has rocked it to sleep. In the same way the soul that has become close to God, and drinks his spiritual goodness, clings to God, and cannot be taken away except by force. If we distract the imagination of such a soul, we pry its intellect loose, it clings by means of the will. If by some violent distraction we compel the will to abandon its hold, the soul continues to look at God with deep longing. The soul can never again be entirely detached from God; and it will return to God at every opportunity.

On the Love of God, Book 7, Chapter 3

Johann Arndt

*T*he Protestant reformers of the early sixteenth century emphasized the importance of faith as the means whereby the individual is justified before God; and thus they stressed personal conversion. Johann Arndt, born nine years after the death of the German reformer Martin Luther, feared that his fellow Protestants were ignoring the progress toward holiness that should take place after conversion.

He was thus the first to develop a specifically Protestant form of spirituality. He recognized that the converted Christian must still fight against temptation, and will still need forgiveness. And he saw prayer as the primary weapon in the fight. His great work, True Christianity, has a robust simplicity that is lacking in much medieval spiritual writing; yet its message is similar—suggesting that at a spiritual level the Protestant and Catholic traditions tend to merge.

The son of a Lutheran pastor, Arndt's first ambition was to become a physician. But illness forced him to abandon his medical studies and he began to study mysticism. In 1583, at the age of twenty-eight, he was himself ordained a pastor, and in the same year he married. In addition to serving his congregation, he devoted himself to trying to resolve the theological quarrels that divided different groups of Protestants. Rather than seeking doctrinal formulae in which all might agree, he urged people simply to pray together, allowing God to unite their minds and hearts.

A SUMMARY OF TRUE CHRISTIANITY

Our great spiritual illness demands a great divine remedy. We cannot bring this about by our own powers; only Christ in his mercy can heal our souls. He has given himself to us completely, so that we can depend on him at all times. He is the gift above all gifts, the all in all....

Christ is the foundation of all human righteousness. This righteousness must be received by grace alone, so that it can penetrate to the core of our beings. Through this grace we turn from ourselves to Christ. The righteousness of Christ becomes ours through faith. This is God's work, not ours; righteousness given by God is eternal, built on the rock of God's truth and permanently bonded to it. We boast in him alone; he is our consolation, honor, wisdom, and victory.

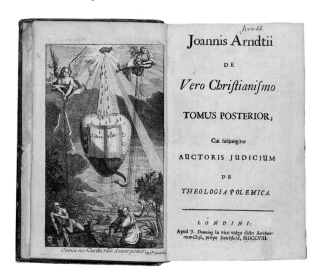

ABOVE *Johann Arndt's True Christianity urged unity between all Christians – God's truth being common to all. "There is no place in the Christian heart for spiritual pride."*

A Christian is not only justified by faith, but also sanctified. The fruits of the Spirit grow within us—although in the early days of faith they are weak. The sign is that we actually want to abide by the laws of God; our hearts are holy, so we behave in a holy fashion. Yet we do not take pride in this, nor condemn the failures of others. Christ has taught us to be forgiving, knowing that we still need forgiveness....

Our perfection and holiness consists in union with God in Christ; this union is eternal. It occurs through faith and by grace; and nothing that we may do can bring it about. We must submit ourselves to God, and deny our own wills. Self-will and self-love are our greatest enemies. Christ must turn us from ourselves to him; we cannot achieve this ourselves.

In every Christian there are two opposing people: Adam and Christ. Adam must die, in order for Christ to live. To overcome Adam we must be vigilant; we must pray earnestly; and we must constantly struggle. If Adam lives in me, I am not God's child, but a child of the devil. We should remember that by nature we are evil in Adam; by grace we attain righteousness in Christ. There is no place in the Christian heart for spiritual pride....

Love is the greatest of all virtues. But we can easily err, particularly in the love of God and of neighbor. Those who love God for the material blessings he bestows love themselves more than God, because they love God and his blessing for themselves. Such impure love brings forth impure fruits. Some love God because they fear his anger; such love is weak. Some love God in order to gain his wisdom. Some love God in order to learn virtue....

True love for God consists in opening ourselves wholly to God in prayer. Such love has four features: we submit our will to God's will; we put aside all enmity; we serve others as Christ served those around him; and we try to imitate Christ in every way—except for the fact that we cannot be sinless. Prayer is impossible without love.

TRUE CHRISTIANITY, BOOK 2

ABOVE *Johann Arndt became interested in mysticism after illness forced him to abandon his medical studies.*

A GUIDE TO PRAYER

ONE
We recognize that Christ shows us the way to holiness and so through him we can become children of God. We seek to follow him by continual prayer.

TWO
We recognize that only through prayer can we obey the commandments of God.

THREE
In prayer we honor God, and listen to his teaching.

FOUR
In prayer alone do we seek victory over the heart and its temptations.

FIVE
In prayer we perceive the wisdom of God, and we sense that he always listens to us, and receives us with love.

SIX
We remember always that we pray not because of our piety, but because of our unworthiness. Without prayer we are nothing.

SEVEN
We do not pray to persuade God of anything, because he has foreseen and ordained all things.

EIGHT
Through prayer we participate in God's grace. As we learn to pray more deeply, so our prayer becomes more silent.

NINE
God wants everyone to pray.

TEN
We do not start praying because we are righteous, nor do we stop praying when we have committed a sin.

TRUE CHRISTIANITY, BOOK 3

Jeremy Taylor

*U*nlike the Protestant leaders in other parts of Europe, most of the reformers in England wished to maintain many of the old medieval traditions, especially in the sphere of worship and prayer. Their main objection to medieval Catholicism was that regular prayer was largely confined to priests, monks, and nuns. Thus their primary aim was to make the practice of prayer more accessible to ordinary people. The greatest writer in this quest, Jeremy Taylor, was the son of a poor barber in Cambridge, who finished his life as a bishop. In his book Holy Living, he sought to show how men and women in the world could be as holy as the most pious members of a monastery or convent; and the key to this holiness is a discipline of prayer. He gave clear, practical instructions as to how this practice of prayer could be achieved.

In 1626, at the early age of thirteen, Jeremy Taylor won a place as a poor scholar at Cambridge University; and seven years later was ordained and elected to a fellowship. He served as vicar of the prosperous town of Uppingham; but as a staunch supporter of the monarchy, he was forced into hiding when King Charles was defeated in the English Civil War. He served as the private chaplain of an aristocratic family in Wales, and it was there that he devoted himself to writing. After the restoration of the monarchy in 1660 the new king promoted him to a bishopric.

ABOVE *The Return of Charles II to Whitehall in 1660 (Alfred Barron Clay, 1867). "The prayers of men have saved cities and kingdoms from ruin..."*

THE PURPOSE OF PRAYER

There is no greater argument in the world of our spiritual danger and unwillingness to religion, than the backwardness which most men have always, and all men have sometimes, to say their prayers; so weary of their length, so glad when they are done, so witty to excuse and frustrate an opportunity; and yet all is nothing but a desiring of God to give us the greatest and the best things we can need, and which can make us happy. It is a work so easy, so honorable, and to so great purpose, God hath not given us a greater argument of His willingness to have us saved, than by rewarding so easy a duty with so great blessings.

Christ hath put it into the hand of men to rescind or alter all the decrees of God by the power of prayers, and the prayers of men have saved cities and kingdoms from ruin; shut the mouths of wild beasts; hath altered the course of nature; caused rain in Egypt and brought in the sea. It cures diseases without physic, and makes physic to do the work of nature, and nature to do the work of grace, and grace to do the work of God; and it does miracles of accident and event.

Yet prayer that does all this is, of itself, nothing but an ascent of the mind to God, a desiring thing fit to be desired, and an expression of this desire to God as we can, and as becomes us. And our unwillingness to pray is nothing else but not desiring what we ought passionately to long for; or if we do desire it, it is a choosing rather to misuse our satisfaction and felicity than to ask for it.

HOLY LIVING, CHAPTER 4

RULES FOR THE PRACTICE OF PRAYER

ONE We must be careful that we never ask anything of God that is sinful, or that directly ministers to sin; for that is to ask God to dishonor Himself, and to undo us. We had need consider what we pray; for before it returns in blessing it must be joined with Christ's intercession, and presented to God. Let us principally ask of God power and assistance to do our duty, to glorify God, to do good works, to live a good life, to die in the fear and favor of God. These things God delights to give; and commands that we shall ask and we may with confidence expect to be answered graciously.

TWO We may lawfully pray to God for the gifts of the Spirit that minister to holy ends, such as are the gift of preaching, the spirit of prayer, good expression, a ready and unloosed tongue, good understanding, learning, opportunities to publish them, etc., with these only restraints: we may not ask them to serve our own ends, but only for God's glory, and then we shall have them, or a blessing for desiring them; we must submit to God's will, desiring Him to choose our employment, and to furnish our persons as He shall see expedient.

THREE Whatsoever we may lawfully desire of temporal things, we may lawfully ask of God in prayer, and we may expect them, as they are promised. Whatsoever is necessary to our life and being is promised to us; food to keep us alive, clothing to keep us from nakedness and shame; so long as our life is permitted to us, so long as all things necessary to our life shall be ministered. We may be secure of maintenance, but not secure of our life; for that is promised, not this. We are not to make accounts by the measure of our desires, but by the measure of our needs.

FOUR Let the words of our prayers be pertinent, grave material, not studiously many, according to our need, sufficient to express our wants. God hears us not the sooner for our many words but much the sooner for an earnest desire.

FIVE Whatever we beg of God, let us also work for it, if the thing be a matter of duty, for God loves to bless labor and to reward it, but not to support idleness.

HOLY LIVING, CHAPTER 4

REMEDIES AGAINST WANDERING THOUGHTS

If we feel our spirit is apt to wander in our prayers, and to retire into the world, or to things unprofitable:

ONE Use prayer to be assisted in prayer; pray for the spirit of supplication, for a sober, fixed, and recollected spirit; and when to this you add a moral industry to be steady in your thoughts, whatsoever wanderings after this do return irremediably are a misery of nature and an imperfection, but no sin, while it is not cherished and indulged in.

TWO In private it is not amiss to attempt the cure by reducing your prayers into collects and short forms of prayer, making voluntary interruptions and beginning again, that the want of spirit and breath may be supplied by the short stages and periods.

THREE When you have observed any considerable wandering of your thoughts, bind yourself to repeat that prayer again with actual attention, or else revolve the full sense of it in your spirit; and possibly the tempter may be driven away with his own art, and may cease to interpose his trifles when he perceives they do but vex the person into carefulness and piety.

FOUR Be sure, with actual attention, to say a hearty Amen to the whole prayer with one united desire, for that desire does the great work of the prayer, and secures the blessing, if the wandering thoughts were against our will, and disclaimed by contending against them.

FIVE Avoid multiplicity of businesses of the world; and labor for an evenness and tranquility of spirit, smooth in all tempests of fortune; for so we shall better tend religion, when we are not torn in pieces with the cares of the world, and seized upon with low affections, passions, and interest.

SIX It helps much if we say our prayers silently, without the voice, only the spirit. For, in mental prayer if our thought wanders we only stand still; when our mind returns we go on again; there is none of the prayer lost, as it is if our mouths speak and our hearts wander.

HOLY LIVING, CHAPTER 4

Angelus Silesius

rotestant Christianity, while teaching that each individual can communicate directly with God, was from the outset suspicious of mysticism, questioning the authenticity of personal visions of God. For this reason, a number of Protestants with mystical inclinations felt compelled to adopt Roman Catholicism. Prominent among these was Johannes Scheffler, who on becoming a Franciscan priest in 1661 took the name Angelus Silesius—the Silesian Angel. His most famous work, The Cherubinic Wanderer, is a series of epigrams in which he proclaims the mystical unity of God with the soul. The book contains no direct teaching; but its joy, serenity, and enthusiasm are wonderfully infectious.

ABOVE *The Blessed Filippo Ciardelli healing a sick man (Bartolomeo di Fredi, Diocesan Museum Montalcino, Siena). "If I see Christ in my neighbor, then I both know Christ and know my neighbor."*

Scheffler grew up in the Silesian capital, Breslau, in a rich, landowning family. His parents, who were devout Lutherans, had been forced to flee from religious persecution in their native Poland. As a young man, he studied medicine in Strasbourg and then in Padua, where he encountered the writings of Ignatius of Loyola. He became physician to a Catholic duke in Germany, and under the guidance of the duke's chaplain, became Catholic. When several years later he had joined the Franciscan order, he returned to Breslau and devoted himself to caring for the poor and sick of the city.

BECOMING LIKE GOD

God is both my final goal and my original source. If I should find God, I would become what he is; I would shine within his radiance; my words would be within his Word. I would be made divine.

MY DWELLING PLACE

Where is my dwelling place? And where can I never stand? Where is my final goal, toward which I should ascend? My dwelling place is the place where I cannot stand; it is beyond all place, and above all place.

GIVING AND RECEIVING

God loves me above all creatures—just as he loves every creature beyond all creatures. I love him above all creatures. I give him as much as I receive from him.

SILENT PRAYER

God is far beyond all words that I can express. I cannot speak to him properly in words; and he does not speak to me fully in words. I speak to him best, and he speaks to me best, in silence. I hear him and I worship him without words.

BLESSING

It is in my hands to determine whether God blesses me. It is within your hands whether God blesses you. All that is required is to give consent, and submit.

CARRYING A BURDEN

As long as you feel yourself to be a distinct individual, you still carry a burden. As long as you have knowledge, and thus are a subject observing objects, you still carry a burden. As long as you possess material things, you still carry a burden. As long as you cherish objects, and yet are not unified with them, you still carry a burden.

GOD IS PURE NOTHING

God is the purest nothing. He is untouched by time and space. He does not exist in the realm of human knowledge. The more you reach out for him, the more he escapes your grasp.

LOVE AND UNITY

To love is very difficult. Yet loving is not enough. We must become love. The subject and the object must become one.

SEEING GOD

God lives in supreme light. There is no path that gives you access to that light. You yourself must become that light; only by becoming supreme light can you see God.

RETURNING TO THE SOURCE

The spirit of God breathed into us to bring us to life; he is the source of life. He invites us to return to him, and immerse ourselves in him; he wants us constantly to inhale him.

EACH IN ITS OWN ELEMENT

The bird flies in the air. The stone rests on the land on the earth. The fish swims in the water. The soul's element is the hand of God.

SPIRITUAL BLOSSOM

If you graft yourself onto God, you will bear green leaves and exquisite blossom. God's Holy Spirit will be your sap, making the leaves and the flowers grow. Your beauty will be his beauty.

LIVING IN CHRIST

God has been born on earth in Jesus Christ; if God is not born in you, then you mock the birth of Christ. God has died on earth in Jesus Christ; if you do not share his death, you mock his sacrifice. God has risen to life in Jesus Christ; if your agony does not become your joy, you mock his resurrection.

HEAVEN AND HELL

Heaven with its joy lives within you, as does hell with its pain. You may choose whether heaven grows in your soul, or hell—whether you are joyful or miserable.

PERFECTION AND POWER

If I were to despair of ever becoming perfect, I would be denying the power of God. I would also be denying his providence, since he wants to make me perfect.

FINDING GOD

Go to where you cannot go; there you will meet God. See what you cannot see; you will look on the face of God. Hear what you cannot hear; you will listen to the words of God.

GOD AND I

God is that which he is; I am that which I am. If I were to know myself well, I would know God. If I were to know God well, I would know myself.

GOD AND MY NEIGHBOR

If I see Christ in my neighbor, then I both know Christ and know my neighbor. I see the divine light which shines in every person; and that light is Christ.

NOISY PRAYER

God does not lack worshipers; the natural sound of every creature is a hymn of praise. The sounds of nature are in perfect harmony; let human voices and spirit also join in perfect harmony.

FROM THE CHERUBINIC WANDERER, BOOK 1

Jean-Pierre de Caussade

At a time of accelerating economic change and social disruption, a number of spiritual writers urged people to adopt a passive attitude to outward events. One group, known as the "quietists," taught that the material world should be ignored, and that spiritual tranquility is all that matters. Others emphasized the presence of God in all creatures, and taught that his will is revealed in the unfolding of events; inner peace is to be found by perceiving God's presence through the eyes of faith, and aligning our will with his. The greatest writer among the latter group was a French Jesuit called Jean-Pierre de Caussade.

He entered the Jesuit order in Toulouse in 1693 at the age of eighteen. Having completed his own training, he began to train others, teaching physics and logic. Then for fifteen years he became an itinerant preacher, touring every region of his native country. The last twenty years of his life were spent in organizing spiritual retreats for fellow Jesuits and for monks and nuns of other orders. His great book, Self-Abandonment to Divine Providence, was written shortly before his death, summarizing all that he had learned and taught.

ABOVE *A Jesuit and his family (Marco Benefiale, Palazzo Barberini, Rome). French Jesuit Jean-Pierre de Caussade asks, "Can the wisdom and goodness of God be wrong?"*

DIVINE HARMONY

The will of God is the essence and power of all things; and the will of God harmonizes all things with the soul. Without the will of God, all is nothingness and emptiness, lies and vanity, the latter without the spirit, husks without kernels, death. The will of God is salvation and health, life to the body and the soul.

The will of God within an object cannot be perceived merely by looking at the object's external appearance; nor can it be perceived by assessing whether the object may be helpful to one's body or soul, because that in itself is utterly unimportant. The will of God is the process by which any object or event forms the image of Jesus Christ with our hearts. We should not desire one thing rather than another, because God can bring all things into unity with us.

Sometimes pleasant ideas fill the mind; sometimes the mind is distracted and confused. Sometimes pleasant emotions fill the heart; sometimes the heart is disturbed and anxious. Sometimes the body is well, sometimes it is sick. Yet in every situation and at every moment the divine will is active, loving you and sustaining you. Without the divine will, bread would be poison; with it, poison becomes nourishment. Without the divine will, books would darken the mind; with it, darkness becomes light. The divine will makes all things good and true. And thus all things become blessings from God.

SELF-ABANDONMENT TO DIVINE PROVIDENCE, CHAPTER 1

DIVINE FULLNESS

The soul that is not attached to the will of God will find neither contentment nor sanctification in worship or in acts of charity. If what God himself chooses for you does not satisfy you, no other hand can serve you as you desire. If you are disgusted with the food which the divine will has prepared for you, every other food will seem even more insipid. A soul can only be truly nourished, strengthened, purified, enriched, and sanctified by the divine fullness of the present moment. What more do you want? Since all good is contained in the present moment, why look elsewhere? Do you know better than God? If he has ordained a particular event, why desire a different event?

Can the wisdom and goodness of God be wrong? Do you think you will find peace by struggling against the Almighty? Is not the resistance to God—which we often make, but rarely admit—the cause of our inner disturbance and discontent?

The soul that refuses to be satisfied by the divine fullness of the present moment will be punished by being unable to find satisfaction elsewhere…. The soul that accepts God's design as it is, and embraces the present moment, finds serenity and peace.

SELF-ABANDONMENT TO DIVINE PROVIDENCE,
CHAPTER 1

DIVINE DESIGN

Once the soul perceives that all things are designed by God, the soul derives spiritual value from all things. Every object, and all that is contained in every object, becomes holy and perfect, everything that the soul sees becomes divine in its sight.

But in order not to stray from the right path, the soul must be careful. It must not follow every inspiration; it should first ensure that the inspiration truly comes from God. The test is whether the inspiration enables the soul to understand the duties appropriate to its state. Nothing is to be preferred to these duties; and there is nothing to be feared in these duties. The moments employed in fulfilling these duties are supremely precious to the soul, because the soul knows it is giving pleasure to God.

Holiness consists in submitting to the designs of God. Nothing must be rejected which he offers; nothing should be sought which is not offered by God. The purpose of reading spiritual books, of listening to the counsels of the wise, of praying out loud, and of quiet meditation, is to instruct us in the ways of God and to unite us to his will.

SELF-ABANDONMENT TO DIVINE PROVIDENCE,
CHAPTER 1

DIVINE WORKINGS

All creatures live in the hands of God. The senses perceive only outward action; but faith perceives the actions of God in every event. Faith knows that Jesus Christ is alive in all things, and operates through the course of history—century by century. Faith knows that the briefest moment and the tiniest atom contain a portion of Christ's hidden life and his mysterious power. Outward activity is a veil concealing the inner workings of God….

Most of us do not possess faith which is sufficiently pure or penetrating to see this clearly; but God sometimes takes us by surprise, drawing back the veil in order to deepen our faith.

SELF-ABANDONMENT TO DIVINE PROVIDENCE,
CHAPTER 2

THE TREASURE OF THE PRESENT MOMENT

If you are able to respond to each moment as the manifestation of God's will, you shall find in each moment everything which the heart can desire. What can be more reasonable and more perfect than God's will? Its infinite value could not be increased by some change in time, place, and circumstance.

If you have discovered the secret of finding God's will at every moment and in every event, you possess the most precious gift on earth. You do not need to desire anything else. You do not need to hanker after more wealth. Everything you truly want at any moment is contained in the events of that moment.

The present moment is always full of infinite treasure. It contains far more than you can possibly hold. Faith is the measure of its riches: what you find in the present moment is according to the measure of your faith. Love also is the measure: the more the heart loves, the more it rejoices in what God provides. The will of God presents itself at each moment like an immense ocean which the desire of your heart cannot empty; yet you will drink from that ocean according to your faith and love.

SELF-ABANDONMENT TO DIVINE PROVIDENCE,
CHAPTER 3

Nikolaus Ludwig von Zinzendorf

Zinzendorf believed that Protestant Christianity was too cerebral, reducing religion to a matter of believing the correct concepts. He regarded spiritual experience as the essence of religion, and believed that people could have authentic experiences of God even though they possess almost no theological understanding.

The foundation of faith, Zinzendorf taught, is a sense of one's own inner distress and misery, and hence the discovery that Christ alone can bring lasting happiness. He wanted every Christian to be an evangelist; thus "implicit faith," in which the individual receives God's love into the heart, should lead to "explicit faith," expressed in words and actions to others.

Zinzendorf inherited a large estate east of Dresden, where he gave refuge to Protestants from Moravia fleeing Catholic persecution. He became their spiritual leader in 1727 and they became known as the Moravian Church. They soon began sending missionaries across the world, and Zinzendorf himself went to Pennsylvania to evangelize the native Americans. In 1732 he outlined his religious philosophy, describing himself as a "German Socrates." Fourteen years later he gave a series of lectures in London, of which the most famous was entitled Saving Faith.

RIGHT *Zinzendorf maintained that theological training was not necessary to understand religion. "If religion depended on reason, theologians would always excel in holiness; experience tells us this is not so."*

CONCEPTS AND EXPERIENCE

Religion can be grasped without reason; otherwise no one could have religion except those with intelligence. Moreover, if religion depended on reason, theologians would always excel in holiness; experience tells us this is not so.

Religion can be grasped through experience, without rational concepts. If this were not so, a deaf, blind, or mentally deficient person could not have the religion necessary for salvation. The first would not be able to hear the truth; the second would not be able to read the truth; and the third would not be able to grasp the truth.

The truth of concepts matters far less than the truth of experience. Errors of doctrine are less important than errors of the heart. An ignorant person is far less evil than a stubborn person.

Understanding reached from concepts changes with time, education, and other circumstances. Understanding reached from experience is not subject to these changes; it simply deepens with time and circumstances.

The experience central to religion is receiving God's revelation of himself. That which God does not want human beings to understand, he does not reveal. That which he does want human beings to understand, he does reveal. It may be useful to express divine revelation in concepts; it is not necessary.

THE GERMAN SOCRATES

IMPLICIT FAITH

We cannot create faith within ourselves. God must work within us, giving us new birth, so that the heart, spirit, mind, and all the faculties are transformed. This transformation is the essence of faith. And if faith is to enter us, it must be preceded with distress, which opens our ears to it.

This distress comes when we recognize ourselves to be spiritually poor, when we see that we have no Savior, when we become palpably aware of our misery. We see our own corruption, and become profoundly anxious because of it. We are like a sick person reaching the crisis of an illness—desperately looking out for someone to help, and willing to accept the first offer of aid without examination or investigation....

What results from this faith-in-distress, from this faith which arises out of a desire for salvation? Thankful love results from it. An unknown man appears. Yet even though we do not know him, the heart says: "He wants to help, he wants to comfort; and he can help and comfort. He is the one I heard about in my youth. They call him the Savior, the Son of God, the Lord Jesus. He must help me. If only he would come to my aid! If only he would take my soul into his care, so that it would not perish! Lord, have mercy!"

SAVING FAITH

EXPLICIT FAITH

Faith-in-distress may be called implicit faith: it operates within the heart alone and is not visible to anyone else.... It must then lead to explicit faith, which unfolds and manifests itself to others. Explicit faith has two parts. The first part consists in learning.... We want to find out about your Savior. We want to know him from head to foot, in heart and body. We want to penetrate his nature, both as he is now and as he was on earth in the flesh. We think deeply about him and his teaching; we instruct ourselves about the truths he taught, one after the other, using both the faculty of reason to understand them in our mind, and the faculty of emotion to grasp them in our heart. We go and speak to those who know and love the Savior....

This faith which we are not learning about and sharing with others is a beautiful thing. We find ourselves falling in love with our Savior, rejoicing in the happiness with which he fills our heart. We take great pleasure in meditating upon him; and our joy is enhanced when through him we encounter the Father and the Holy Spirit.

FAITH-IN-DISTRESS

Faith is no great art. Faith grows out of misery and distress. Only those who are so blinded by pride refuse to admit their distress. Any sensible and honest person recognizes their distress, and so yearns for faith to alleviate it.

God, in his patience and mercy, knowing people better than they know themselves, requires only this faith-in-distress in order to begin the process of salvation. Horror at our own sin and corruption is the foundation of saving faith. We find ourselves saying: "He who appears before my heart, who has such a bloody appearance, who is said to have died for me—it will be he who saves me. Yes, yes!" Then our horror turns into happiness. We are invited into the eternal kingdom.

Now comes the second part of explicit faith. Having learned about our faith, we now want to tell others about it. We want to proclaim the wounds of Christ, from which God's power flows; we want to proclaim his wounded heart, from which God's love flows. And our faith is so vibrant that we are able to speak with conviction and assurance. Our faith flows out of us with divine power and love, pouring itself at the feet of all we meet.

SAVING FAITH

John of Cronstadt

During the nineteenth century the Russian Orthodox Church experienced a spiritual revival, which enabled the laity, as well as the priests, to withstand the corrosive cynicism and persecution of the Communist revolution in the twentieth century.

The man who, more than anyone, stimulated this revival was a simple parish priest called John, serving the fortress town of Cronstadt. He believed that attendance at church services is useless unless it is complemented by private prayer; and he encouraged everyone, from the Czar down to the lowliest artisan, to have a discipline of daily prayer. He described prayer as standing in the spiritual sunshine in which the heart is softened and the mind enlightened. He also recognized the spiritual weariness and darkness that occasionally accompanies prayer, but said simply that perseverance soon dispels them.

He was the son of a village deacon in a remote village in the far north of Russia. He won a place at the theological academy in St. Petersburg, and in 1855 at the early age of twenty-six, he was appointed priest at Cronstadt, which was only a short distance away from the city. His life was quiet and uneventful; but through transcripts of his sermons his reputation steadily grew. Two Czars sought his counsel and one called him to his deathbed.

He refused all offers of promotion, but had a weakness for silk cassocks and gold pectoral crosses, which admirers gave him. His enduring reputation depends on his spiritual diary, entitled My Life in Christ, which is a series of short reflections, mainly on prayer.

STANDING IN THE SUNSHINE

Prayer is the living water by which the soul quenches its thirst. When you pray, think of yourself as alone before God; and bring all your concerns into your relationship with God. Think of God in the world, as your soul is in the body—though he is infinitely higher than the world, and is not limited by it. Your body is small, and is wholly penetrated by your small soul; the world is large, and is wholly penetrated by the infinite greatness of God.

For those who are pious and who love God, there is a constant and invisible intercourse between the soul and God. Like a father or a teacher, God sometimes approves, and sometimes condemns our thoughts, desires, and intentions. At one moment he says that something is good; then later he says that another thing is bad. Thus through prayer the soul receives moral, emotional, and spiritual guidance.

Although God knows all our needs, prayer is necessary for the cleansing and enlightenment of the soul. To pray is to stand spiritually in the sunshine, feeling the warmth of God, and seeing the world in his light. If we are truly to enjoy life on earth, then through prayer we must learn to see heaven in all earthly things. Then we shall both be fully involved in earthly activities and simultaneously transcend life on earth, rising upward to our true and eternal dwelling place.

Prayer is necessary for our cold hearts to be warmed, for our hearts hardened by vanity to be softened by humility.

MY LIFE IN CHRIST, CHAPTER 1, SECTION 1

THE BREATH AND FOOD OF THE SOUL

When you are praying, convince yourself that the Lord is present, beside you and within you, and that he is hearing every word and sensing every emotion. Speak to God with your whole heart; do not try to justify feelings and attitudes which are wrong. Have faith that God will have mercy upon you, that your sincere repentance will evoke his forgiveness. I know this to be true.

It is easy to breathe the air around us, and easy to eat the food that is put before us. It is even easier for the faithful soul to receive every spiritual gift from the Lord. Prayer is the breathing of the soul; it is the food by which the soul is nourished.

Prayer is founded on faith. Firstly it requires faith that God exists, that he is omnipotent, that he holds all creatures in the palm of his hand, that he gives creatures voices by which to communicate with each other—although he does not give himself an audible voice. Secondly, prayer requires faith that my prayer will reach him—or, more precisely, that my prayer will go directly from my heart to his ears.

MY LIFE IN CHRIST, CHAPTER 1, SECTION 2

HONOR AND HUMILITY

Prayer is a natural activity. It is the means by which I identify myself with my Creator; and it is the means by which my Creator answers me of his blessings. God created me from nothing. But God in his mercy has imbued me with reason, with emotions, and with free will. Thus with my reason, as an act of free will, I can direct my emotions toward him, and become his loyal servant. I can acknowledge my total dependence upon him, and look to him for all my needs, both spiritual and material.

Prayer reminds me day by day that I am the image of God; that by humbly prostrating myself before God, he uplifts me and bestows upon me great spiritual blessings: that prayer is the means by which I can grow in every kind of virtue. To be able to pray, to be able to communicate with God, is the greatest honor which God could bestow on me. Yet, while honoring me, prayer also reminds me of my nothingness: I am nothing and I have nothing, so I have to ask God for everything.

MY LIFE IN CHRIST, CHAPTER 1, SECTION 3

WEARINESS AND DARKNESS

It must be admitted that sometimes we grow weary of praying. Why? It is because the image of ourselves as reflections of God grows dim in our minds; thus we feel alienated from him. Thus to overcome this weariness, we must strive to look at ourselves afresh, recognizing anew that God made us in his image....

ABOVE *A Religious Procession (I M Pryanishnikov, 1840-94, State Russian Museum, St Petersburg). Parish priest John of Cronstadt led the way in Russia's spiritual revival in the nineteenth century.*

People sometimes say that if you feel no inclination to pray, it is better not to pray. This is crafty sophistry. If you only prayed when you wanted, you would eventually stop praying at all, because your heart would rebel against prayer. In prayer the heart sacrifices itself to God; the heart dies daily as we pray. And as we persist in prayer, the heart is raised up to new life. To repeat this process of death and resurrection day by day requires self-discipline and perseverance.

During prayer there are sometimes moments, and also long periods, when the soul plunges into deadly darkness, and experiences great anguish. Do not despair when this occurs. Remember that, although the divine light has ceased to be visible to your soul, it still shines in many other souls, and shines throughout the natural world.

This assures you that God has not deserted you, but merely that you have become temporarily blinded to him. Indeed the darkness is a good reminder of your inner sinfulness and corruption, and hence your dependence on him. So let the darkness be an opportunity for even greater and more fervent repentance—and soon your spiritual eyes will open again, and the light will be even brighter.

MY LIFE IN CHRIST, CHAPTER 1, SECTIONS 5 AND 6

Friedrich von Hügel

Early in the twentieth century a devout Catholic layman, Friedrich von Hügel, recognized that for most people traditional religious doctrines were no longer credible. Yet he also saw that the human need for religion is natural, and therefore remained as strong as ever. He thus concluded that spirituality, which fulfills this need, rather than belief, must be the essence of modern faith.

He sought to develop a spirituality that was loyal to the finest Christian traditions, but required only minimal theological assent. In this he was one of the pioneers of a spiritual movement that has steadily grown in the final century of the second millennium; and its theological liberalism has been allowed to embrace other religious traditions across the world.

His father was an Austrian aristocrat in the diplomatic service, and his mother was British. He grew up in Vienna, but in 1867, when he was fifteen, his parents retired to Torbay in southwest England. In 1873 he married into the English aristocracy, and settled near Hampstead Heath in London. Since he had sufficient money to live without working, he became a private scholar. He devoted the last two decades of the nineteenth century to the study of Christian mysticism; and then in the twentieth century as he approached old age, he began to lecture and write prolifically, based on both his studies and his personal experience.

THE NEED FOR RELIGION

Man's personality, the instrument of all his fuller and deeper apprehensions, is constituted by the presence and harmonization of a whole mass of energies and intimations belonging to different levels and values; and not one of these can (in the long run and for mankind at large) be left aside or left unchecked by the others, without grave drawback to that personality.

Religion is indeed the deepest of energizings and intimations within man's entirety, but it is not the only one; and though through religion alone God becomes definitely revealed to man as self-conscious Spirit, as an object, as the object, of direct, explicit adoration, yet those other energies and intimations are also willed by God and come from him, and (in the long run and for mankind at large) are necessary to man's health and balance even in religion itself.

So also the esthetic sense alone conveys the full and direct intimations of the beautiful; yet it nevertheless requires for its healthy, balanced functioning, the adequate operation of numerous other energies and intimations, from the senses up to mental processes, in the man who apprehends the beautiful.

ESSAYS AND ADDRESSES

THREE ESSENTIALS OF RELIGION

Like all living realities, living religion possesses a sovereign spontaneity and rich simplicity which seem to render all attempts at analysis an insult. Indeed, religion in particular possesses three essentials, which continually bring expansion and simplicity to its tension and complexity.

Religion is essentially social horizontally; in the sense that each several soul is therefore unique because intended to realize just this post, function, joy, effect within the total organism of all souls. Hence no soul is expected to be a "jack-of-all-trades," but only to develop fully its own special gifts and attributes, within and through, and for, that larger organism of the human family, in which other souls are as fully to develop their own differing gifts and attributes, as so many supplements and compensations to the others. The striving of any one soul can thus be peaceful, since limited in its range to what this particular soul, at its best, most really wants and loves.

And religion is essentially social vertically—indeed here is its deepest root. It is unchangeably a faith in God, a love of God, an intercourse with God; and though the soul cannot abidingly abstract itself from its fellows, it can and ought frequently to recollect itself in a simple sense of God's presence. Such moments of direct preoccupation with God alone bring a deep refreshment and simplification to the soul.

And religion, in its fullest development, essentially requires not only this, our little span of earthly years, but life beyond. Neither an eternal life that is already fully achieved here below, nor an eternal life to be begun and known solely in the beyond, satisfies these requirements. But only an eternal life already begun and truly known in part here, though fully to be achieved and completely to be understood hereafter, corresponds to the deepest longings of man's spirit as touched by the prevenient Spirit, God.

ESSAYS AND ADDRESSES

ABOVE *Early 20th-century pioneer, Friedrich von Hügel, recognized the need for individual, spontaneous spirituality rather than unquestioning faith in established religious dogma.*

SPIRITUAL DRYNESS

If then, spiritual dryness is indeed inevitable in the life of prayer, we will be much helped to bear these desert stretches, by persistent recognition—hence also indeed especially in our times of fervor—of the normality and the necessity of such desolation. We will thus come to treat desolation in religion as we treat the recurrence of the night within every twenty-four hours of our physical existence; or as bodily weariness at the end of any protracted exertion in our psychic life.

When desolation is actually upon us, we will quietly modify, as far as need be, the kind and the amount of our prayer—back, say, from prayer of quiet to ordinary meditation, or to vocal prayer—even to but a few uttered aspirations. And, if the desolation is more acute, we will act somewhat as the Arab caravans behave in the face of a blinding sandstorm in the desert. The men dismount,

throw themselves upon their faces in the sand; and there they remain, patient and uncomplaining, till the storm passes, and until, with their wonted patient endurance, they can and do continue on their way.

There are generally a weakness and an error at work within us at such times, which considerably prolong the trouble, and largely neutralize the growth this very trouble would otherwise bring to our souls. The weakness lies in that we let our imagination and sensitiveness be directly absorbed in our trouble.

We contemplate, and further enlarge, the trouble present in ourselves, instead of firmly and faithfully looking away, either at the great abiding realities of the spiritual world, or if this is momentarily impossible for us, at some other, natural or human, wholesome fact or law. And the error lies in our lurking suspicions that, for such trials to purify us, we must feel them fully in their tryingness—that is, we must face and fathom them directly and completely.

Such a view overlooks the fact that such trials are sent us for the purpose of preoccupying us with our smaller selves; and again, it ignores the experience of God's saints across the ages, that, precisely in proportion as we can get away from direct occupation with our troubles to the thought and love of God, to the presence of him who permits all this, in the same proportion do and will these trials purify our souls.

ESSAYS AND ADDRESSES

RELIGION AND NATURE

If there is one danger for religion—if there is any one plausible, all-but-irresistible trend which, throughout its long rich history, has sapped its force, and prepared the most destructive counter-excesses, it is just that—that allowing the fascinations of grace to deaden or to ignore the beauties and duties of nature. What is nature? I mean, all that, in its degree, is beautiful, true, and good in this many-leveled world of the one stupendously rich God.

SELECTED LETTERS

ABOVE *Illumination from the*
opening word of St. Matthew's Gospel.

Part Two

TESTIMONY

Of all forms of Christian literature,
testimonies transport the reader
most vividly into the period and place
that the writer lived; and so the relationship
between faith and culture is most explicit.

Introduction

When Jesus walked around Galilee preaching to the common people, he urged them to repent—to change the direction of their lives—and the New Testament is filled with the stories of individuals and groups changing direction in response to Christ, or in some cases refusing to change direction.

Luke's account starts at the time of Christ's birth, when the shepherds are drawn by angels into the stable, and are filled with joy. It continues three decades later, when many thousands are overwhelmed by the authority of his teachings, and others are healed in body and spirit by his touch. Then we hear how, after the death of Christ, his Spirit transforms the disciples gathered in Jerusalem, prompting them to form a community in which his teachings are applied to every aspect of daily life. And soon afterward we learn of the most famous conversion, that of Paul on the road to Damascus.

These stories are to be called testimonies, and have formed a crucial element in Christian writing and preaching. They give encouragement and guidance to those who already believe in Christ's message, and they convey to others the experience of becoming and being a disciple. Sometimes their testimonies are told by observers, or by later writers who have collected evidence. The four Gospels, testifying to the life of Christ himself, are of this form, and so are the Acts of the Apostles, telling the story of the first churches.

In the second and third centuries, eyewitness accounts of Christian martyrdom strengthened the hearts of others in danger of a similar fate, and also forced outsiders to investigate the faith that gave such joy to men and women facing death. Thereafter, for over a millennium, the spiritual biographies of saints were by far the most popular form of Christian literature; and the more vivid stories from the biographies were depicted on the walls of cathedrals and parish churches.

In the New Testament, Paul refers obliquely to his conversion and frequently uses his own experiences to illustrate spiritual and theological points. And writers in the early centuries sometimes followed Paul's example, especially when they, like Paul, composed letters to be read aloud at church worship. But with a few sparkling exceptions, full-blooded personal testimonies, in which individuals describe in depth their own spiritual progress, were comparatively rare until the Reformation of the sixteenth century.

Then personal testimony took over from the biography of a saint as the most avidly read form of Christian writing, initially in the Protestant churches, and later in the Roman Catholic Church also. These were often presented as journals, giving the impression of having been written on the very day each experience occurred—although in some cases they were composed several years later in more tranquil circumstances.

There is a third type of testimony, in which the writer projects personal experiences onto fictional characters and situations. Arguably the Book of Revelations, at the end of the New Testament, may be interpreted in this way. But certainly from the second century right up to the present day, there have been clear examples. They enable the particularities of the writer's life to be given universal application.

Of all forms of Christian literature, testimonies transport the reader most vividly into the period and place that the writer lived; and so the relationship between faith and culture is most explicit. Not surprisingly, over the centuries large changes have occurred in the ways in which religious experience is expressed; and in the past few hundred years significant variations in words and phrases have appeared between the denominations.

Sadly, Christians are sometimes tempted to doubt the validity of experiences described in different terminology from their own. Yet if readers can penetrate the linguistic differences,

they cannot help but be struck by the similarities of faith across the centuries and across the continents. In other aspects of culture, such as technology and politics, the gulf between Palestine two thousand years ago and the circumstances of most later Christians has been so wide as to be virtually unbridgeable. But in spiritual matters, the gulf narrows spectacularly, and bridges can be crossed in all directions. That is why testimonies written in any period and place in the Christian world remain so vivid and so immediate.

"Of all forms of Christian literature, testimonies transport the reader most vividly into the period and place that the writer lived; and so the relationship between faith and culture is most explicit."

RIGHT *The Apostles St. Peter and St. Paul (El Greco, 1541–1614, Hermitage, St. Petersburg). Testimonies from contemporaries of Christ and later collectors of evidence form a vital part of Christian teaching.*

Luke

*A*lthough not a direct witness to most of the events
*he described, Luke was the most assiduous collector
of other people's testimonies, recording them in
language that was vivid and compelling. The Christmas story
comes to us largely from Luke's pen; and this has captured the
popular imagination across the world more than any other
religious tale. The coming of the Holy Spirit at Pentecost, which
turned bewildered disciples into a vibrant community, is
conveyed with Luke's gift for apt imagery. And the conversion
of Paul on the road to Damascus, an event that began the
process of turning a Jewish sect into a universal church,
is also recorded by Luke—Paul himself
barely mentions it.*

*For many people, especially in
modern times, Luke's descriptions of
events stretch credibility. Yet Luke was
not primarily concerned with factual
accuracy; he wished to draw his reader
into the spirit of what occurred. We need
not believe that an army of angels
literally filled the night sky and began to
sing, to acknowledge that this is how
those shepherds experienced the joy of
Christ's birth. And spiritual writers
since Luke have frequently likened the
Spirit to heat within their breasts
without thinking that a fire was
actually blazing.*

THE COMING OF THE HOLY SPIRIT

On the day of Pentecost all the believers
came together in one place. Suddenly a
noise from the sky, like a violent wind, filled
the whole house where they were sitting. They
saw flames like tongues of fire, which spread
out and touched every person. They were all
filled with the Holy Spirit, and began to speak
in different languages, as the Spirit gave them
power of expression.

Devout people, from every nation under
heaven, were staying in Jerusalem; and when
they heard the noise, a large crowd of them
gathered. They were excited because each one
heard his own language spoken. In amazement
and wonder they exclaimed: "Surely all these
people speaking are Galileans! How is it that all
of us hear them speaking in our own native
languages? We are from Parthia, Media, and
Elam; from Mesopotamia, Judaea, and
Cappadocia; from Pontus and Asia, from Phrygia
and Pamphylia, from Egypt and the regions of
Libya near Cyrene.
Some of us are visitors
from Rome, both Jews
and Gentiles converted
to Judaism, and some
are from Crete and
Arabia. Yet all of us hear
them speaking in our
own languages about the
great things which God
has done." They were all
astonished and
bewildered, and asked
one another: "What does
this mean?"

Some, however,
mocked the believers.
"These people are
drunk," they said.

ACTS 2

ABOVE *17th-century Russian icon of
St. Luke the Evangelist (Frankfurt, private
collection). St. Luke used compelling
imagery in his testimonies to emphasize
the wonder of the events he was describing.*

THE CONVERSION OF SAUL

Saul still threatened to murder the Lord's disciples. He went to the high priest and asked for letters addressed to the synagogues in Damascus, authorizing him to arrest any followers of the new way whom he found, both men and women, and bring them to Jerusalem. While Saul was on the road to Damascus, approaching the city, suddenly a light from the sky flashed all around him. He fell to the ground and heard a voice saying: "Saul, Saul, why are you persecuting me?"

"Tell me, Lord," he replied, "who are you?"

The voice said: "I am Jesus, whom you are persecuting. Get up and go into the city, and you will be told what you must do."

The men traveling with Saul stood speechless; they heard the voice, but could see no one. Saul rose from the ground, but when he opened his eyes he could see nothing; so they had to lead him to Damascus by the hand. He was blind for three days, and did not eat or drink.

ACTS 9

ABOVE *The Holy Family (El Greco, 1560, Museum of Santa Cruz, Toledo). The story of the Nativity may not have played such a large part in the Christian calendar without the writings of St. Luke.*

THE BIRTH OF CHRIST

At this time Caesar Augustus ordered that a census be made of the whole Roman Empire. This was the first census, and took place when Quirinius was governor of Syria. Everyone went to his hometown to be registered.

Joseph set out from the town of Nazareth in Galilee to Bethlehem in Judaea, the birthplace of David, since he was a descendant of David, in order to register with Mary, who was promised in marriage to him. Mary was pregnant, and while they were in Bethlehem, the time came for her to have her baby. She gave birth to a son, her firstborn. She wrapped him in swaddling clothes, and laid him in a manger, because there was no room for them at the inn.

In the countryside near to Bethlehem there were shepherds out in the fields, keeping watch through the night over their flock. An angel of the Lord appeared to them, and the glory of the Lord shone around them. They were terrified, but the angel said: "Do not be afraid. I come to you with good news, which will bring great joy to all the people. Today in the town of David your savior has been born, Christ the Lord. This is a sign for you: you will find a baby wrapped in swaddling clothes, lying in a manger."

Suddenly with the angel a great company of heaven's angels appeared, singing praise to God: "Glory to God in the highest heaven, and on earth peace to all in whom he delights."

When the angels had left them and returned to heaven, the shepherds said to one another: "Let us go to Bethlehem, and see this event which the Lord has made known to us."

They hurried off and found Mary and Joseph, and the baby lying in a manger. When they saw the child, they related what they had been told about him; and all who heard it were astonished at what the shepherds said. Mary treasured all these things and pondered them in her heart. The shepherds went back, singing praises to God for all they had heard and seen, just as the angel had told them.

LUKE 2

Ignatius of Antioch

*T*he letters of Ignatius, bishop of Antioch at the start of the second century, were written in the course of his journey to Rome, under armed guard, where he expected to be thrown to the wild beasts in the amphitheater. He referred frequently to his own impending martyrdom, begging that his fellow Christians take no steps to prevent it. And through his words the psychology of the martyr—the peculiar mixture of eagerness and fear—is expressed with chilling clarity. In offering guidance for the future, he insisted on the authority of the local bishop, to whom the faithful should submit in all moral and spiritual matters, even asking his approval for the choice of a spouse.

Ignatius was condemned for his faith in his own city, probably in 108, and then put in chains. The purpose of taking him to Rome was probably to create greater publicity. But no record exists of his actual death; and some scholars have suggested that he was spared, or died before arrival.

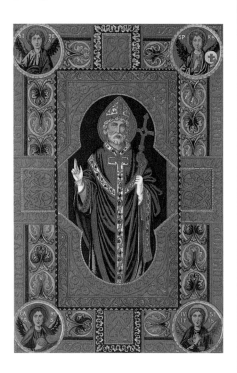

ABOVE *Condemned to death for his faith, St. Ignatius of Antioch wrote: "Many people fail to see how tenaciously evil clings to the soul; but I perceive clearly that I am fighting a formidable enemy."*

DESIRE FOR MARTYRDOM

I am writing to all the churches, to assure them that I truly wish to die for God. So do not put any obstacles in my way; do not try to be kind to me. I beg you to let me be a meal for the animals, because they can be my path to God. I am God's wheat; and I shall be ground into fine flour by the lions' teeth, to make the purest bread for Christ.

Better still, let these animals be my tomb; let them consume every scrap of my flesh, so I cause not trouble to anyone after I have died. When no trace of my body remains visible, then I shall surely be a disciple of Jesus Christ. So pray to him for me, that the animals may make me a sacrifice for God. But I am not issuing orders to you, as if I were Peter or Paul. They were apostles, while I am a condemned criminal. They were free men, while I am still a slave—though if I suffer, Jesus Christ will set me free, and I shall rise with him to share his liberty. The chains that now bind me are teaching me to abandon all earthly desires.

The soldiers who accompany me on my journey from Syria to Rome are like wild animals. On land and on sea, by night and by day, I feel as though I am chained to ten savage leopards, who respond to my kindness with insolence. But their ill-treatment helps me to become a better disciple—although I know this will not ensure my salvation. How I look forward to the real lions which are waiting for me! I merely pray that they may be swift in their work. I will invite them to come to me.

They have refused to touch some more wretches; but I shall urge them to devour me with all speed. And if they are still reluctant, I shall force them to eat me. Please forgive me for saying these things, but I know what is best for myself. This is the first stage of my discipleship. Let no power, seen or unseen, grudge me this path to Jesus Christ.

THE EPISTLE TO THE ROMANS, CHAPTERS 4 AND 5

THE WEAPON OF HUMILITY

God has filled my head with many insights. But I do not want pride to bring me down, so I constantly remind myself of my own limitations. I should be feeling apprehension; and I should be indifferent to those who seek to flatter me. The words of flatterers are like whips to me; although I yearn for martyrdom, I am very uncertain of whether I am worthy of it. Many people fail to see how tenaciously evil clings to the soul; but I perceive clearly that I am fighting a formidable enemy. So I greatly need the virtue of humility, which is the only weapon capable of defeating the prince of this world.

No doubt I could write to you on elevated spiritual matters. But I do not think this would help you, because you are spiritual infants. You would not be able to digest my words; they would stick in your throat, and I would have to ask your forgiveness. I am bound in chains for my faith. I am able to understand many heavenly secrets. I am familiar with the hierarchies of angels and other heavenly powers. I am an expert in spiritual things, both seen and unseen. Yet despite all this, I do not count myself yet a true disciple. We need to recognize our shortcomings, if we are not to fall short of God.

THE EPISTLE TO THE TRALLIANS, CHAPTERS 4 AND 5

ABOVE *An extract from the letters of St. Ignatius of Antioch, written during his imprisonment by the Romans.*

LIFE OR DEATH

All things must come to an end. We face two alternatives, life and death; and each of us will go in one direction or the other. It is as if there are two different currencies in circulation, God's and the world's, each with its own distinctive features. Unbelievers carry the stamp of the world; while believers, who follow the law of love, bear the stamp of God the Father, through Jesus Christ. Unless we are ready and willing to share in his death, we cannot share his life.

I have been able to meet you all, discerning the quality of faith in each one of you. I urge you to be united in mind and spirit in all you do. Let the bishop preside over your affairs, representing God, with clergy acting as a council of apostles; and let my special friends, the deacons, be entrusted with their particular ministry in the name of Jesus Christ, who was with the Father through all eternity, and in these final days has been revealed. Everyone should try to conform to God's will. Show the utmost consideration for one another. Never let your emotions mar your attitude to a neighbor; simply love one another with the loyal spirit of Jesus Christ. Do not allow anything to cause divisions among you. Be obedient to your bishops and leaders; and let them be an example to others.

THE EPISTLE TO THE MAGNESIANS, CHAPTERS 5 AND 6

SUBMISSION TO AUTHORITY

Your behavior and customs you must conform closely to the mind of the bishop. Indeed your clergy, whom you justly respect and who are a credit to God, are attuned to their bishop like the strings of a harp. Their thoughts and their emotions are in perfect harmony, so that together they are a living hymn of praise to Jesus Christ. I beg you to come and join this choir, every one of you. May you become a symphony of souls. Together take your note from God, and sing aloud to the Father with one voice through Jesus Christ. The Father will hear you, and know by your good works that you are members of His Son's body.

THE EPISTLE TO THE EPHESIANS, 2,3, AND 4

The Shepherd of Hermas

Many early Christian teachers believed that it was possible for disciples to lead perfect and sinless lives; and some held that a sin committed by a baptized Christian could not be forgiven. The author of The Shepherd of Hermas wanted to uphold the spiritual and moral ideals of the gospel, but recognized that Christians remain prey to sinful impulses. The book describes a series of visions, in the first of which he encounters a beautiful woman called Rhoda, whom he desires. This desire is taken to represent not only sexual sin, but all sin; and it is used to indicate the root of sin that lies in our feelings and emotions. The most significant vision is of a beautiful man dressed as a shepherd, who gives a series of commandments. These are in sharp contrast to the ten commandments given to Moses: whereas the commandments to Moses focus primarily on outward actions, the shepherd's commandments concern the psychology of sin and righteousness.

The author is entirely unknown. The book appeared in some early canons of scripture, but was eventually dropped because there was no evidence of apostolic connections. It was probably written over a period of years, after about 125.

THE BEAUTIFUL WOMAN

I saw a woman called Rhoda bathing in the River Tiber in Rome. I gave her my hand and helped her out of the river. When I saw how lovely she was, I thought, "I would be delighted to have a wife of such beauty and character." That was my only thought; I had no other, not one.

Some time later, when walking to Cumae, enjoying the glory, splendor, and strength of God's creation, I began to feel sleepy. I lay down and fell into a deep slumber. A spirit seized me, and took me through a region without paths, where the ground was rocky. I came to a stream, and waded across. The ground was level on the other side. I knelt down, and began to pray and confess my sins. While I prayed, Heaven opened, and I saw the woman whom I had desired. She greeted me, calling out to me.

I looked at her, and asked: "What are you doing here?"

She answered: "I was taken up to Heaven to accuse you of sin before the Lord."

"Are you accusing me now?" I asked.

"No," she said, "but listen to what I am going to say to you. God who dwells in Heaven, who created out of nothing all that exists, who causes all things to increase and multiply, and who brought into being his holy Church—God is angry with you because you sinned against me."

I said: "Did I sin against you? In what place? When did I speak an evil word to you? Did I not respect you as a sister? Why do you charge me falsely with wickedness and impurity?"

She laughed, and replied: "The desire of wickedness rose up in your heart. Do you not think that an evil desire is itself an evil deed? Yes, and evil desire is a sin, a great sin. Righteous people have righteous intentions; so Heaven respects them and assists them in all their actions. But those who have evil intentions in their hearts, who desire what they do not possess, who lust after wealth and earthly pleasures, and who are indifferent to all future blessings—these people are slaves, and bring death upon themselves. They may try to repent; but their position is hopeless, because they have abandoned their real selves, the inner source of life itself. But if you pray to God, he will heal you."

THE SHEPHERD OF HERMAS, VISION I

THE BEAUTIFUL MAN

While I was sitting on my bed at home and praying, a man entered my room. He was quite beautiful. He was dressed like a shepherd, his body covered with white goatskin, a bag on his shoulders and a staff in his hand. He greeted me, and I greeted him in return.

He immediately sat down beside me and said: "I have been sent by the most holy angel to live with you for the rest of your life."

I thought he had come to tempt me, and I asked: "Who are you? Why have I been handed over to you?"

He said: "Do you not recognize me?"

"No," I replied.

"You have been handed to me, so that I can be your shepherd." While he was still speaking, his appearance changed, and I recognized him; I knew that I had been truly handed over to him. I was seized with fear; and I felt ashamed at the way I had spoken to him.

"Do not be afraid," he said; "but be strong in the commandments I am about to give you. I have been sent to remind you of things you already know, to enable you to remember what really matters. Write down my commandments and parables; write down whatever I show you.... If you have my commandments and keep them, doing so with a pure heart, you shall receive from the Lord all he has promised. But if you hear them and do not repent, continuing to add to your sins, you will be punished by the Lord."

FIRST COMMANDMENT

Believe that there is one God, who made all things out of nothing, who perfects all things, who contains all things, and who is himself uncontained. Fear him, and in your fear control your wicked passions.

SECOND COMMANDMENT

Be simple and innocent. Be like a child who does not know that wickedness destroys people's lives. Speak evil of no one, and do not listen to those who speak evil of others. By listening to the evil of others, you share in their sin.... Do good to others with a simple heart; give to those who seek help, without casting doubt on their sincerity. Remember that all you give comes from God; and the recipients will have to render an account to God for what they received.

THIRD COMMANDMENT

Love truth, and let only truth come from your mouth. The soul which God has put within your flesh, must always be honest. In this way the Lord who lives in you will be glorified, for the Lord always speaks the truth and never lies. Those who lie show contempt for the Lord and defraud him, not returning to him the truth which they received from him.

FOURTH COMMANDMENT

Be pure in heart. Do not allow yourself to think about another man's wife. Do not think about fornication or any other kind of immorality. Even thinking about sin, dwelling in its pleasures, is sinful. But if your thoughts are confined to your wife, you will not sin.

FIFTH COMMANDMENT

Be both courageous and calm, and you shall have power over evil, always doing what is righteous. If you are courageous, you will be able to respond fully to the guidance of the Holy Spirit who dwells within you. The Holy Spirit will not be constrained by evil, but will be fully active, and you will feel joyful, happy, and healthy, serving God with a glad heart. But if you become bad tempered, then the Holy Spirit, who is delicate, becomes oppressed, and unhappy within you, and wants to leave.

SIXTH COMMANDMENT

Be straightforward in all you do. Do not try to be devious. Walk in a straight path, never take a crooked path. The crooked path is rough, with many stumbling blocks, and it is steep and thorny. So those who walk in it suffer great harm. The straight path is smooth, without stumbling blocks, and has no thorns.

THE SHEPHERD OF HERMAS, VISION 5

Polycarp of Smyrna

If Eusebius had not compiled his History of The Church, almost all the records of the first three centuries would have been lost. He toured libraries and sacristies throughout the Christian world, copying down accounts of terrible persecutions and martyrs' deaths, doctrinal and personal disputes that split congregations, and acts of charity performed by ordinary church members.

One of the earliest and most inspiring documents he preserved is the description of the trial and death of Polycarp, bishop of Smyrna in the middle of the second century. Indeed, it is the most ancient surviving account of a Christian martyrdom outside the New Testament. Polycarp was already a very old man at the time of his arrest; and when he refused to renounce his faith, he was sentenced to death by burning.

RIGHT *Christian Martyrs (Byzantine manuscript, Biblioteca Nazionale, Turin). Polycarp of Smyrna met a similar fate: " ...Thus he appeared not like burning flesh, but like gold or silver being refined in a furnace."*

THE MARTYRDOM OF POLYCARP

When Polycarp, the wonderful old Bishop of Smyrna, first heard news of persecutions he was quite unperturbed, remaining calm and relaxed. He wanted to stay in the city, but his friends begged and pleaded with him to escape.

Eventually he agreed to go as far as a small farm a short distance away. In the company of a few friends, he devoted himself night and day to constant prayer to the Lord, asking and imploring God, as he had always done, to grant peace to the churches throughout the world. Those hunting him were relentless in their pursuit. And in their love and devotion for him, his friends compelled him to move to another farm. But he was soon discovered. Two of his servants were found; and under torture they revealed his whereabouts.

Late in the evening the soldiers arrived; Polycarp was upstairs in bed. He might easily have moved to another house, but he had refused, saying: "May God's will be done." When Polycarp heard the soldiers arrive he came downstairs, and greeted them in the most cheerful and kindly manner. Never having seen him before, they were astonished to be confronted with a man of such advanced years and such quiet, serene confidence. Why, the soldiers wondered, were the authorities so eager to arrest an old man like this?

Polycarp ordered that a table be laid for them, and invited them to eat as much as they wished, asking them in return to be allowed to pray for a further hour without interruption. The soldiers agreed; and to the amazement of everyone present, Polycarp stood up and began to pray, shining with divine grace as he did so.... When the hour was over, the soldiers set Polycarp on an ass, and led him into the city.

It was Passover Saturday. He was met by Herod, the chief of police, and his father Nicetes, and he was transferred into their carriage. They sat beside him, and tried to persuade him to abandon his faith.

"What harm," they asked, "is there in making a sacrifice to the emperor? Then you would be safe."

At first Polycarp remained silent. But when they persisted, he replied: "I have no intention of doing what you suggest."

They now began to threaten him; and when this failed, they threw him out of the carriage. He scraped his shin as he fell; but without looking around, as if nothing had happened, he set off cheerfully and swiftly to the stadium.

When he arrived at the stadium, the roar was so loud that many could not hear what was going on. As he entered into the arena, a voice from heaven spoke to him: "Be strong, Polycarp, and play the man."

No one saw the speaker, but many heard the voice. As his presence was announced, a tremendous roar went up. People gasped, exclaiming: "Polycarp has been arrested!"

Eventually, when he stepped forward, the proconsul asked if he really was Polycarp.

"Yes," Polycarp replied.

The proconsul urged him to deny the charge. "Respect your years," the proconsul said, and added the appeals regularly made on these occasions: "Swear by the emperor. Change your attitude, and cast away your godless religion."

Polycarp was unmoved. He looked around the crowd, waved his hand toward them, looked up to heaven, and cried out: "Cast away their godless religion!"

The proconsul pressed him further: "Deny Christ, and I will set you free."

"For eighty-six years," Polycarp replied, "I have been Christ's servant, and he has never done me wrong. How can I turn against the king who saved me?"

The proconsul asked him again to swear by the emperor.

"If you imagine," Polycarp retorted, "that I will swear by the emperor, as you put it, pretending not to know who I am, I will tell you plainly: I am a Christian. If you wish to study Christian teaching, choose a day and you will hear it."

"I have wild animals," said the proconsul; "if you do not change your attitude, I will throw you to them."

"Call your wild animals," replied the old man; "I cannot change my attitude, if it means changing from better to worse. But it is a splendid thing to change from cruelty to justice."

"If you make light of the wild animals," exclaimed the proconsul, "I will have you destroyed by fire—unless you change your attitude."

"The fire which you threaten," replied Polycarp, "burns for a time, and then goes out. There is a fire which you know nothing about. It is the fire of future judgment and of eternal punishment, the fire reserved for the ungodly. Why do you hesitate? Do what you want."

Logs and fagots were now collected from workshops and public baths. When the pyre was ready, Polycarp took off all his outer garments and loosened his belt. He tried to remove his shoes, but he was not accustomed to this, as each of the faithful strove all the time to be first to touch him. Indeed even before his hair had turned gray, his manifest virtue had inspired people to honor him. The wood had been placed around him with a stake at his back. He showed no fear. They were about to nail him to the stake, but he begged them to leave him free: "He who enables me to endure the fire, will enable me to remain on the pyre without shrinking."

So they bound him to the stake without nailing him, tying his hands behind his back. He was like a noble ram from a great flock being presented as a burnt offering to please almighty God....

Polycarp said a final prayer. When he had finished, the men in charge lit the fire, and a great flame shot up. Then we witnessed a wonderful sight—we who were privileged to be present, and have been spared to tell others. The fire took the shape of a vaulted room, or a ship's sail filled with wind, and it surrounded the martyr's body. Thus he appeared not like burning flesh, but like gold or silver being refined in a furnace. We became aware of a marvelous fragrance, like that of frankincense or some other costly spice.

Finally, when people realized that the body would not be consumed by the fire, one of the soldiers came forward, and ran his sword through Polycarp.

The History of the Church, 15.9–15.40

Anthony of Egypt

*I*n the fourth and fifth centuries, as the Christian church grew in wealth and power, large numbers of both men and women retreated into the depths of Egypt and Syria, to devote themselves without distraction to God. Some lived alone; while others formed loose-knit communities usually centered on a monk renowned for his spiritual wisdom.

The person traditionally credited with starting this exodus was a wealthy young man called Anthony, born in Upper Egypt in about 251. And his Life, written in the middle of the following century by the great bishop of Alexandria, Athanasius, played a major part in encouraging others to follow Anthony's example. After hearing the call, Anthony initially lived in a tomb near his own home. Then at the age of thirty-five he went into the heart of the desert, where he lived in a disused fortress. After another twenty years entirely alone, his admirers eventually compelled him to form a community, as others could benefit from his insights. Anthony, like later monks, was seen as conducting a battle against the devil, not only on his own behalf, but for the sake of all humanity.

HEARING THE CALL

Anthony was aged about eighteen or twenty when his parents died; and he found himself responsible both for the home and for his young sister. Six months later, as he was on his way to church, he reflected on how the apostles gave up everything to follow the Savior; and how the members of the first church sold their possessions, and laid the proceeds at the feet of the apostles to distribute to those in need. Anthony thought about the wonderful reward in heaven for those who displayed such faith.

He was still pondering these things when he entered church. As he walked through the door the gospel was being read, and he heard the Lord saying to the rich young man: "If you wish to be perfect, go and sell what you possess and give it to the poor, and you will have treasure in heaven."

He knew God had planned that he should reflect on the apostles, and then hear the passage. Immediately Anthony left the church and gave to the people of the town the wealth he had inherited, which was three hundred acres of fertile and beautiful land. He then sold all that was portable, and gave the money to the poor, keeping a little for his sister.

THE LIFE OF ANTHONY,
CHAPTER 2

RIGHT *Anthony of Egypt lived a hermit's life in the desert for many years, before his followers persuaded him to form a community, centered around his great spiritual insight.*

FIGHTING THE DEVIL

Guarding himself against the devil, Anthony went to the tombs that were some distance from the village. He asked one of his friends to bring him bread from time to time. Anthony went into one of the tombs, and the friend closed the door behind him.

The devil knew that Anthony might attract many others with his self-discipline, and draw them out with him into the desert. So with an army of demons the devil entered the tomb, and hit him with such force that he fell to the ground, speechless with agony. Anthony later said that the pain was so severe that it could not have been inflicted by humans. But God never abandons those who put their trust in him. The next day Anthony's friend came bringing bread, and saw him sprawled out, as if dead; and he carried him back to the church in the village, laying him on the floor. Relatives and others in the village gathered to look at him.

Around midnight Anthony came to his senses. He saw everyone asleep, with only his friend keeping watch. He beckoned to his friend, and

asked him to carry him back to the tomb, waking no one. The friend did as Anthony asked, and closed the door of the tomb behind him. Again Anthony was alone inside. He was still too weak to stand up, so he prayed lying down. Then he yelled out: "Here I am—Anthony! I do not flee from your attacks. Even if you attack again and again, I shall not be separated from the love of Christ."

THE LIFE OF ANTHONY, CHAPTERS 8 AND 9

SHINING WITH HOLINESS

Anthony spent almost twenty years in the fortress, pursuing the ascetic life alone. A growing number of people wanted to emulate his asceticism; and eventually they tore down the barricade which Anthony had put across the fortress door.

Anthony emerged, as if from a shrine, radiating the mysterious love of God. This was the first time since he had entered the fortress that anyone had seen him. The people were astonished that his body looked so healthy: he was neither fat from lack of exercise, nor thin from fasting and fighting demons, but just as they had known him prior to his withdrawal. His soul was utterly pure: not tense with anxiety, nor relaxed with pleasure, nor overwhelmed by elation or depression. And when he saw the crowd that had gathered to welcome him, he was neither annoyed nor excited, but calm and tranquil. He was a person in total harmony with his own nature.

Through Anthony the Lord healed many in the crowd who had bodily illnesses, and he drove demons out of those who were mentally disturbed. The Lord also gave Anthony the grace of speech, so he consoled those who mourned, and reconciled those who were in conflict. He urged everyone to prize the love of Christ above all things.

THE LIFE OF ANTHONY, CHAPTER 14

Maria the Harlot

From the earliest days of the desert monks, they occasionally had children living with them. In some cases the child had felt called to the ascetic life, and had run away from home. In other cases the child was an orphan, and the hermit a relative.

The most famous instance was that of Abraham, a much revered spiritual master, and his orphaned niece Maria. The story of her seduction by another monk, her subsequent life in a brothel, and Abraham's dramatic rescue, was written down by a disciple of Abraham called Ephrem, probably a Syrian. It was subsequently translated into numerous other languages, and retold by other writers. Different writers drew different morals. To Ephrem it signified the beauty and power of holiness, and the possibility of even the worst sinner repenting. To others, however, it showed the folly of trying to deny all bodily needs, as the young Maria tried to do—and hence the virtue of moderation.

MARIA'S TALE

Abraham the hermit had a natural brother whose wife had died. Then the brother himself died, leaving a daughter called Maria, aged seven. Friends brought the girl to her uncle. Abraham built a room on the outside wall of his hermitage for her. There was a window

between two cells; and through it he taught her the Psalter and the rest of the Scriptures. She kept vigil with him, and joined in singing praise to the Lord; she imitated him in all his ascetic practices. Soon she became very proficient at these practices, and virtue grew in her soul. The holy man prayed for her constantly, that she should not become entangled with the affairs of the locals.... She spent twenty years with him in this way, living like an unspotted lamb or a pure white dove.

A certain monk used to come and visit Abraham, claiming to seek his spiritual guidance. This man could not see Maria because the external window of her cell was too high. But he spoke to her, and was filled with lust for her.

ABOVE AND LEFT *The Hermit and the sleeping Maria (1626–28, Rubens, Kunsthistorisches Museum, Vienna). "The old man prayed for her constantly, that she should not become entangled with the affairs of the locals."*

Gradually over the course of a year his words softened her heart. One day he climbed up to her window, and she allowed him to climb into her cell. Immediately he took off her clothes and had intercourse with her. Afterward she was utterly disgusted with herself. When she had put on her clothes, she beat her face with her hands, appalled at the magnitude of her sin. Yet passionate lust still surged in her body. She decided she had no choice but to leave her cell. She ran away to a city, and began to work as a prostitute in a brothel.

Abraham was told in a dream what had happened. He prayed constantly, day and night, to the Lord for her. After two years he asked a friend to go and look for her. The man found her; and, his heart filled with pity, he told Abraham what he had seen. At once Abraham asked his friend to obtain for him a horse and a soldier's uniform, so that he could go and see Maria without being recognized. In addition to the uniform Abraham put on a large hat to hide his face. He took a pound's weight of coins, climbed onto the horse, and rode through the countryside to the city.

He went into the brothel, and looked around for Maria. He was anxious not to reveal his purpose, so he said to the brothel-keeper, with a smile on his face: "My friend, I hear you have a very beautiful girl here; if I may, I would like to have her."

The brothel-keeper could see that he was very old; and in order to stir his lust she replied: "As you say, I have a girl whose beauty is quite exceptional, excelling everything that nature can create."

The old man asked the name of this girl, and the brothel-keeper assured him that she was called Maria.

Smiling with joy, Abraham said: "I beg you to take me to her at once, so that I can enjoy her— I have heard countless people praise this girl."

The brothel-keeper summoned Maria. When her uncle saw her in the garb of a prostitute he was overcome with grief, and sadness almost drove the smile from his face. By a great effort of will he held back the tears, fearful that the brothel-keeper would guess his motive and force him to leave. When they had sat together and drunk a little, the astonishing man began to fondle her. He even got up, put his arms around her, and kissed her neck. When his lips touched her skin, Maria smelled his sweet aroma of asceticism coming from his body; and she remembered the days when she too had lived as an ascetic. As if a spear had pierced her heart she gave a loud cry; and realizing her own wretched condition, she burst into tears.

Abraham and Maria had a meal together. Then Maria invited Abraham into her chamber, in order to lie on her bed.

Abraham agreed, saying: "Let us go in." He saw the bed , and sat on it, pretending to be eager.

Maria said to him: "Let me unfasten your trousers."

Abraham replied: "First close the door carefully, and lock it."

The girl wanted to undress him first, but he would not let her. When she had locked the door, the old man said: "Mistress Maria, come close to me." She came to him, he held her firmly with one hand, as if he were about to kiss her. Then with the other hand he snatched the hat off his head.

In a voice breaking with tears, he cried: "Do you not know me, Maria my child? Am I not the one who took care of you?" Maria became like a stone in his arms, overcome by both shame and fear.

As he wept, Abraham pleaded with her to speak to him: "Tell me that you will come home with me, my child. Throw your sin onto my shoulders, my daughter, and on the day of judgment I will give an account of it to the Lord; I am responsible for what has happened."

When morning came, Abraham said to her: "Get up, my daughter, and let us go home." She asked him what she should do with the gold she had accumulated, and with her clothes.

Abraham replied: "Leave them here, Maria, because they are tainted with evil." So they got up and went out. He placed her on the horse, and walked in front. He felt like the shepherd who had found a lost sheep, and was carrying it home on his shoulders. When they arrived, they swapped cells: he put her into the inner cell, while he lived in the outer cell. From that moment she wore a hair shirt next to her skin.

Augustine of Hippo

Augustine was the first great writer to explore in depth the process of his own conversion. In his Confessions he described with transparent honesty the intellectual, spiritual, and sexual confusions of his early life and showed how God was guiding him through these muddles. The book is a poignant mixture of anguished conversations with God, accounts of actual events, and relentless self-questioning. The record of the moment of conversion has a curiously anti-climatic quality, which gives it even greater power.

Born in North Africa in 354, his father was pagan and his mother Christian. His intellectual brilliance won him the post of professor of rhetoric in Milan. He had a mistress who bore him a son; but this liaison deeply disturbed his conscience. He embraced Christianity as the only means of assuaging guilt and self-loathing. After his conversion Augustine returned to North Africa, where he founded a monastery. In 396 he became bishop of the town of Hippo.

LEFT *Augustine of Hippo recorded in detail his own conversion to Christianity: "In an instant, as I reached the end of the sentence, the light of faith shone into my heart and all the darkness of doubt was dispelled."*

THE RESTLESS HEART

To praise you, Lord, is the deepest desire of a human being. You stir people to take pleasures in praising you because you have made us for yourself. Our heart is restless, until it rests in you.

Who will enable me to find rest in you? Who can help me to receive you into my heart, intoxicating it, so that I can forget all the wrongs I have done, and embrace you, my only source of goodness? What are you to me? Help me to find the right words to express myself to you. What am I to you, that you command me to love you; and that, if I fail to love you, you are angry with me and threaten me with terrible sufferings? If I do not love you, what harm does that do? What a wretch I am! In your mercy, Lord God, tell me what you are to me? Say to my soul that you are my salvation. Speak to me, that I may hear. The ears of my heart are before you, Lord. Open them, and say to my soul that you are my salvation. After you have spoken I shall run to you, and cling to you.

Do not hide your face from me. Let me die, if that is the only way I may see you. The house of my soul is too small for you to come in. Enlarge it, so you may enter.

CONFESSIONS, BOOK 1

THE ENLIGHTENED HEART

I probed the hidden depths of my soul, and squeezed out its miserable secrets. And when I could see those secrets clearly, a great storm broke within me, bringing a great deluge of tears. I rose and left Alypius, so that in solitude I could weep freely.... I flung myself down beneath a fig tree, and gave way to the grief which now overwhelmed me. My tears were like a sacrifice offered to God. I spoke openly to God, crying out: "Lord, will you never be content? Must I always taste your anger? Or will you forgive the sins of my past?"

I felt I was the prisoner of my sins, and in my misery I kept exclaiming: "How long must I wait? Why not now? Why not blot out my ugly sins at once?"

I was asking these questions, my heart filled with bitter sorrow, when I heard the lilting voice of a child in a nearby house. Whether the voice belonged to a boy or a girl I cannot say; but again and again it seemed to say: "Take it and read, take it and read."

I looked up, wondering if these were chanted in some game; but I could not remember hearing them before. I stemmed the flow of tears and stood up, telling myself that this could only be a divine command to open the book of scripture, and read the first passage on which my eyes should fall....

I had left the book containing Paul's Epistles where Alypius was sitting. I hurried back there, seized the book, and opened it. In silence I read the passage: "Not in reveling and drunkenness, not in lust and wantonness, not in quarrels and rivalries. Instead, arm yourselves with the Lord Jesus Christ; think no more about the flesh and the appetites of the flesh." I had neither need nor wish to read more. In an instant, as I reached the end of the sentence, the light of faith shone into my heart, and all the darkness of doubt was dispelled.

CONFESSIONS, BOOK 8

LOVING GOD

What do I love when I love God? Not material or temporal beauty; not some brilliant light that brightens my eyes; not a sweet song captivating my ears; not the fragrance of flowers, perfume, and spices; not henna or honey; not a body that one longs to embrace. It is not these that I love when I love God.

And yet when I love him, I love a certain kind of beauty, a voice, a smell, an embrace. But they come not from outside; they are within myself. My soul is bathed in a light which is not binded by space; it listens to a sound that never dies away; it breathes a fragrance that is not carried away on the wind; it tastes food that is not consumed by eating; it enjoys an embrace from which it is never severed by the fulfillment of desire. This is what I love when I love God.

CONFESSIONS, BOOK 10

RIGHT *St. Augustine preaching to his disciples (Biblioteca Medicea-Laurenziana, Florence). After converting to Christianity, Augustine left Milan and founded a monastery in North Africa.*

I was asking these questions, my heart filled with bitter sorrow, when I heard the lilting voice of a child in a nearby house. Whether the voice belonged to a boy or a girl I cannot say; but again and again it seemed to say: "Take it and read, take it and read."

I looked up, wondering if these were chanted in some game; but I could not remember hearing them before. I stemmed the flow of tears and stood up, telling myself that this could only be a divine command to open the book of scripture, and read the first passage on which my eyes should fall....

Patrick

S.COLVMBA   S.PATRICIVS   S.BRIGIDA

Between his landing on the northeast coast of Ireland around 435, and his death a quarter of a century later, Patrick took the gospel to every corner of Ireland, establishing churches and ordaining priests. His method was to win over a local chief, and through him convert the people; then he would persuade the chief to let one of his sons join his mission, and to provide gifts to take to the next chief. But near the end of his life some of the priests he had ordained turned against him, accusing him of keeping gifts for his own benefit. This charge induced him to write his Confession, in which he defended himself by recounting the story of his life. It is a document of great excitement and insight.

Patrick grew up in a Christian family on the west coast of Britain, and was kidnapped by pirates and taken as a slave to Ireland. While tending sheep on a mountain he had a series of intense religious experiences. He eventually escaped and returned home. But he heard a voice calling him back to Ireland. He probably received training in Gaul, before embarking on his mission.

ABOVE *Persistent spiritual voices finally compelled St. Patrick to return to Ireland and spread the word of Christ. "But I did not give way to the Spirit's promptings until I was utterly exhausted."*

A SLAVE IN IRELAND

I, Patrick, a sinner, am the most unlearned, and the lowest of all the faithful, utterly despised by many. My father was Calpornius, a deacon, and my grandfather Ptitus, a priest. I was brought up near the town of Bannaven Tiburnnia. At the age of sixteen, before I knew God, I was taken captive and shipped to Ireland, along with thousands of others.

When I arrived in Ireland I was sent to tend sheep. I used to pray many times each day; and, as I prayed, I felt God's love fill my heart and strengthen my faith. Soon I was saying up to a hundred prayers each day, and almost as many at night. I had to stay all night in the forests and on the mountains, looking after the sheep, and I would wake to pray before dawn in all weathers, snow, frost, and rain; I felt no fear, nor did I feel sleepy, because the Spirit was so fervent within me.

It was there one night, while I was asleep, that I heard a voice speaking to me: "You do well to fast and pray, for soon you shall be returning to your home country."

And shortly afterward I heard another voice: "See, your ship is ready." The ship was not near, but was two hundred miles away in a place where I knew nobody and had never visited. I immediately fled from the man who had enslaved me for six years, and in the strength of God traveled to the coast. During the whole journey I met no dangers whatever.

FAR RIGHT *Patrick's faith was strengthened during his captivity in Ireland: "I and my companions have at times been arrested and put in irons, and our captors have been eager to kill us; yet the Lord has always set us free."*

THE CALL OF IRELAND

At last I reached my home, and spent the next few years with my family. They begged that now, after suffering so many hardships, I should never leave them again. But one night in a dream I saw a man coming from Ireland, whose name was Victoricus, carrying countless letters. He gave one of them to me, and I read the heading: "The Voice of the Irish."

And as I looked at these words, I heard a voice coming from the Forest of Foclut in the far west of Ireland, calling me: "We implore you, young man, to return and walk among us."

My heart seemed to be breaking and I could read no more.

During another night I heard a voice—I do not know whether it was within me or beside me, God only knows—whose words I could not understand, except the final sentence:

"He who lay down his life for you, it is he that speaks within you."

And I awoke full of joy. And sometime later I saw him praying within me: I was, as it were, inside my own body and I could hear his voice. He was praying most powerfully. I was dumbfounded, wondering who it could be praying within me; but at the end of the prayer he said that he was the Spirit.

And then I awoke, remembering the apostle's words: "The Spirit helps us in our weakness; for we do not know how to pray as we ought, but the Spirit himself intercedes for us with sighs too deep for words."

Finally I knew I must go to Ireland. But I did not give way to the Spirit's promptings until I was utterly exhausted. The Lord thus broke down my stubbornness, and molded me according to his will, making me fit to do work which once had been far beyond me. I could now dedicate myself to the salvation of others, whereas once I had been indifferent even to my own salvation.

I have baptized many thousands of people, but never asked as much as a halfpenny in return. Despite being such an unexceptional person myself, I have trained and ordained priests throughout the country; but I have never asked even the price of a shoe as reward. Instead, I have spent whatever money I possessed for the benefit of the common people.

I have traveled in the remotest regions of the country, where no Christian has ever been before, and there I have baptized and confirmed people, and ordained priests; and I have done so with a joyful heart and tireless spirit. I have given presents to kings and persuaded them to release slaves; and I have inspired the sons of kings to travel with me on my missions. I and my companions have at times been arrested and put in irons, and our captors have been eager to kill us; yet the Lord has always set us free.

But I now see that in this present world I am exalted above my true merit, and I am more privileged than I deserve. I am more suited to poverty and adversity than to riches and luxury— for the Lord Christ was poor for our sakes. Yet in truth I have no wealth of my own, and every day I expect to be killed, betrayed, or reduced to slavery. I am frightened of none of these things, because my heart is set on the riches of heaven.

THE CONFESSION

Kevin

A recurring theme of Celtic literature is the close relationship that forms between holy people and the animals and birds among whom they live. A typical pattern was for a man or woman to go and live as a hermit in some remote spot. As the hermit grew closer to God, animals and birds offered their services, and the hermit ministered to them. Eventually the hermit may even have formed a community of animals and birds, each performing a different role.

These stories were handed down, and doubtless embellished through the generations, and finally written down. The Irish hermit Kevin, who lived in a valley near the east coast, is the hero of several of the most enchanting tales. They were collected and committed to paper in roughly the tenth century, about three hundred years after Kevin's death—reputedly in 618 at the age of one hundred and twenty.

RIGHT *The Creation of Birds and Animals (St. Florentin, nr Auxerre). Stories of Kevin record his close relationship with animals: "For company he had the wild animals, who would come and drink water from his cupped hands."*

KEVIN AND THE COW

Walking alone through remote regions of Ireland, Kevin came one day to a valley, with a beautiful, clear stream running down the mountains into two blue lakes. Kevin decided to stay near the upper lake, drinking its water, gathering herbs to eat from around its shore, and sleeping in the hollow of an old tree nearby.

Some nearby herdsmen took their cows to graze each day in this valley. Since God wanted to reveal Kevin to other people, he caused one of the cows to visit Kevin daily. The cow would eat the cut grass near Kevin's tree, drink from the lake, and nuzzle up to Kevin, licking his

rough clothes; then in the evening, when the cow heard the herdsmen shouting at the cattle to drive them home, she would hurry back to the herd.

Every day as the herd entered the valley, the cow would steal away up to Kevin. To the herdsmen's amazement she began to give abundant milk, far greater in quantity and far richer than that of the other cows. The herdsmen reported this to their master, who said to them: "Keep a close eye on her, and discover the pasture where she grazes."

So the next day one of the herdsmen followed the cow up to the valley to Kevin's tree. And when he saw the cow licking Kevin's clothes he was filled with an irrational anger—as if Kevin's holiness was a judgment on himself. He started to insult Kevin and beat the cow, and finally drove the cow back down the valley, thrashing it with a stick.

That evening at the farm all the cows and calves fell into a frenzy, foaming at the mouth; and the cows became so wild that they began to butt their own calves with their heads. The herdsman who had insulted Kevin ran to his master to say what was happening; and, after questioning the herdsman, the master ordered the herdsman to go to Kevin and seek forgiveness, begging him to heal the cattle.

The herdsman ran to the valley, and fell on his knees before Kevin. Kevin blessed him, then he fetched some water from the lake, and blessed that also, ordering the herdsman to take it to the cows and sprinkle it over them. The herdsman did as Kevin told him, causing the frenzy to cease instantly; and the cows began to lick their calves with love.

And Kevin's fame spread across the whole region.

KEVIN AND THE WILD BOAR

Gradually other men came to join Kevin at the lake, and a large monastery grew up around the tree where Kevin lived. At length Kevin grew weary of the bustle of community life; and, leaving the monastery under the charge of others whom he trusted, Kevin went up the valley for about a mile, building himself a small hut at the top. He ordered the monks not to bring him food, nor to come to him, except in dire emergency. For company he had the wild animals, who would come and drink water from his cupped hands. Kevin also constructed out of branches and leaves a small chapel where he could pray.

One day a wild boar came running through the woods, panting with fright, and hid in Kevin's chapel. A few moments later a cruel huntsman called Brandub, notorious for killing both animals and humans merely for pleasure, arrived with a pack of snarling hounds. The hounds went up to the entrance of the chapel, but refused to go in, falling silent and bowing their heads. Brandub just about to yell at the hounds, accusing them of cowardice, when he saw Kevin nearby, standing under a tree; birds were perched on Kevin's arms and were flying around his head, singing with joy.

Then a wind arose, and the leaves in the tree became a chorus of the birds' song, rustling in the perfect harmony. The cruel huntsman was filled with fear, and fell off his horse onto the ground. Then he crawled to Kevin, and begged his blessing. From that day onward Brandub never again killed either people or animals, and lived instead on wild herbs.

KEVIN AND THE BLACKBIRD

Kevin devoted part of each day to reading the Scriptures, sitting in his hut, with arms stretched out through the window reaching up to heaven. One day, while he was reading, a blackbird, thinking the arm was a branch, settled on Kevin's open hand. There it made a nest and laid some eggs.

When Kevin saw what was happening he was so filled with love for the bird that he did not move. Instead he remained in that same position until the eggs were hatched and the young birds could fly.

THE LIFE OF ST. KEVIN

Brendan

he Voyage of Brendan the Navigator was one of the most popular books in Europe in the early Middle Ages, appearing not only in the original Latin, but translated into all the main vernacular languages. Its authorship is unknown, and it was probably written about three centuries after Brendan's death, based on stories that had been transmitted orally. It recounts an astonishing journey by coracle across the North Atlantic, via the Faroes and Iceland, to Newfoundland, and then back via the Azores. Although Brendan and his companions often rowed, their route was mainly determined by the winds and currents. It also records that others had made the journey previously, since Brendan meets various Irish hermits.

Brendan was born in the late fifth century in southwest Ireland, and became abbot of Clonfert in the center of the country. One Lent he returned home, and spent the whole season on a high mountain overlooking the Atlantic. He held the common belief that an "island of promise" lay beyond the horizon; and as he prayed and fasted, he decided to set out to find it. He recruited fourteen other monks to join him, and together they built a boat out of ox-hides tanned with oak bark.

ABOVE *Brendan comforted his fellow monks:
"Have no fear, brothers, for God is our captain and our pilot."*

BRENDAN SETS SAIL

Brendan chose fourteen from his community, took them to the chapel, and made this proposal to them: "My beloved fellow soldiers, if it be God's will, I want to seek out the Island of Promise of which our forefathers have spoken. Will you come with me? What are your feelings?"

As soon as he had finished speaking, the monks replied with one voice: "Father, your desire is ours also. Have we not forsaken our parents and abandoned our property in order to put ourselves totally into your hands? We are ready to go with you, for better for worse, so long as it is God's will."

During the next forty days Brendan and his companions took food only every third day, to prepare themselves physically and spiritually for their journey. Then they bade farewell to their community, and set off to the coast. There, in a narrow cove, they made a coracle, using iron tools. The ribs and frame were carved out of wood, and then covered with ox-hide, tanned in oak bark. They smeared the seams with grease to make them waterproof, storing extra hides and grease in the coracle for repairs. Then a mast was erected, with a simple sail attached, and food for forty days was loaded into the vessel.

When all was ready Brendan ordered his monks aboard, the sail was hoisted, and the coracle was swept out to sea. For the next two weeks the wind was fair, so that they did no more than steady the sail. But then the wind fell, and they had to row, day after day.

When their strength eventually failed, Brendan comforted them: "Have no fear, brothers, for God is our captain and our pilot; so take in the oars, and set the sail, letting him blow us where he wills."

So they stopped rowing and again hoisted the sail. From time to time the wind blew, but they had no idea in what direction they were sailing.

THE FAROE ISLANDS

At last they sighted an island on the horizon. A fair wind sprang up which carried them to its shore, and Brendan ordered them to disembark. Walking around the island they saw great streams of water gushing down from the hills, teeming with all kinds of fish. And there were numerous flocks of sheep, all pure white and so enormous that they seemed to blot out the ground from view.

The day of their arrival was Good Friday, and Brendan ordered the brethren to take one of the sheep to symbolize the Lamb of God. So they chose the finest animal, and one of the monks tied a cord around its horn so he could lead it like a pet. Then suddenly a man appeared, carrying a basket of bread baked in hot ashes and other food, which he laid at Brendan's feet. With tears in his eyes, he cried: "O precious pearl of God, what have I done to deserve this honor, of providing food and drink for you with my own hands in this holy season?"

"My son," Brendan replied, "our Lord Jesus Christ has decided that this is the place where we shall remember his redeeming death."

NEWFOUNDLAND

After many days Brendan and his fellow warriors in Christ saw land in the distance, and this inspired them to row faster. "Do not exhaust your strength," Brendan urged them. "God will bring us to land in his own good time."

When they reached the shore the cliffs were so steep that they could see no place to land. So they sailed around until they found a small creek, just wide enough for the prow of the coracle. Brendan got out first, and climbed up the cliff. At the top he found two caves facing one another. From the mouth of one cave a tiny spring gushed

ABOVE *St. Brendan (E R Frampton, 1908). The Voyage of Brendan the Navigator relates how a group of monks sailed from Ireland by humble coracle across the North Atlantic and beyond.*

forth, and inside the other cave was a hermit. The hermit came out to greet Brendan, embracing him; and then the hermit asked Brendan to invite the other monks up to join them.

As the monks reached the top of the cliff, the hermit kissed each one, and called them by name. The monks were astonished at this prophetic gift of knowing their names, and also were amazed at the hermit's appearance: he had no clothes, but was covered from head to toe with thick, white hair. The hermit introduced himself as Paul. Brendan asked how he came to this remote place, and how long he had lived there.

Paul replied: "For forty years I belonged to St. Patrick's monastery in Ireland, where I was in charge of the cemetery. One day Patrick himself appeared to me in a vision, ordering me to go down to the shore where a small boat would be waiting for me. The next morning I walked to the beach, and there indeed was a boat. I got in, and the wind carried me straight here. Once I had arrived I know that this was where God wanted me to live. So I pushed the boat away with my feet."

THE VOYAGE OF ST. BRENDAN

John Moschus

T he most popular book about the desert monks of
Egypt and of Syria was the collection of stories by
John Moschus. His imagination was stirred not by
epigrams expressing the desert wisdom, but by tales that
illuminated it. As a young man, in about 575, he joined a
monastic community near Jerusalem, built around the cave
where the three wise men were said to have hidden from
Herod's anger.

Some time later he traveled throughout Palestine and
Syria, visiting monastic groups and hermits. By this time the
monastic movement had accumulated countless stories, handed
down from one generation of monks to the next, about the great
spiritual mentor. The issue of factual accuracy never concerned
John Moschus or the monks who spoke to him; spiritual truth
was the measure of a story's value.

The most famous story is of the lion and the donkey. Some
centuries later the same story became attached
to St. Jerome; but in its original form the human hero is called
Gerasimus. The spiritual
truth outlined in the
story concerns the
relationship between
human holiness and the
animal kingdom.

LEFT *St. Jerome
(Pietro Perugino,
1445–1523, Musée Des
Beaux Arts, Caen). One
of John Moschus's most
famous tales is that of
St. Jerome, the lion, and
the donkey.*

GERASIMUS AND THE LION

The monastery named after the great spiritual leader, Gerasimus, lay about a mile from the River Jordan. When we arrived there, the monks told how Gerasimus had once met a lion on the banks of the river. The lion was roaring with pain because the sharp point of a reed was stuck in his paw, and the paw was swollen and full of pus. When the lion saw the old man, he showed him his paw with the thorn in it; the lion was weeping and seemed to be pleading for help.

Gerasimus took pity on the lion. He sat down on the bank, held the paw in one hand, and gently drew out the thorn with the other. He then squeezed out the pus, cleansed the wound with water from the river, and bound it with a rag. The old man waved at the lion to go away, but the lion refused. Instead the lion followed Gerasimus wherever he went, like a disciple following a master. The old man marveled at the gratitude of the wild beast. From that time onward the old man fed the lion, giving him bread flavored with herbs.

At that time the monastery had a donkey to draw water from the Jordan for the monks needs. Gerasimus ordered the lion to guard the donkey. The lion went everywhere with the donkey, even watching the donkey grazing. One day, while the lion was dozing, the donkey wandered off. At that moment a camel driver from Arabia came past, and stole the donkey.

When the lion awoke and could not find the donkey, he was utterly distraught. He returned to the monastery with his head drooping low. Gerasimus thought that the lion had eaten the donkey; and the lion had no words to explain himself.

"As a punishment for devouring the donkey," Gerasimus declared, "you shall now do the work which the donkey did." So four large jars were tied to the lion; and the lion's task, day by day, was to dip the jars in the river, fill them with water, and carry them back to the monastery.

One day a soldier came to the monastery to ask for Gerasimus" blessing. The soldier saw the lion carrying the jars, and learned the reason. He felt sorry for the lion, and gave three coins to the old man to buy a donkey, and so relieve the lion.

Some time later the camel driver passed the monastery again, on his way to sell barley in Jerusalem. When he had crossed the river, he caught sight of the lion, and in terror ran away. The lion recognized the donkey, and roared with joy. He bound up the donkey, put the halter in his mouth, and led him, along with the three camels, back to Gerasimus.

The old man realized that he had accused the lion falsely. He decided to call the lion Jordan, and let the lion stay by his side all the time. For the next five years the lion was always with the old man as he ministered to his brethren.

Finally the old man died. At the burial the lion was nowhere to be found. A little later the lion reappeared, and began looking for his old master. One of the monks said to the lion: "Jordan, our old master has passed to the Lord, and left us orphans. Come and eat with us." But the lion refused to eat, and instead wandered around the monastery looking for his old master. When he realized that Gerasimus was no longer there, he roared with sadness.

The monk who had offered him food ruffled his mane, and said again: "The old master has gone to God and left us." And other monks caressed him and tried to console him. But nothing could assuage his grief. His roars grew louder, and tears fell from his eyes.

The monk said to him: "Come with me, and I will show you our master's grave; then you will believe us."

He led the lion to the place where Gerasimus had been buried; it was about five yards from the church. The monk pointed to the grave, and then knelt beside it. The lion lay on top of the grave, and beat his head on the grave, giving out a low roar. He would neither move nor eat; and that is where he died.

PRATUM SPIRITUALE

Cuthbert

he most popular
Celtic figure is
Cuthbert, whose
continuing fame rests on the
masterly biography of him by
Bede. Aidan from Iona had
established a monastery at
Lindisfarne, an island linked to
the northeastern coast of
England by a sandbank; and
this monastery became a center
of education and evangelism.
Cuthbert was a successor to
Aidan as bishop of Lindisfarne.
But both before and after
holding this office he lived as a
hermit on a tiny island several
miles out to sea. There,
according to Bede, he turned an
initial conflict with local birds into a joyful friendship. Bede
also records an earlier part of Cuthbert's life when otters used
to dry Cuthbert's body, after he had spent the night in prayer
standing in water.

Cuthbert died in 687, and his body was eventually laid to
rest at Durham. Bede was born in 673, and spent his life as a
monk at nearby Jarrow. Much of our knowledge of the Celtic
period come from his History of the English Church and
People. This includes a brief account of Cuthbert's life, which
he explains in his biography. Bede too was buried at Durham;
that city's magnificent cathedral was built in response to the
hordes of pilgrims that came to visit these two tombs.

ABOVE Cuthbert's life and deeds
were recorded by Bede in his magnificent biography of the saint: "He
showed to everyone that good fortune and bad fortune alike are
transitory, and that true and permanent happiness can only be
found through faith in God."

NIGHT PRAYER

When he was at home in the monastery,
Cuthbert rose from his bed each night,
and went out to pray; he returned just in time
for morning prayers. Usually none of the monks
saw him, because they were asleep. But one
night one of the monks was lying awake, and
noticed Cuthbert creeping out of the dormitory.
This monk decided to get up and follow him.
Cuthbert went down to the river and waded into
the water until his entire body up to his
shoulders was submerged. He remained there,
praying and singing psalms, until the first light
of dawn.

Then he came out and knelt down on the
bank. Two otters also came out, and lay down
beside him, warming his feet with their breath,
and trying to dry his body with their fur. When
the sun had risen, Cuthbert blessed the otters,
and they slipped back into the water. He walked
home, and joined the other monks in church.
Later that day the monk who had watched
Cuthbert was so overwhelmed with guilt that
he threw himself at Cuthbert's feet and
confessed what he had done. "I will forgive
you," said Cuthbert, "but you must promise not
to tell anyone, while I am still alive, of what you
have seen."

CHAPTER 10

RETREAT TO FARNE

For many years Cuthbert had yearned to live
as a hermit, and he had prayed that one day
God would make this possible. He believed that
a monk should spend the first part of his life in
the active service of his brethren and the
common people; and he regarded solitude as the
reward for such service.

Eventually Cuthbert sailed to Farne Island
to be a hermit. This lies a few miles to the
southeast of Lindisfarne, and to its east lies the
limitless ocean. There he built a small oratory
for prayer, and a hut in which to live. Both
buildings were circular, constructed from rough
stones and peat which he found on the island
itself; their roofs were made from rough-hewn
timbers and straw.

Near the landing-place he made a larger house for guests. There was no fresh water on the island, so a group of young monks came from Lindisfarne to dig a well.

CHAPTERS 17 AND 18

THE BIRDS AND THE SEED

At first monks from Lindisfarne brought bread for Cuthbert to eat. But he decided that he should live by his own labor. So he asked them to bring seeds and a spade with which to dig the land. In the spring he sowed the seeds, which were wheat; but by mid-summer none had grown. "It's either the nature of the ground," he said to his brethren, "or the will of God. I will try barley instead. If that fails, I will return to the monastery. It would be better to eat by my own labor there, than stay here depending on the labor of others."

So, although it was late in the year, the monks brought him barley seeds, which he planted immediately. And these quickly sprang up, bearing a good crop. However, as soon as the barley began to ripen, birds flew down and set about devouring it. Cuthbert came out and spoke to the birds: "Why are you eating crops which you did not sow? Perhaps you have greater need for them than I have. If God has given you permission, then do as he bids. If not, stop stealing my food and go away." The birds seemed to understand Cuthbert's words, and flew away. Never again did they eat crops which Cuthbert had sown.

CHAPTER 19

RAVENS AND THE GUESTHOUSE ROOF

Ravens had long inhabited the island which Cuthbert now made his home. One day Cuthbert saw them tearing the straw from the guesthouse, and taking it away to build their nests. Cuthbert rebuked them; and with a wave of his right hand told them to leave his property alone. The ravens ignored him, and continued tearing the straw.

"How dare you defy me!" Cuthbert shouted; and he ordered them to leave at once. They were frightened he would attack them, so they flew away.

Afterward the ravens felt guilty at what they had been doing. And three days later one of them returned. Cuthbert was digging, and the bird flew down to his feet and stood before him; it spread out its wings and bowed its head. Cuthbert realized that it was apologizing and begging for his forgiveness.

Cuthbert was overjoyed at the raven's repentance and invited all the ravens to return. They came back, carrying in their beaks a lump of pig's lard, to offer as a gift. Cuthbert put the lard in the guesthouse. The ravens stayed on the island, building their nests with grass and twigs which they found for themselves. Cuthbert invited guests to grease their shoes with the lard, telling them how he had obtained it. "None of us is too virtuous to learn lessons from the birds," he would add.

CHAPTER 20

VISITORS TO FARNE

Once the brethren from Lindisfarne had helped Cuthbert to build his hermitage, he lived completely alone. But countless visitors rowed across the choppy waters from the mainland to see Cuthbert and to ask his advice on spiritual matters. When he saw a boat arrive, Cuthbert went down to the landing-place to welcome the visitors. He took them into the guesthouse and washed their feet in warm water. Then he led them one by one to the oratory, where they could each speak to him in private. They confessed their sins to him, and confided in him the temptations they faced, asking for his guidance on how to overcome them.

No one left Farne Island disappointed; all were able to lay at Cuthbert's feet the spiritual and moral burdens with which they had arrived, and to return light of heart. Those who were beset with worry and anxiety, he filled with peace and tranquility. He showed to everyone that good fortune and bad fortune alike are transitory, and that true and permanent happiness can only be found through faith in God. He also taught that the devil does not only catch wicked men and women in his net; all those who are merely lukewarm in their love are susceptible to the devil's tricks.

CHAPTERS 18–22

Francis of Assisi

ithout doubt the most popular Christian figure of all time, apart from Jesus himself, is Francis of Assisi. He was hugely loved in his lifetime, and this affection has never waned. He was not a great or prolific writer; yet his Canticle of Brother Sun is very powerful, and has frequently been set to music. But he inspired great writing. In the decade after his death several biographies were written by those who joined his order, and these contain passages of sublime beauty and charm.

He was born in Assisi in about 1182, and as a young man enjoyed a riotous social life at the expense of his father, a wealthy cloth merchant. But when he turned to religion, and gave up all material possessions, his father was furious. His exuberant personality, and his passion for nature, soon attracted others, and he formed the Friars Minor—the Little Brothers. Before his death in 1226 they numbered several thousand, and in the following decade the order continued to multiply.

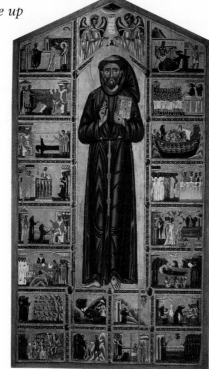

ABOVE *Altarpiece with life of St. Francis of Assisi, Santa Croce, Florence (Tuscan school, 13th century). St. Francis of Assisi is one of the most popular Christian saints of all time.*

CANTICLE OF BROTHER SUN

Most high, all-powerful, good Lord, All praise is yours, my Lord, through all you have made, Especially my Lord Brother Sun, Who brings the day, and gives us your light. How beautiful he is, and radiant in his splendor. He bears a likeness of you, most high God.

All praise is yours, my Lord, through Sisters Moon and Stars. In heaven you formed them, bright, precious, and fair.

All praise is yours, my Lord, through Brothers Wind and Air. In their various moods, severe or stormy, You sustain all the creatures you have made.

All praise is yours, My Lord, through Sister Water, Useful and humble, and precious and pure.

All praise is yours, my Lord, through Brother Fire, By him you brighten up the night. How beautiful and playful he is, robust and strong.

All praise is yours, my Lord, through Sister Earth; Our mother who feeds and governs us, Who gives us fruits and flowers, and herbs.

All praise is yours, my Lord, through all who love and forgive, Through all who endure sickness and trial in peace. By you, most high, they will be crowned.

All praise is yours, my Lord, through Sister Death, From whose embrace no living creature can escape. We grieve for those who die in mortal sin. Happy are those whom she finds doing your will; The second death can do them no harm.

Praise and bless my Lord, and give him thanks, And serve him with great humility.

CANTICLE OF BROTHER SUN

THE CALL TO POVERTY

One day Francis walked by the church of St. Damian. The building was old, and in such a poor state that it was about to collapse. Prompted by the Spirit, Francis went inside to pray. He fell prostrate in front of an image of Christ on the cross, and he felt the warmth of God's grace enter him. His eyes filled with tears as he gazed at the crucifix. Then he heard a voice coming from the crucifix, saying to him three times: "Francis, repair my house which is falling into ruin."

Francis rose to his feet, made the sign of the cross, and went to a nearby town to sell the cloth he had been carrying. He even sold the horse he had been riding. Then he returned to the church. The poor priest who served the church was now there. Francis greeted the priest with reverence, and offered him the money he had obtained, to be used for repairing the church and helping the poor; he also asked if he could stay in the church for a time. The priest allowed him to stay, but would not accept the money, for fear of the anger of Francis's parents. Demonstrating his contempt for wealth, Francis threw the money into the windowsill, valuing it little more than dust.

When his father learned what he had done, he flew into a rage, and hurried to the church. Francis headed toward Assisi to meet him. The townspeople were shocked to see his dirty face and unkempt hair, and they thought he had gone mad. They picked up stones and lumps of mud, and threw them at him, shouting insults. But Francis walked in, indifferent to the violence and deaf to the abuse. His father, hearing the noise, ran toward Francis, not to save him but to destroy him. Casting aside all compassion, he dragged Francis home, venting his anger with both words and blows, even striking him with a chair. But this simply strengthened Francis's resolve....

His father then took Francis to the bishop of the town, with the purpose of compelling Francis to return all his possessions to his family. Francis now loved poverty, so he was eager to comply. He hurried with his father to the bishop's house; and as soon as he entered, he tore off all his clothes, and handed them to his father—revealing a hair shirt next to his skin. Drunk with fervor, he even took off his underwear, stripping himself completely naked. The bishop was amazed, and tears welled up in his eyes. He stood up and embraced Francis, and covered him with his own cloak. He then ordered his servant to find clothes for Francis. At Francis's request, they brought him the rough woolen tunic of a peasant. Francis accepted it gratefully, and with a piece of chalk marked a cross on the front.

BONAVENTURE'S LIFE OF FRANCIS, CHAPTER 2

SERMON TO THE BIRDS

Francis saw some trees beside the road, in which a great multitude of different birds were perched. Another huge flock was in the field beside the trees. Francis was enchanted by the sight, and he felt the Spirit of God come upon him. He said to his companions: "Wait for me here on the road, while I go and preach to our sisters the birds." And he went into the field where the birds were on the ground. As soon as he began to preach the birds in the trees flew down to him. All the birds remained still and quiet, while he moved among them, brushing some of them with his tunic. Not a single bird moved—as Francis's companions can testify.

Francis said: "My sisters the birds, you have received much from God. You should always praise him for your ability to fly freely, for your feathers lying thickly over your bodies, for the beautiful colors of your plumage, for the food that you can find without working, for the songs that you can sing to your Creator, for your vast numbers, for the preservation of your species in the ark, and for the air in which you move. You neither sow nor reap. Yet God gives you food to eat; rivers and streams in which to drink; mountains, hills, rocks, and crags in which to hide; and tall trees in which to nest. And since you can neither spin nor weave, he gives lovely garments for you and your chicks to wear. All these blessings are signs that your Creator loves you. So take care, dear sisters of mine, always to give thanks to God, singing his praises."

THE LITTLE FLOWERS OF ST. FRANCIS, CHAPTER 16

RIGHT *St. Francis of Assisi is remembered most for his deep love of nature. "All the birds remained still and quiet while he moved among them."*

Margery Kempe

Her contemporaries could not agree whether Margery Kempe was a saint or a woman possessed by an evil spirit. And reading her spiritual autobiography today, it is hard to avoid the conclusion that she was mentally unbalanced. She frequently heard melodies of great sweetness, which she believed came from Christ. And on one occasion she was convinced that Jesus visited her. She also saw the face of the child Jesus in every child she met. These spiritual experiences were in constant conflict with her intense sexual and material desires. And eventually, to his great sadness, she eventually rejected all further physical relationships with her husband.

Born in about 1373 into a wealthy family of merchants in King's Lynn, a port on the east coast of England, she married a comparatively poor man, who could not afford her expensive tastes. She started various businesses to boost their income, all of which collapsed. After her religious experiences began she traveled widely, after criticizing the bishops and clergy she met for their lack of religious devotion. She eventually returned home, to nurse her ailing husband. Her book is the first autobiography written in English. Though its style is often crude—she herself was illiterate, and dictated the text to a priest—its unrestrained honesty compels admiration.

THE HEAVENLY MELODY

One night, as this creature lay in bed with her husband, she heard a melody so sweet and delightful that she thought she had been taken to paradise. Immediately she jumped out of bed, and declared: "How terrible that I have been a sinner! It is so happy in heaven."

This melody was so lovely that it was beyond comparison with any music heard in the world. Afterward, whenever this creature heard any joyful tune, she found that her spiritual feelings were stimulated, because she was reminded of the bliss of heaven; this caused her to burst loudly into tears—and also to have contempt for this wretched world.

Hearing this melody she was drawn closely to God. And from that moment on, she was constantly thinking of the joy and beauty of heaven. When she was in the company of others, she often said: "It is so happy in heaven." Those who had known her previous behavior were surprised to hear her talk so much of the bliss of heaven, and said to her: "Why do you speak in this way? You don't know heaven; you haven't been to heaven any more than we have." They were also angry with her because she would not hear or talk about worldly matters, as she had done previously.

A further effect of this experience was that she no longer wanted to have sexual intercourse with her husband. Paying the debt of matrimony had become so abominable to her, that she felt she would prefer to eat the ooze and muck of the gutter than to consent to intercourse. But she had no choice but to obey her husband. So she said to him: "I am not allowed to deny you my body. But all the love and affection of my heart is withdrawn from all earthly creatures, and set on God alone." He continued to assert his will over her, and she obeyed with much weeping and wailing.

CHAPTER 3

TRANQUILITY AND TEMPTATION

For the first two years after this creature was drawn to the Lord, her spirit was very tranquil, and was free from all temptations. She could endure fasting; it did not trouble her.

She hated the pleasures of the world, so her flesh did not rebel. She thought herself to be so strong, that she no longer feared the devil in hell. She performed great bodily penances. She felt that she loved God more than he loved her. She was struck by the deadly blow of spiritual pride, but she was not aware of it. Many times she yearned that Christ would loosen his hands from the cross and embrace her, as an expression of love.

Our merciful Lord Jesus Christ, seeing this creature's pride, sent her three years of great temptations.… In particular he laid before her the snare of lust. Even though she thought that all physical desire had been quenched within her, physical desire overwhelmed her for a long time. She found herself unable to suppress it. She frequently confessed her sins, she wore a hair shirt, she did great bodily penances, and she wept many bitter tears. She often prayed to our Lord that he should uphold and restrain her, so that she would not succumb to temptation; she felt she would prefer to be dead than to fall. Yet throughout this time she had no desire to have intercourse with her husband, who was utterly repugnant to her.

Chapter 4

JESUS' VISIT

One Friday before Christmas this creature was kneeling in the chapel of St. John, within the church of St. Margaret in Lynn, weeping a great deal, and begging mercy and forgiveness for her sins and transgressions.

ABOVE *The wealthy Margery Kempe married a poor man; she claimed that Christ had spoken to her through a series of melodies.*

Our blessed and merciful Lord Jesus Christ embraced her spirit, and said to her:

"Daughter, why are you weeping so bitterly? I, Jesus Christ, have come to you. I suffered bitter pains and died on the cross for you. I, the same God, forgive every one of your sins. You shall never go to hell or to purgatory; when you leave this world, you shall pass at the blink of an eye to the bliss of heaven. I am the same God that reminded you of your sins, and prompted you to confess them. I grant you forgiveness to the end of your life.

"Therefore I command you to be bold, and call me Jesus, your dearest love. I am your dearest love, and shall remain so without end. Daughter, you have a hair shirt on your back. I want you to stop wearing it. I will give you a hair shirt in your heart which will please me much more than all the hair shirts in the world. Also, my beloved daughter, I want you to give up the thing which you love best, the eating of meat. Instead of meat you shall eat my body and blood, the sacrament of the altar. I want you to receive my body every Sunday; and I shall cause such grace to flow into you that people will marvel at it.

"You shall be bitten and gnawed by the people of the world, just as rats gnaw dried fish. Do not be afraid, daughter, for you shall be victorious over all your enemies. I shall give you grace to reply to every cleric who questions you; you shall respond in a spirit of divine love. I swear to you by my Lordship that I shall never forsake you, whether in happiness or in sorrow."

Chapter 5

FACES OF CHRIST

This creature felt such love for the humanity of Christ, that when she saw women carrying children in their arms, she looked to see whether they were boys; and, if they were, she would cry, roar, and weep as if she had seen Christ as a child. And if she saw a handsome man, she observed him closely, hoping to see in him the man who was God. She often cried when she encountered a handsome man, weeping and sobbing profusely as she went about the streets.

Chapter 35

Teresa of Avila

n her gripping autobiography, Teresa of Avila related her mystical teaching directly to her own experience. She described the different stages by which her soul had grown closer to God, in language that is vivid and at times erotic; and she then drew out general theological lessons. Learning the art of mystical prayer took the first half of her adult life. And having obtained a degree of inner peace, she devoted the rest of her life to reforming her religious order, the Carmelites, opening several new convents.

Her grandparents were Spanish Jews who converted to Christianity. As a teenager Teresa, one of ten children, was so unruly that her father sent her to a boarding school in Avila, in the hope that the priests and nuns running it would instill discipline. They were so successful that in 1535, at the age of twenty, she became a nun—against her father's wishes.

In the early years she suffered various symptoms of psychological disturbance, including paralysis. When she finally reached the higher stages of mystical prayer, she quickly became renowned for her ecstatic trances; and by her own account she even left the ground on several occasions, and had to be held down by other nuns.

ECSTATIC PRAYER

In the highest stage of prayer the soul is conscious that it is fainting away in a kind of swoon; it feels very calm, and full of joy. The breath and the bodily powers progressively fail, so that you cannot move even the hands without great effort. The eyes close involuntarily; and if they remain open, they see almost nothing. If you try to read in such a state, you can scarcely make out a single letter—you see that there are letters, but you cannot read them, even if you try. You hear, but you do not understand what you hear.

Your senses serve no purpose; you cannot even distinguish pleasure from pain. Your tongue cannot form a single word, nor would it have the strength to pronounce one. The strength of the body vanishes. As a result the strength of the soul increases, to enjoy its bliss to the full. This one joy is so great that bystanders can see it.

This state of ecstatic prayer does no harm, however long it lasts. At least it has never harmed me. Even when I have been ill, I can never recall any bad effects from ecstatic prayer; on the contrary, it has always left me feeling much better. What harm could such a blessing do? The effects are so manifest that it is obvious to any observer that a wonderful thing is happening. At the time it robs you of your bodily strength; but afterward your strength has increased.

In fact ecstatic prayer usually lasts only a very short time. It is so quick that the external signs are not always obvious at the time. But once it is over, you are so radiant that it seems the sun is shining from your soul.

THE AUTOBIOGRAPHY OF TERESA, CHAPTER 18

THE RISING OF THE SOUL AND BODY

In ecstatic prayer the Lord catches the soul, just as the clouds gather up the morning mists on earth; and the Lord carries the soul right out of itself, just as the clouds—so I am told—carry the mist toward the sun. The Lord takes the soul in the direction of heaven, to show the kingdom that he has prepared. I do not know whether this happens literally, but this is how it seems. In these raptures the soul no longer seems to be in the body; and the body's heat diminishes, so the flesh grows cold....

When the Lord begins to carry the soul upward, at first you feel afraid; so this level of prayer requires great determination and courage. You must risk everything, and put yourself entirely in God's hands. You must allow yourself to be carried wherever God wants to take you. You might try to resist, and use all your strength to do so. In fact I have myself wanted to resist, especially when I am in a public place, because I feel worried about causing embarrassment to others; I have even resisted in private because I am afraid of delusions. At times my struggle has been successful; but it has been like fighting a great giant, leaving me utterly exhausted. At other times resistance has proved impossible; my soul has been carried away, and usually my head as well, without my being able to stop it. Occasionally my entire body has been lifted off the ground.

Bodily levitation has happened rarely. Once, however, it occurred when I was with the other nuns in church; I was on my knees, ready to take Communion. I felt very distressed when I realized that my body was rising up, because I knew it would cause entertainment, and arouse talk. So I asked the sisters not to mention it to outsiders. On another occasion my body was raised so high that my sisters had to hold me down.

The Autobiography of Teresa, Chapter 20

ABOVE *St. Teresa of Avila formed the religious order of Carmelite nuns which is still in existence today. Her practice of mystical prayer led to ecstatic trances.*

THE PURPOSE OF ECSTATIC PRAYER

We may speak of love and humility as the true flowers of spiritual growth; and they give off a wonderful scent which benefits all who come near. The purpose of ecstatic prayer is to enable these flowers to bloom. Unless you have experienced ecstatic prayer, you can never imagine how much the Lord can accomplish through it, in such a short time. Of course, ecstatic prayer is not essential for spiritual growth; people who over many years follow the rules and principles of prayer, given by spiritual writers over the centuries, will eventually bear these beautiful flowers. But it is hard work, and takes much time. In ecstatic prayer, without any effort, the Lord raises the soul from the earth and lifts it to heaven.

The souls which receive the gift of ecstatic prayer are not more deserving than those that do not. Certainly my soul has not merited this gift. The Lord bestows the gift of ecstatic prayer according to his pleasure. No soul is ever prepared for it; but God makes the soul ready as and when he wishes.

The Autobiography of Teresa, Chapter 21

AN EROTIC VISION

In a state of ecstatic prayer I saw an angel. He was not tall, but short, and very beautiful. His face glowed like a fire.... In his hands I saw a great golden spear, and the iron tip seemed to be burning. He plunged the spear into my heart several times, so deep that it penetrated my entire body. Then he pulled the spear out, he seemed to take my inner organs; and I was left utterly consumed with the love of God. I was also in great pain; and it was so severe that I moaned out loud. The pain induced a feeling of joy so extreme that I wanted it to last forever.

The Autobiography of Teresa, Chapter 29

William Bradford

*T*he men and women whom Americans regard as their founders came from an obscure corner of northeast England. They were inspired by religious zeal; and their style of Christianity, which was strictly puritan, suffered severe persecution in the early years of the seventeenth century. Thus they decided to emigrate, first to Holland, and then to America, in order to practice their religion freely. And as they sailed across the Atlantic they signed the Mayflower Compact, committing themselves to democratic government.

The main chronicler of this historic expedition was one of the young members, William Bradford. He led the leading party that chose the site for the colony, and he served for thirty years as its governor, setting it on a firm political and economic foundation. He had no formal education, learning as a boy only the skills of farming. But his artless style seems appropriate to record the actions of a group who prized simplicity and frugality in all things material.

ABOVE *"A band of exiles moor'd their bark on the wild New England shore" (from Our Island Story). William Bradford recorded the journey of the founding fathers from England to America.*

REASONS FOR MIGRATING TO AMERICA

This Proposition being made public and coming to the scanning all, it raised many variable opinions among men, and caused many fears and doubts among themselves.

Some, from their reasons and hopes conceived, labored to stir up and encourage the rest to undertake and prosecute the same. Others again, out of their fears, objected against it and sought to divert from it: alleging many things, and those neither unreasonable, nor unprobable.

That it was a great design and subject to many unconceivable perils and dangers, etc. Besides the casualties of the seas, which none can be freed from; the length of the voyage was such as the weak bodies of women, and other persons worn out with age and travail, as many of them were, could ever be able to endure.

And yet if they should, the miseries of the land, which they should be exposed unto, would be too hard to be borne; and likely some, or all of them together, to consume and utterly to ruinate them. For there they should be liable to famine, and nakedness, and the want of all things. The change of air, diet, and drinking of water would infect their bodies with sore sicknesses and grievous diseases.

And also those which should escape, or overcome, these difficulties, should yet be in continual danger of the savage people. Who are cruel, barbarous, and most treacherous; being most furious in their rage, and merciless where they overcome: not being content only to kill and take away life; but delight to torment men in the most bloody manner that may be—flaying some alive with the shells of fishes: cutting off the members and joints of others by piecemeal; and, broiling them on the coals, eat the collops of their flesh in their sight, whilst they live: with other cruelties horrible to be related.

And surely it could not be thought but the very hearing of these things could not but move the very bowels of men to grate within them; and make the weak to quake and tremble. It was further objected, that it would require greater sums of money to furnish such a voyage and to fit them with necessaries, than their consumed estates would amount to: and yet they must as well look to be seconded with supplies as presently to be transported.

Also many precedents of ill success and lamentable miseries that had befallen others in the like designs, were easy to be found; and not forgotten to be alleged. Besides their own experience in their former troubles and hardships in their removal into Holland: and how hard a thing it was for them to live in that strange place, though it was a neighboring country, and a civilized and rich commonwealth.

It was answered, that all great and honorable actions are accompanied with great difficulties; and must be both enterprised and overcome with answerable courage. It was granted the dangers were great, but not desperate; the difficulties were many, but not invincible. For though there were many of them likely; yet they were not certain. It might be that sundry of the things feared might never befall; others, by provident care and the use of good means, might in a great measure be prevented: and all of them, through the help of God, by fortitude and patience, might either be borne, or overcome.

True it was, that such attempts were not to be made and undertaken without good ground and reason; not rashly, or lightly, as many have done for curiosity, or hope of gain, etc. But their condition was not ordinary. Their ends were good and honorable; their calling lawful and urgent: and therefore they might expect the blessing of God in their proceeding. Yea, though they should lose their lives in this action: yet might they have comfort in the same; and their endeavors would be honorable.

They lived in Leiden but as men in exile, and in a poor condition: and as great miseries might possibly befall them in this place. For the twelve, or rather, ten, years of truce were now out: and there was nothing but beating of drums and preparing for war; the events whereof are always uncertain. The Spaniard might prove as cruel as the savages of America; and the famine and the pestilence as sore here as there; and their liberty less to look out for remedy.

After many other particular things answered and alleged on both sides; it was fully concluded by the majority to put this design in execution; and to prosecute it by the best means they could.

BRADFORD MANUSCRIPT, FOLIOS 51–55

DEPARTING FOR AMERICA

And the time being come that they must depart, they were accompanied with most of their brethren out of the city of Leiden unto a town sundry miles off, called Delfshaven; where the ship lay ready to receive them. So they left that goodly pleasant city, which had been their resting place nearly twelve years: but they knew they were pilgrims and looked not much on these things; but lifted up their eyes to the heavens, their dearest country, and quieted their spirits.

When they came to the place, they found the ship and all things ready: and such of their friends as could not come with them, followed after them; and sundry also came from Amsterdam to see them shipped, and to take their leave of them. That night was spent with little sleep by the most; but with friendly entertainment, and Christian discourse, and other real expressions of true Christian love. The next day, the wind being fair, they went aboard and their friends with them; when truly doleful was the sight of that sad and mournful parting.

To see what sighs and sobs and prayers did sound among them; what tears did gush from every eye, and pithy speeches pierced each heart; that sundry of the Dutch strangers, that stood on the quay as spectators, could not refrain from tears. Yet comfortable and sweet it was to see such lively and true expressions of dear and unfeigned love.

But the tide, which stays for no man, calling them away that were thus loath to depart; their Reverend Pastor, falling down on his knees, and they all with him, with watery cheeks, commended them, with most fervent prayers, to the Lord with his blessing. And then, with mutual embraces and many tears, they took their leaves one of another: which proved to be the last leave to many of them.

BRADFORD MANUSCRIPT, FOLIOS 91–93

"He had no formal education, learning as a boy only the skills of farming. But his artless style seems appropriate to record the actions of a group who prized simplicity and frugality in all things material."

George Fox

hree decades after his conversion George Fox, the founder of the Quakers, composed a Journal describing his personal spiritual development and his ministry. He recorded how as a young man he sought the truth from the priests of the Church of England, but was disgusted by their spiritual laxity; and how he at last discovered the light of Christ with his own soul. He found he had a gift for preaching, and began to win converts; then climbing Pendle Hill, in the northwest of England, he had a vision of great masses of people discovering Christ's light with themselves.

He believed passionately in human equality, and recounted the trouble he caused by not raising his hat to people of distinction. Fox was also a prolific letterwriter; and in a famous letter to Oliver Cromwell, who was the military dictator of England, he urged pacifism.

The son of a humble weaver, George Fox won disciples in every class of society, who shared his abhorrence of elaborate rituals and complex doctrines. He was a brilliant organizer, establishing groups throughout England, which met each week in silence to wait for the Holy Spirit's guidance. Despite vicious persecution—Fox himself was jailed several times—the Quakers continued to grow. By the time of his death in 1691, one in a hundred of the English population were Quakers, and the movement was spreading to America.

ABOVE *The Childhood of George Fox by P. Cauley-Robinson. "Great things did the Lord lead me into, and wonderful depths were opened unto me, beyond what can by words be declared…"*

ON PENDLE HILL

Thus the work of the Lord went forward, and many were turned from the darkness to the light within the compass of these three years, 1656, 1647, and 1648. And divers meetings of Friends, in several places, were then gathered to God's teaching, by his light, spirit, and power; for the Lord's power brake forth more and more wonderfully.

Now was I come up in spirit through the flaming sword into the paradise of God. All things were new, and all creation gave another smell unto men than before, beyond what words can utter. I knew nothing but pureness, and innocency, and righteousness, being renewed up into the image of God by Christ Jesus, so that I saw I was come up to the state of Adam which he was in before he fell.

The creation was opened to me, and it was showed me how all things had their names given them according to their nature and virtue. And I was at a stand in my mind whether I should practice physics for the good of mankind, seeing the nature and virtues of the creatures were so opened to me by the Lord. But I was immediately taken up in spirit, to see into a state in Christ Jesus, that should never fall.

And the Lord showed me that such as were faithful to him in the power and light of Christ should come up into that state in which Adam was before he fell, in which the admirable works of the creation, and the virtues thereof, may be known, through the openings of that divine Word of wisdom and power by which they were made.

Great things did the Lord lead me into, and wonderful depths were opened unto me, beyond what can by words be declared; but as people come into subjection to the spirit of God, and grow up in the image and power of the Almighty, they may receive the Word of wisdom, that opens all things, and come to know the hidden unity in the Eternal Being.

THE JOURNAL OF GEORGE FOX

THE RAGE AND SCORN

Oh, the rage and scorn, the heat and fury that arose! Oh, the blows, punchings, beatings, and imprisonments that we underwent for not putting off our hats to men! For that soon tried all men's patience and sobriety, what it was. Some had their hats violently plucked off and thrown away so that they quite lost them. The bad language and evil usage we received on this account are hard to be expressed, besides the danger we were sometimes in of losing our lives for this matter, and that, by the great professors of Christianity, who thereby discovered that they were not true believers. And though it was but a small thing in the eye of man, yet a wonderful confusion it brought among all professors and priests. But, blessed by the Lord, many came to see the vanity of that custom of putting off the hat to me, and felt the weight of Truth's testimony against it.

THE JOURNAL OF GEORGE FOX

TO OLIVER CROMWELL

I who am of the world called George Fox, do deny the carrying or drawing of any carnal sword against any, or against thee, Oliver Cromwell, or any man.

In the presence of the Lord God I declare it. God is my witness, by whom I am moved to give this forth for the Truth's sake, from him whom the world calls George Fox; who is the son of God who is sent to stand a witness against all violence and against all the works of darkness, and to turn people from the darkness to the light, and to bring them from the occasion of the war and from the occasion of the magistrate's sword, which is a terror to the evildoers who act contrary to the light of the Lord Jesus Christ, which is a praise to them that do well, a protection to them that do well and not evil.

Such soldiers as are put in that place no false accusers must be, no violence must do, but be content with their wages; and the magistrate bears not the sword in vain. From under the occasion of that sword I do seek to bring people. My weapons are not carnal but spiritual, and "my kingdom is not of this world," therefore with a carnal weapon I do not fight, but am from those things dead; from him who is not of the world, called of the world by the name George Fox. And this I am ready to seal with my blood.

LETTER, 1654

ABOVE *The Quakers rejected the sacraments and an ordained ministry. They preached pacifism and adherence to the inner light of Christianity.*

John Bunyan

hile languishing in prison for his Christian activities, Bunyan turned his own life into a long allegory, in which the hero is portrayed as a pilgrim journeying to the Celestial City. The vivid, and often disturbing, imagery of Pilgrim's Progress made it the most popular spiritual book ever written in English. And the names he gave to the places and people whom the hero encountered, such as Vanity Fair and the Slough of Despond, Valiant-for-Truth and Great-Heart, have passed into common English parlance. Even the poorest Christian households in Britain and America have usually possessed a copy of Bunyan's masterpiece, alongside the Bible.

The son of a tinker, Bunyan spent his early adult years plying the family trade, traveling from village to village repairing pots and pans. He fought in Cromwell's army in the Civil War, and afterward returned to his home county of Bedfordshire with a firm Protestant faith. After receiving baptism by total immersion, he became an itinerant preacher, visiting congregations that had split from the Church of England. After the restoration of the monarchy in 1660, in common with many other independent Christians, he suffered continual persecution.

ABOVE *John Bunyan wrote Pilgrim's Progress while in jail for preaching his own style of Christianity.*

CHRISTIAN LOSES HIS BURDEN

Now I saw in my dreams that the highway up which Christian was to go was fenced on either side with a wall that was called Salvation. Up this way, therefore, did burdened Christian run but not without great difficulty, because of the load on his back. He ran thus till he came to a place somewhat ascending; and upon that place stood a cross, and a little below, in the bottom, a sepulcher.

So I saw in my dream that, just as Christian came up to the cross, his burden loosed from off his shoulders, and fell from off his back, and began to tumble, and so continued to do till it come to the mouth of the sepulcher, where it fell in, and I saw it no more.

Then was Christian glad and lightsome, and said with a merry heart, "He hath given me rest by his sorrow, and life by his death." Then he stood still awhile to look and wonder: for it was very surprising to him that the sight of the cross should thus ease him of his burden. He looked, therefore, and looked again, even till the springs that were in his head sent the water down his cheeks.

Now, as he stood looking and weeping, behold, three Shining Ones came to him, and saluted him with, "Peace be to thee."

So the first said to him. "Thy sins be forgiven thee," the second stripped him of his rags, and clothed him with a change of raiment; the third also set a mark on his forehead, and gave him a roll with a seal upon it, which he bade him look on as he ran, and that he should give it in at the celestial gate: so they went their way. Then Christian gave three leaps for joy.

PILGRIM'S PROGRESS, PART 1

VANITY FAIR

As in other fairs of less moment there are several rows and streets under their proper names, where such and such wares are vended; so here likewise you have the proper places, rows, streets (namely, countries and kingdoms) where the wares of this fair are soonest to be found. Here are the Britain Row, the French Row, the Italian Row, the Spanish Row, the German Row, where several sorts of vanities are to be sold. Now, the way to the Celestial City lies just through this town where this lusty fair is kept. So these pilgrims must needs go through this fair. Well, so they did, but, behold, even as they entered into the fair, all the people in the fair were moved, and the town itself, as it were, in a hubbub about them and that for several reasons.

First, the pilgrims were clothed for such kind of raiment as was diverse from the raiment of any that traded in that fair. The people, therefore, of the fair, made a great gazing upon; some said they were fools; some, they were bedlams; and some, they were outlandish men.

Secondly, as they wondered at their apparel, so they did likewise at their speech; for few could understand what they said. They naturally spoke the language of Canaan; but they that kept the fair were the men of this world. So that from one end of the fair to the other, they seemed barbarians each to the other.

Thirdly, that which did not a little amuse the merchandisers was that these pilgrims set very lightly by all their wares. They cared not so much to look upon them; and if they called upon them to buy, they would put their fingers in their ears and look upward, signifying that their trade and traffic were in heaven.

One chanced, mockingly, beholding the carriage of the men, to say unto them, "What will you buy?"

But they, looking gravely upon him, said, "We buy the truth." At that there was an occasion taken to despise the men the more; some mocking, some taunting, some speaking reproachfully, and some calling on other to smite them.

PILGRIM'S PROGRESS, PART 1

THE CELESTIAL CITY

They came up to the gate. Now, when they were come up to the gate, there was written over it in letters of gold; "Blessed are they that do his commandments. That they may have the right to the tree of life, and may enter in through the gates into the city."

Then I saw in my dream that the Shining Men bid them call at the gate: the which when they did, some from above looked over the gate, to

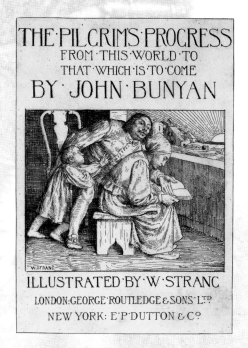

ABOVE *Bunyan's renowned Pilgrim's Progress symbolized his own spiritual journey through religious persecution.*

wit, Enoch, Moses, and Elijah, to whom it was said, "These pilgrims are come from the City of Destruction, for the love that they bear to the King of this place."

And then the pilgrims gave in unto them each man his certificate, which they had received at the beginning; those therefore were carried in to the King, who, when he had read them, said, "where are the men?" To whom it was answered, "They are standing without the gate." The King then commanded to open the gate, "that the righteous nation, which keepeth the truth, may enter in."

Now, I saw in my dreams that these two men were in at the gate; and lo, as they entered, they were transfigured, and they had raiment put on that shone like gold. There were also those that met them with harps and crowns, and gave them to them—the harps to praise withal, and the crowns in token of honor. Then I heard in my dreams that all the bells in the City rang again for joy! Now, just as the gates open to let in the men, I looked in after them, and behold, the City shone like the sun; the streets also were paved with gold; and in them walked many men with crowns on their heads, palms in their hands, and golden harps to sing praises withal.

PILGRIM'S PROGRESS, PART 1 z

John Wesley

*J*ohn Wesley was certainly the most influential, and possibly the most energetic, Christian that England has produced. In the course of his ministry he traveled a quarter of a million miles on horseback; he delivered about forty thousand sermons, typically preaching three or four times a day; and he wrote well over two hundred books and tracts, mostly composed in the saddle. By the end of his life there were about a hundred thousand members of the Methodist Societies he founded; and today the denomination that grew out of them has about twenty million adherents across the world. Moreover the evangelical movement, which continues to influence almost every Christian church, looks back to Wesley as one of its primary sources of inspiration.

His most famous written work is his Journal. In it he described his spiritual anguish, leading up to his conversion in 1738, in which he entrusted himself to Christ as his savior. He grew up in the rectory at Epworth in Lincolnshire, under the strict discipline of devout parents. In 1719, at the age of sixteen, he went to Oxford University, where he and his brother Charles organized the Holy Club, a group of young men who imposed on themselves a rule of prayer and charity. He was ordained a priest, and set sail for Georgia as a missionary to the native Americans. Yet despite his efforts to serve God, he was beset by guilt, regarding himself as an unredeemed sinner. It was only when a Moravian minister from London, Peter Boehler, taught him to open his heart to Christ that he experienced peace and joy—and his true ministry began.

ABOVE *John Wesley, founder of the Methodist Society, which is today an international denomination with around 20 million followers.*

EARLY LIFE

I believe, till I was about ten years old, I had not sinned away that washing of the Holy Ghost which was given me in baptism, having been strictly educated and carefully taught that I could only be saved by universal obedience, by keeping all the commandments of God in the meaning of which I was diligently instructed.

And those instructions, so far as they respected outward duties and sins, I gladly received and often thought of. But all that was said to me of inward obedience or holiness I neither understood nor remembered. So that I was indeed as ignorant of the true meaning of the law as I was of the Gospel of Christ.

The next six or seven years were spent at school, where, outward restraints being removed, I was much more negligent than before, even of outward duties, and almost continually guilty of outward sins which I knew to be such, though they were not scandalous in the eye of the world.

However, I still read the scriptures and said my prayers, morning and evening. And what I now hoped to be saved by was (1) not being so bad as other people; (2) having still a kindness for religion; and (3) reading the Bible, going to church, and saying my prayers. Being removed to the university for five years, I still said my prayers both in public and in private, and read with scriptures several other books of religion, especially comments on the New Testament.

Yet I had not all this while so much as notion of inward holiness; nay, went on habitually, and for the most part very contentedly, in some or other known sin indeed, with some intermissions and short struggles, especially before and after the Holy Communion, which I was obliged to receive thrice a year. I cannot well tell what I hoped to be saved by now, when I was continually sinning against that little light I had, unless by those transient fits of what many divines taught me to call "repentance."

THE JOURNAL

BUILDING ON SAND

In 1730 I began visiting the prisons, assisting the poor and sick in town, and doing what other good I could by my presence or my little fortune to the bodies and souls of all men. To this end I abridged myself of all superfluities, and many that are called necessaries of life. I soon became a byword for so doing, and I rejoiced that my name was cast out as evil.

The next spring I began observing the Wednesday and Friday fasts commonly observed in the ancient Church, tasting no food till three in the afternoon. And now I knew not how to go any further. I diligently strove against all sin. I omitted no sort of self-denial which I thought lawful. I carefully used, both in public and private, all the means of grace at all opportunities. I omitted no occasion of doing good. I for that reason suffered evil.

And all this I knew to be nothing unless as it was directed toward inward holiness. Accordingly this, the image of God, was what I aimed at in all, by doing his will, not my own. Yet when, after continuing some years in this course, I apprehended myself to be near death, I could not find that all this gave me any comfort or any assurance of acceptance with God. At this I was then not a little surprised, not imagining I had been all this time building on the sand.

THE JOURNAL

LACKING FAITH

January 1738, being in imminent danger of death and very uneasy on that account, I was strongly convinced that the cause of that uneasiness was unbelief and that the gaining a true, living faith was the one thing needful for me. But still I fixed not this faith on its right object: I meant only faith in God, not faith in or through Christ. Again, I knew not that I was wholly void of this faith but only thought I had not enough of it.

So that when Peter Bœhler, whom God prepared for me as soon as I came to London, affirmed of true faith in Christ (which is but one) that it had those two fruits inseparably attending it, "dominion over sin, and constant peace from a sense of forgiveness," I was quite amazed and looked upon it as a new Gospel. If this was so, it was clear I had not faith. But I was not willing to be convinced of this. Therefore I disputed with all my might and labored to prove that faith might be where these were not, especially where the sense of forgiveness was not.

THE JOURNAL

ABOVE *Wesley preaching on his father's tomb — from Wesley's Journals, 1742.*

CONVERSION

In the evening, I went very unwillingly to a society in Aldersgate Street, where one was reading Luther's Preface to the Epistle to the Romans. About a quarter before nine, while he was describing the change which God works in the heart through faith in Christ, I felt my heart strangely warmed. I felt I did trust in Christ, Christ alone for salvation; and an assurance was given me that he had taken away my sin, even mine, and saved me from the law of sin and death. I began to pray with all my might for those who had in a more especial manner despitefully used me and persecuted me. I then testified openly to all there what I now first felt in my heart.

THE JOURNAL

Jonathan Edwards

Protestant Christianity, with its emphasis on personal commitment, is marked by periodic revivals, in which large numbers of people in a particular area experience a spiritual renewal. One of the most spectacular revivals, which came to be called the Great Awakening, began in the Massachusetts town of Northampton in 1735.

Starting with the conversion of a young woman, renowned for her wild social life, it rapidly spread from person to person, until almost the entire population was caught up in religious fervor. The Northampton revival remains famous through the gripping account of that time penned by the minister of the Congregational Church.

Jonathan Edwards was the son of a minister in Connecticut. After graduating from Yale University, he was invited to Northampton in 1727, at the age of thirty-four. His congregation was wealthy and cultured, and appreciated the deep theological scholarship that underpinned his sermons. Although his faith was firm, it lacked passion; and he was as astonished as anyone at the sudden spiritual eruption that occurred. So the title he gave to his description, Faithful Narrative of the Surprising Works of God, reflected his own reaction to the revival.

THE GREAT AWAKENING

And then it was, in the latter part of December, that the Spirit of God began extraordinarily to set in, and wonderfully to work among us. There were, very suddenly, one after another, five or six persons who were to all appearance savingly converted, and some of them wrought upon in every remarkable manner.

Particularly, I was surprised with the relation of a young woman who had been one of the greatest company-keepers in the whole town. When she came to me, I had never heard that she was become in any wise, serious, but by the conversation I then had with her it appeared to me that what she gave an account of was a glorious work of God's infinite power and sovereign grace. God had given her a new heart, truly broken and sanctified. I could not then doubt of it, and have seen much in my acquaintance with her since to confirm it.

Though the work was glorious, yet I was filled with concern about the effect it might have upon others. I was ready to conclude (though too rashly) that some would be hardened by it. But the event was the reverse, to a wonderful degree. God made it, I suppose, the greatest occasion of awakening to others of anything that ever came to pass in the town.

I have had abundant opportunity to know the effect it had, by my private conversation with many. The news of it seemed to be almost like a flash of lightning upon the hearts of young people all over the town, and upon many others. Those among us who used to be the farthest from seriousness, and that I most feared would make an ill improvement of it, seemed greatly to be awakened with it.

Many went to talk with her concerning what she had met with: and what appeared in her seemed to be to the satisfaction of all that did so. Presently upon this, a great and earnest concern about the great things of religion and the eternal world became universal in all parts of the town, and among persons of all degrees and all ages.... There was scarcely a single person in the town, old or young, left unconcerned about the great things of the eternal world.

Those who were wont to be the vainest and

loosest, and had been most disposed to think and speak slightly of vital and experimental religion, were now generally subject to great awakenings. The work of conversion was carried on in a most astonishing manner, and increased more and more. Souls did as it were come by flocks to Jesus Christ.

From day to day, for many months together, might be seen evident instances of sinners brought out of darkness into marvelous light, with a new song of praise to God in their mouths. The work of God, as it was carried on, and the number of true saints multiplied, soon made a glorious alteration in the town, so that in the spring and summer following in 1735, the town seemed full of the presence of God; it never was so full of love, nor of joy, and yet so full of distress, as it was then.

There were remarkable tokens of God's presence in almost every house. It was a time of joy in families on account of salvation being brought to them: parents rejoicing over their children as newborn, and husbands over their wives, and wives over their husbands.

The doings of God were seen in His sanctuary. God's day was a delight, and his tabernacles were amiable. Our public assemblies then were beautiful. The congregation was alive in God's service, everyone earnestly intent on the public worship, every hearer eager to drink in the words of the minister. The assembly were from time to time in tears while the Word was preached: some weeping with sorrow and distress, others with joy and love, others with pity and concern for the souls of their neighbors. Our public praises were then greatly enlivened.

Our congregation excelled all that ever I knew in the external part of the duty, before (the awakening), the men generally carrying three parts of music regularly and well, and the women a part of themselves. But now they were evidently wont to sing with unusual elevation of heart and voice, which made the duty pleasant indeed.

On whatever occasion persons met together, Christ was to be heard of and seen in the midst of them. Our young people, when they met, were wont to spend their time in talking of the excellency and dying love Jesus Christ, the glory of the way of salvation, the wonderful, free, and

sovereign grace of God, His glorious work in the conversion of a soul, the truth and certainty of the great things of God's Word.

Even at weddings, which formerly were mere occasions of mirth and jollity, there was now no appearance of any but spiritual mirth. Many who before had labored under difficulties about their own state, had now their doubts removed by more satisfying experience, and more clear discoveries of God's love, (being) renewed with fresh and extraordinary incomes of the Spirit of God; though some much more than others, according to the measure of the gift of Christ....

> "There were remarkable tokens of God's presence in almost every house. It was a time of joy in families on account of salvation being brought to them: parents rejoicing over their children as newborn, and husbands over their wives, and wives over their husbands."

These awakenings, when they have first seized on persons, have had two effects. One was, that they have brought them immediately to quit their sinful practices. The looser sort (of people) have been brought to forsake and dread their former vices and extravagances. When once the Spirit of God began to be so wonderfully poured out in a general way through the town, people had soon done with their old quarrels, backbitings, and intermeddling with other men's matters.

The other effect was, that it put them on earnest application to the means of salvation, reading, prayer, meditation, the ordinances of God's house, and private conference.

Their cry was, "What shall we do to be saved?" The minister's house was thronged far more than ever the tavern had been wont to be.

FAITHFUL NARRATIVE OF THE SURPRISING WORKS OF GOD

David Brainerd

*I*n his early twenties David Brainerd's spiritual gifts were so widely recognized that he was offered the pastorship of two of the leading churches in America. But he turned both down in order to preach the gospel to the native Americans. He traveled beyond the frontier, entrusting himself to their generosity for food and shelter. The tribes he visited admired his courage and warmed to his gentle manner, and he won many souls. But from childhood his body had been frail and sickly, and in 1747, at the age of twenty-nine, he succumbed to the rigors of his calling.

His Diary relates in bold, unadorned prose his missionary labors, describing both the discomforts and the successes. In addition to physical weakness, he also fought a constant battle against depression. He found solace in the simple, undemanding friendships he made among his converts.

ABOVE *David Brainerd traveled throughout the country preaching Christianity to native Americans. "Some of the white people, who came out of curiosity to 'hear what this babbler would say' to the poor ignorant Indians, were also much awakened."*

GOING BEYOND THE FRONTIER

*W*ednesday, March 9, 1743—Rode sixteen miles to Montauk, and had some inward sweetness on the road, but something of flatness and deadness after I came there and saw the Indians. I withdrew and endeavored to pray, but found myself awfully deserted. However, I went and preached from Isaiah 53:10. Had some assistance, and I trust something of the divine presence was among us. In the evening also I prayed and exhorted among them. May the God of all grace succeed my poor labors in this place.

FRIDAY, APRIL 1

I rode to Kaunaumeek, near twenty miles from Stockbridge (near Albany, New York), where the Indians live with whom I am concerned, and there lodged on a little heap of straw.

LORD'S DAY, APRIL 10

Rose early in the morning and walked out; spent considerable time in the woods in prayer and meditation. Preached to the Indians, both forenoon and afternoon. They behaved soberly in general. Two or three in particular appeared under some religious concern, with whom I discoursed privately; and one told me her heart had cried ever since she heard me preach first.

WEDNESDAY, MAY 18

My circumstances are such that I have no comfort of any kind but what I have in God. I live in the most lonesome wilderness; have but one single person to converse with that can speak English (his Indian interpreter, John Wauwaumpequunnaunt). I live poorly with regard to the comforts of life. Most of my diet consists of boiled corn, hasty-pudding, etc. I lodge on a bundle of straw, and my labor is hard and extremely difficult. I have little appearance of success to comfort me. The Indians" affairs are very difficult, having no land to live on but what the Dutch people lay claim to and threaten to drive them off from. They (the Dutch) have no regard to the souls of the poor Indians, and by what I can learn, they hate me because I come to preach to them (the Indians).

THE JOURNAL, 1743

A DAY OF GOD'S POWER

AUGUST 8

In the afternoon I preached to the Indians; their number was now about sixty-five persons, men, women, and children. I discoursed from Luke 14:16-23,6 and was favored with uncommon freedom in my discourse. There was much visible concern among them while I was discoursing publicly; but afterward when I spoke to one and another more particularly, whom I perceived under much concern, the power of God seemed to descend upon the assembly like a rushing mighty wind, and with an astonishing energy bore all before it.

I stood amazed at the influence which seized the audience almost universally. Almost all persons of all ages were bowed down with concern together. Old men and women, who had been drunken wretches for many years, and some little children, not more than six or seven years of age, appeared in distress about their souls, as well as persons of middle age. The most stubborn hearts were now obliged to bow. A principal man among the Indians, who with a great degree of confidence the day before told me he had been a Christian more than ten years, was now bitterly repentant.

Another man, considerable in years, who had been a murderer, a Powwow or conjurer, and a notorious drunkard, was likewise brought to cry for mercy with many tears.

Some of the white people, who came out of curiosity to "hear what this babbler would say" to the poor ignorant Indians, were also much awakened, and some appeared to be wounded with a view of their perishing state. Those who had lately obtained relief were filled with comfort; they appeared calm and composed, and seemed to rejoice in Christ Jesus.

Some took their distressed friends by the hand, telling them of the goodness of Christ and the comfort that is to be enjoyed in Him, and invited them to come and give up their hearts to Him. A young Indian woman, who I believe never knew before she had a soul, hearing that there was something strange among the Indians, came to see what was the matter. Earlier she had laughed and mocked at me, but I had not proceeded far in my discourse before she felt effectually that she had a soul.

She seemed like one pierced through with a dart, and cried out incessantly. After the service was over I hearkened to hear what she said, and perceived the burden of her prayer to be, Guttummaukalumneh mechaumeh kmeleh Ndah, "Have mercy on me, and help me to give Thee my heart." Thus she continued praying for many hours together. This was indeed a surprising day of God's power, and seemed enough to convince an atheist of the truth, importance, and power of God's Word.

THE JOURNAL, 1743

THE POWER OF GOD'S WORD

AUGUST 26

Being fully convinced it was now my duty to take a journey far back to the Indians on Susquehanna River, I asked (my people) if they could not be willing to spend the remainder of the day in prayer for me. They cheerfully complied, and continued praying all night till nearly break of day. This day an old Indian, who had all his days been an obstinate idolater, was brought to give up his rattles (which they use for music in their idolatrous feasts and dances) to the other Indians, who quickly destroyed them. This was done without any attempt of mine in the affair. It seemed to be nothing but the power of God's Word. May the glory be ascribed to Him who is the sole Author of it!

THE JOURNAL, 1743

Their hearts were engaged and cheerful in duty. Love seemed to reign among them. They took each other by the hand with tenderness and affection as if their hearts were knit together. Several other Indians, seeing and hearing these things, were much affected and wept bitterly, longing to be partakers of the same joy and comfort.

John Woolman

At a time when even enlightened white people in America regarded black slavery as part of the natural order, this modest, self-taught shopkeeper set about opposing it. After his conversion he found himself no longer able to accept that black people were mentally and spiritually inferior. On the contrary, he believed that God had laid upon him a duty to proclaim the equality of white and black. He became a Quaker, and spoke of his beliefs at Quaker gatherings. But Woolman's main work was in talking to the slave owners and attempting to persuade them of the error of their practice.

Born in Northampton, New Jersey, he trained as a tailor, and then opened a shop. He was a highly successful trader, but in 1757, at the age of thirty-seven, he sold his business, and used the proceeds to finance his mission, traveling from place to place. In the following fifteen years until his death his patient efforts began to change the climate of opinion. And two years later the Quakers in Philadelphia voted to abolish slave owning among their members.

ABOVE *John Woolman stood alone in his belief that slavery was incompatible with Christianity.*

FIRST ENCOUNTER WITH SLAVERY

All this time I lived with my parents and worked on the plantation, and having had schooling pretty well for a planter, I used to improve it in winter evenings and other leisure times. Being now in the twenty-first year of my age, a man in much business at shopkeeping and baking asked me if I would hire with him to tend shop and keep books. I acquainted my father with the proposal, and after some deliberation it was agreed for me to go. After a while my former acquaintances gave over expecting me as one of their company, and I began to be known to some whose conversation was helpful to me.

About the twenty-third year of my age I had many fresh and personal revelations in respect to the care and providence of the Almighty over His creatures in general, and over man as the most noble among those which are visible. My employer having a Negro woman, sold her, and desired me to write a bill of sale, the man being waiting who bought her.

The thing was sudden; and though the thoughts of writing an instrument of slavery for one of my fellow-creatures felt uneasy, yet I remembered I was hired by the year. It was my master who directed me to do it, and it was an elderly man, a member of our Quaker Society, who bought her.

So through weakness I gave way and wrote; but at the executing of it I was so afflicted in my mind that I said, before my master and the Friend, that I believed slave-keeping to be a practice inconsistent with the Christian religion. This in some degree abated my uneasiness.

Yet as often as I have reflected seriously upon it, I thought I should have been clearer, if I had desired to have been excused from it as a thing against my conscience; for such it was. And some time after this a young man of our Society spoke to me to write a conveyance of a slave to him, he having lately taken a Negro into his house.

I told him I was not easy to write it; for though many of our Meeting and in other places kept slaves, I still believed the practice was not right, and desired to be excused from it. I spoke to him in goodwill, and he told me that keeping slaves was not altogether agreeable to his mind, but that the slave being a gift to his wife, he had accepted of her.

THE JOURNAL OF JOHN WOOLMAN

CONFRONTING A SICK MAN

In the year 1753, a person at some distance was lying sick and his brother came to me to write his will. I knew he had slaves, and asking his brother, was told he intended to leave them as slaves to his children. As writing is a profitable employ, and as offending sober people was disagreeable to my inclination, I was straitened in my mind. But as I looked to the Lord, He inclined my heart to His testimony, and I told the man that I believed the practice of continuing slavery to this people was not right. I told him I had a scruple in my mind against doing writings of that kind; that though many in our Society kept them as slaves, still I was not easy to be concerned in it, and desired to be excused from going to write the will.

THE JOURNAL OF JOHN WOOLMAN

DEBATING WITH A COLONEL

On the eleventh day of the fifth month in the year 1757, we crossed the rivers Potomac and Rappahannock and lodged at Port Royal. On the way, we happening in company with a colonel of the militia who appeared to be a thoughtful man, I took occasion to remark on the difference in general betwixt a people used to labor moderately for their living, training up their children in frugality and business, and those who live on the labor of slaves.

The former, in my view, I felt was the most happy life; with which he concurred. He mentioned the trouble arising from the untoward, slothful disposition of the Negroes, adding that one of our laborers would do as much in a day as two of their slaves. I replied that free men, whose minds were properly on their business, found a satisfaction in improving, cultivating, and providing for their families; but Negroes, laboring to support others who claim them as their property, and expecting nothing but slavery during life, had not the like inducement to be industrious.

After some further conversation, I said that men having power too often misapplied it; that though we made slaves of the Negroes, and the Turks made slaves of the Christians, I believed that liberty was the natural right of all men equally. Which he did not deny, but said the lives of the Negroes were so wretched in their own country that many of them lived better here than there. I only said there are great odds in regard to us, on what principle we act; and so the conversation on that subject ended.

THE JOURNAL OF JOHN WOOLMAN

A

JOURNAL

OF

THE LIFE,

GOSPEL LABOURS, AND CHRISTIAN EXPERIENCES

OF THAT FAITHFUL

𝔐inister of 𝔍esus 𝔠hrist,

JOHN WOOLMAN,

LATE OF MOUNT HOLLY, IN THE PROVINCE OF NEW JERSEY, NORTH AMERICA.

TO WHICH ARE ADDED

HIS WORKS,

CONTAINING HIS LAST EPISTLE, AND OTHER WRITINGS.

A NEW EDITION.

" *The work of righteousness shall be peace; and the effect of righteousness quietness and assurance for ever.*" —ISAIAH xxxiii. 17.

LONDON:

PRINTED AND SOLD BY WILLIAM PHILLIPS, GEORGE-YARD, LOMBARD-STREET.

1824.

ABOVE *Although a simple, self-taught shopkeeper, John Woolman played an important part in changing people's attitudes, leading to the eventual abolition of slavery in America.*

Leo Tolstoy

After achieving worldwide success as a novelist, Tolstoy became deeply dissatisfied with both himself and modern life. Although he accepted the doctrines of Christianity, in which he had been brought up, they gave him no solace. Finally, through the influence of the peasants living on his family estate, he decided that the actual words of Christ, in the Gospels, provide a precise guide for living; and he strove to put those words into practice. The essence of Christ's teaching, he came to believe, lay in the words "Resist not evil"; and these imply rejecting the security and comfort provided by political institutions, and becoming self-sufficient. For the rest of his life he dressed as a peasant, grew his own food, and even made his own boots.

Tolstoy was born in 1828 into the Russian nobility, and as a young man served as an officer in the Crimean War. He returned to manage the family estate, where he started a successful school for the peasants. After his conversion he wrote numerous books and pamphlets on religious and moral matters, including What I Believe, published in 1883 and banned the following year by the Russian Orthodox Church—which later excommunicated him. In his final years he was regarded by many as a prophet, receiving visitors from across the world.

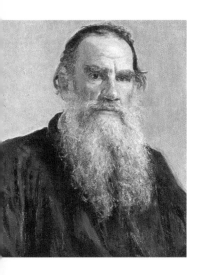

ABOVE A portrait of Leo Tolstoy painted in 1887 by Ilya Efimovitch Repin. (State Tretyakov Gallery, Moscow).

RESIST NOT EVIL

When I understood that the words "Resist not evil" did indeed mean "Resist not evil," my whole understanding of Christ's teaching was suddenly changed; I was appalled at the peculiar way in which I had understood it until then. I knew—we all know—that the meaning of the Christian teaching lies in love for other people.

To say, "Turn your cheek, love your enemies," is to express the very essence of Christianity. I had known all this since childhood, but why had I not understood these straightforward words in a straightforward manner? Why had I searched instead for some allegorical meaning in them? "Do not resist him that is evil" means "Do not ever resist him that is evil, do not commit acts of violence, acts that are contrary to the spirit of love."

And if you are insulted, then suffer the insult and still do not commit acts of violence. It is impossible to say any of this more clearly and straightforwardly than Christ did. How would I, who believed, or at least tried to believe, that the man who had said these words was God—how could I say that I lacked the strength to act on these words? It is as though my master were to say, "Go and chop wood," and I were to reply that I did not have the strength.

What I Believe

THE ERROR OF INSTITUTIONS

From childhood I had been taught that Christ was God and His teaching divine, but I had also been taught to respect the institutions which used violence to insure my safety from evil people. I had even been taught to see these institutions as holy. I was taught that it was shameful and degrading to submit to a doer of evil, to suffer under him, and that it was praiseworthy to resist him. I was taught to judge and to punish. Then I was taught to be a soldier, that is, to resist the doers of evil by the act of murder.

The army of which I was a member was called a Christ-loving army; its acts were sanctioned by a Christian blessing. From childhood to manhood, I was taught what directly contradicts the law of Christ: to resist someone who injures men and to revenge myself through violence for any insult to myself, my family, or my nation. Far from incurring disapproval, these principles were instilled into me; I was taught that they were splendid and in no way contradictory to the law of Christ.

Everything around me, my tranquility, the security of myself and my family, my property, was based on a law that Christ had repudiated, the law of a tooth for a tooth.

Church teachers taught me that Christ's teaching was divine, that human frailty made it impossible to adhere to, and that only Christ's blessing could enable us to accomplish it. And our whole way of life implied what my secular teachers admitted openly: that Christ's teaching was impracticable, a mere fantasy. Through word and deed they taught what was contrary to it. This admission of the impracticability of the Lord's teachings was instilled into me so gradually, came to seem so normal, and harmonized so completely with my own desire, that I was never aware of the contradiction into which I had fallen.

I did not see that it was impossible to profess Christ, the basis of whose teaching was non-resistance to evil, and at one and the same time to work calmly and consciously for the establishment of property, law courts, government, and armies; impossible to establish a life that was contradictory to Christ's teaching and at one and the same time to pray to Christ for the fulfillment of the law of forgiveness and non-resistance to evil.

What now seems so obvious never even entered my head: that it would be considerably simpler to establish a life on the basis of Christ's law and then—if they are indeed so necessary to

ABOVE *Portrait of Leo Tolstoy (I E Repin, 1887, Tretyakov Gallery, Moscow).*

our well-being—to pray for law courts, executions, and wars. In the end I realized how my error had arisen: from an acceptance of Christ in word and a denial of Him in deed.

Non-resistance to evil is the commandment that unifies the whole teaching, but not if it is a mere saying, only if it is a rule that is obligatory for everyone, a law.

It truly is a key that opens everything, but only if it is pushed into the lock. To see this commandment as a mere saying, a saying that cannot be followed without supernatural help, is to destroy the whole of the teaching. And a teaching from which the basic, unifying commandment has been removed cannot seem anything but impossible. To unbelievers it seems simply ridiculous, and it cannot appear otherwise. We have installed an engine, heated up the boiler, set it in motion, but not attached the transmission belt—this is what we have done to the teaching of Christ by saying that it is possible to be a Christian without fulfilling the commandment of non-resistance to evil.

What I Believe

ABOVE *Tolstoy was a prolific writer on his religious beliefs and many regarded him as a prophet. However, What I Believe was banned by the Russian Orthodox Church.*

Charles Haddon Spurgeon

ABOVE *Tens of thousands flocked to hear Spurgeon's weekly sermons.*

purgeon's weekly sermons were heard and read by more people than those of any other preacher, prior to the advent of electronic communication. On a typical Sunday six thousand people crammed into his tabernacle in north London; and his sermon was immediately printed, and circulated throughout the English-speaking world. Yet those texts today seem oddly dry and lifeless, while his gentler, more personal pieces, written near the end of his life, remain compelling. One of the most delightful is a meditation given on vacation in southern France, to members of his congregation who had come to join him. Taking as his text a verse from Psalm 17, "Thou hast visited me in the night," he recounts visits he had received at night from God, describing their effects on him.*

He grew up in a small cottage in an Essex village, receiving minimal education. After a sudden and intense experience of conversion on the eve of his fifteenth birthday, he became convinced that God was calling him to preach. Two years later, in 1852, his voice barely broken, he became minister of a tiny church near Cambridge. From there he went on to London, where he took over a derelict chapel in the midst of slums. Within a year the congregation was too large, and he held services in a music hall; he then built a vast tabernacle. He also founded a College for Pastors, where he trained four hundred young men—all of whom, like him, were from poor families with little schooling.

THE FIRST VISIT

I remember well when God first visited me; and assuredly it was the night of nature, of ignorance, of sin. His visit had the same effect upon me that it had upon Saul of Tarsus when the Lord spake to him out of heaven. He brought me down from the high horse, and caused me to fall to the ground; by the brightness of the light of His Spirit He made me grope in conscious blindness; and in the brokenness of my heart I cried "Lord, what wilt Thou have me to do?"

I felt that I had been rebelling against the Lord, kicking against the pricks, and doing evil even as I could; and my soul was filled with anguish at the discovery. Very searching was the glance of the eye of Jesus, for it revealed my sin, and caused me to go out and weep bitterly. As when the Lord visited Adam, and called him to stand naked before Him, so was I stripped of all my righteousness before the face of the Most High. Yet the visit ended not there; for as the Lord God clothed our first parents in coats of skins, so did He cover me with songs in the night. It was night, but the visit was no dream; in fact, I there and then ceased to dream, and began to

LEFT *On the eve if his fifteenth birthday, Charles Haddon Spurgeon claimed that God called upon him to preach.*

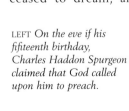

deal with the reality of things.

I was half inclined to cry with the demoniac of Gadara, "What have I to do with Thee, Jesus, Thou Son of God most high?" That first discovery of His injured love was overpowering; its very hopefulness increased my anguish, for then I saw that I had slain the Lord who had come to save me. I saw that mine was the hand which made the hammer fall, and drove the nails that fastened the Redeemer's hands and feet to the cruel tree....

This is the sight which breeds repentance: "They shall look upon Him whom they have pierced, and mourn for Him." When the Lord visits us He humbles us, removes all hardness from our hearts, and leads us to the Savior's feet.

LATER VISITS

Since those early days, I hope that you and I have had many visits from our Lord. Those first visits were, as I said, sharply searching; but the later ones have been sweetly solacing. Some of us have had them, especially in the night, when we have been compelled to count the sleepless hours. "Heaven's gate opens when this world's is shut."

The night is still; everybody is away; work is done; care is forgotten: and then the Lord Himself draws near. Possibly there may be pain to be endured, the head may be aching and the heart may be throbbing; but if Jesus comes to visit us, our bed of languishing becomes a throne of glory.

Though it is true "He giveth His beloved sleep," yet at such times He give them something better than sleep, namely, His own presence, and the fullness of joy which comes with it. By night upon our bed we have seen the unseen. I have tried sometimes not to sleep under an excess of joy, when the company of Christ has been sweetly mine....

Do you ask me to describe these manifestations of the Lord? It were hard to tell you in words: you must know them for yourselves. If you had never tasted sweetness, no man living could give you an idea of honey. Yet if the honey be there, you can "taste and see." To a man born blind, sight must be a thing past imagination; and to one who has never known the Lord, His visits are quite as much beyond conception.

For our Lord to visit us is something more than for us to have the assurance of our salvation, though that is very delightful, and none of us should rest satisfied unless we possess it. To know that Jesus loves me is one thing: but to be visited by Him in love is more.

THE EFFECTS

When the Lord visits us in the night, what is the effect upon us? When hearts meet hearts in fellowship of love, communion brings first peace, then rest, and then joy of soul. I am speaking of no emotional excitement rising into fanatical rapture; but I speak of sober fact when I say the Lord's great heart touches ours, and our heart rises into sympathy with Him. First, we experience peace. All war is over, and a blessed peace is proclaimed; the peace of God keeps our heart and mind by Christ Jesus.

At such a time there is a delightful sense of rest; we have no ambitions, no desires. A divine serenity and security envelop us. We have no thought of foes, or fears, or afflictions, or doubts. There is a joyful laying aside of our own will. We are nothing, and we will be nothing: Christ is everything, and His will is the pulse of our soul. We are perfectly content either to be ill or to be well, to be rich or to be poor, to be slandered or to be honored, so

ABOVE *Charles Haddon Spurgeon was an engimatic preacher: "When hearts meet hearts in fellowship of love, communion brings first peace, then rest, and then joy of soul."*

that we may but abide in the love of Christ. Jesus fills the horizon of our being.

At such a time a flood of great joy will fill our minds. We shall half wish that the morning may never break again, for fear its light should banish the superior light of Christ's presence. We shall wish that we could glide away with our Beloved to the place where He feedeth among the lilies. We long to hear the voices of the white-robed armies, that we may follow their glorious Leader whithersoever He goeth. I am persuaded that there is no great actual distance between earth and heaven: the distance lies in our dull minds.

Thérèse of Lisieux

ne of the most popular books of modern times was the autobiography of a young French nun, who died in 1897 at the age of only twenty-four. Written at the request of the Reverend Mother of her community, it describes her "little way" toward sanctity. She regarded herself as very ordinary and insignificant, and wanted to become a saint through responding in a Christlike manner to the everyday demands of convent life. Since a community of nuns has much in common with both a family and a typical place of work, her simple, honest descriptions of her own behavior have resonances far beyond the convent walls.

The youngest of nine children, her mother died when Thérèse was aged four. Her father, a successful watchmaker, was intensely pious, and was delighted when his two eldest daughters entered the Carmelite convent at Lisieux. Thérèse was eager to follow, and at a papal audience asked permission to become a nun when she turned fifteen—earlier than was normally allowed. This was granted. Much of her autobiography was composed when she was dying of tuberculosis.

WISHING TO BE A SAINT

I have always wished to be a saint. But whenever I used to compare myself with saints, I was aware of the sad difference: they were like high mountains, their heads shrouded by clouds. While I was only an insignificant grain of sand, lying beneath people's feet. But I refused to be discouraged. I said to myself: "God would not put ambitions in people's heads that could not be accomplished. Clearly I can never be a great or important person. So it must be possible for me to become saintly in a very small and insignificant fashion. I shall accept myself as I am, with all my limitations; and then I shall find a little way, all of my own, which will be a shortcut to Heaven."

I continued my musings: "We live in an age of inventions. Nowadays rich people do not even climb stairs, but go by elevator instead. I am not big enough to climb the steep stairway to perfection. Is there not an elevator which will take me up to Jesus?"

CHAPTER 31

MISUNDERSTOOD INTENTIONS

Sometimes an action which seems wrong is in fact praiseworthy—it depends on the intention. I learned this through a trivial incident, and it taught me that you should never pass judgment on others. It happened during recreation. The doorbell had been rung twice, indicating that workmen had arrived bringing some trees for the Christmas crèche. I was bored by the needlework I was doing, and thought I would enjoy lending a hand.

The Mother Sub-Prioress spoke to me and the sister sitting beside me, telling one of us to go and help the workmen. I started to fold up the needlework. But then I thought the sister beside me might get particular pleasure from helping the workmen. So I folded the needlework slowly, to let her finish first. The Mother Sub-Prioress was looking with a smile, and as I got up she said: "Just like you—slow and lazy. There are no extra jewels for your crown today!" And of course everyone else must have silently agreed with her.

I cannot tell you how much good this incident did to me. It made me kinder about other people's faults. And it pricked my vanity. When people speak well of me, I say to myself: "My efforts to do good are often marked down as faults. So the actions that are marked well may really be faults."

CHAPTER 34

DEALING WITH IRRITATION

There is one sister in the community who constantly irritates me. Her mannerisms, her way of speaking, and her whole character repel me. But I recognize that she is very holy, so God loves her dearly. I strived to suppress my feelings toward her. I reminded myself that love is not a matter of pleasant emotions, but of good actions. Thus I decided to behave as if she was the most lovable person I knew. Every time I encountered her, I prayed for her, commending her to God for all her virtues. I felt certain that Jesus would enjoy such progress, because all artists like to hear their work praised.... But I did not confine myself to praying; I also took every opportunity to be kind to her. When I felt tempted to put her down with an unkind remark, I smiled at her and changed the subject....

She was utterly unaware of my true emotions, and never realized why I acted in this way. To this day she believes that her personality attracts me. Once at recreation she came over to me, with a broad smile, and said: "I wish you would tell me why you are especially fond of me; whenever you see me, you give me a sweet look." In truth I had become fond of her that time, because I had learned to see Jesus in the depths of her soul.

CHAPTER 34

DEPENDING ON PRAYER

I depend completely on prayer. It is my only source of strength; it is the irresistible weapon which our Lord has put into my head. Again and again I've observed my prayers touching people's hearts—far more effectively than any words I could say directly to them. The power of prayer is astonishing. Like a queen, prayer always has access to the King, and can obtain whatever it asks. It is a great mistake to think that prayers could only work if they are taken from a book. If that were true, I should be in a terrible position. I can never face the strain of searching through books of prayers, looking for the one designed to meet my present need—it makes my head spin.

I just do what children have to do before they have learned to read. I tell God in my own words what I want, without any splendid turn of phrase; and somehow he always manages to understand me. For me prayer is like a ship being launched into the sea; in prayer I am carried toward God.

CHAPTER 37

ABOVE *The Silent Life (Dora Noyes, 1880). "I depend completely on prayer. It is my only source of strength."*

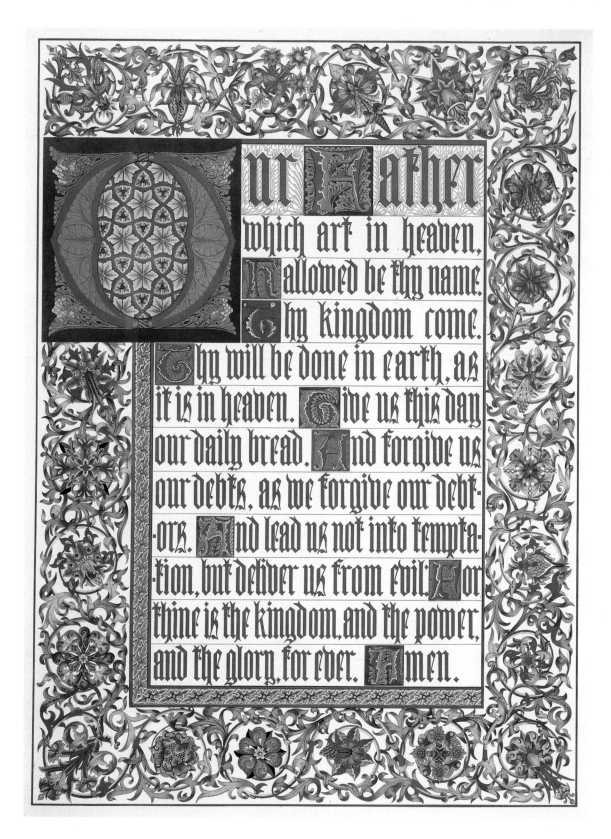

ABOVE *An illumination of The Lord's Prayer*
(anonymous, English, c.1870)

Part Three

❧

PHILOSOPHY

I would be much more afraid of rejecting religious faith, and later finding out it were true, than of embracing religious faith, and later finding out it were false.

BLAISE PASCAL, PENSÉES 241

Introduction

Prior to the Resurrection there is little in the Gospels indicating that Jesus saw himself as the founder of a new religion or philosophy. He specifically denied that he had come to do away with the Law of Moses and the teachings of the prophets; his purpose was to fulfill them, making them come true in his own time. Only after he had risen from the dead did he commission his disciples to carry his message to other lands.

But even then the disciples were reluctant to break out of the Jewish community; and at first the Christian Church seemed little more than a Jewish sect with a modest program for reform. It was the great apostle Paul who began the process of giving this tiny sect a distinct spiritual philosophy, and so set it on the path to becoming one of the major religions of the world. Although he may possibly have seen Jesus and even heard him preach, Paul did not know Jesus personally, and was initially very hostile to the Christians.

And after his conversion on the road to Damascus, he seems by his own account to have made no contact with the leaders in Jerusalem for several years—and so did not receive any firsthand reports of the earthly ministry of Jesus. To Paul the personality of Jesus, and to a great extent his teaching, were insignificant. The key to Christianity in Paul's eyes was the nature of Jesus in relation to God—which in turn determines his power to serve humanity.

Thus in the letters of Paul, we find the central themes of Christian philosophy, which have continued to be debated ever since. In the first verses of the letter to the Romans he writes of Jesus Christ as simultaneously human and divine. In the fifth chapter he shows how the death of this God-man can reconcile sinful human beings with God; and a chapter later he explores how individuals can experience this reconciliation—their old selves die with Christ on the cross, in order that they might be raised with him to new life.

This proved a highly effective policy. But once Christianity began to spread among the gentiles, Paul's philosophy came under severe challenge; and a new type of Christian writer emerged, steeped in the philosophical ideas of the ancient Greeks, which continued to mold moral and spiritual cultures throughout the Roman Empire.

To the Greek mind, the Christian notion of God entering human affairs, and even becoming a human being, was utterly absurd; the infinite and eternal nature of God could not in their view be allied to that which is finite and temporal.

In different ways, most of the great Christian writers of the first millennium grappled with this conundrum and its ramifications; and in the process they developed a religious philosophy of astonishing depth and beauty. Paradoxically, the major philosophical challenge to early Christianity became, at the start of the second millennium, the main stimulus to Christian thought. Through the translations and commentaries of Muslim scholars in Spain, the original works of the classical Greek philosophers, especially Aristotle and Plato, once again became available in Western Europe.

In the medieval period, the Christian theologians used the intellectual framework provided by Aristotle and Plato to restate traditional doctrines with greater precision and force. This in turn led many to feel that Christian teaching was failing to meet people's spiritual needs—and the great Protestant reformers of the sixteenth century attempted to set this right. But this debate, mostly conducted with great passion, honed Christian thought to meet its greatest challenge, the rise of science.

By its nature, scientific inquiry involves skepticism, in which every statement is open to question. Thus at first Christian leaders reacted with hostility, even condemning some scientific thinkers as heretics. And in one respect these leaders have been proved right. For over a thousand years the basic tenets of Christianity had barely been questioned, so philosophical debate was largely a matter of interpreting these tenets.

But scientific skepticism undermined this intellectual dominance, gradually causing Christianity to be seen as one philosophical view among many. The decline in attendance at Christian worship is in part a consequence of this. Nonetheless, from the seventeenth century onward, the brightest Christian writers embraced skepticism as a tool for exploring the deepest religious truths. And through their genius Christianity continued to be respected as intellectually credible—and exciting.

ABOVE *God As Christ, The Word Made Flesh. Paul introduced the central themes of Christian philosophy, describing Jesus Christ as simultaneously human and divine.*

In different ways, most of the great Christian writers of the first millennium grappled with this conundrum and its ramifications; and in the process they developed a religious philosophy of astonishing depth and beauty.

Paul

*I*n his letters, probably written or dictated in haste between preaching engagements or during arduous journeys, Paul makes no attempt to present a systematic Christian philosophy. Yet he was a man of the highest intelligence, who was familiar with Greek philosophical ideas as well as Jewish theology. Thus, scattered through his letters are all the philosophical and theological themes that later Christian thinkers have taken up and debated.

He discusses at length the significance of the death and resurrection of Christ, both for the universe as a whole, and for the individual believer. He agonizes over the relationship between external moral laws and the inner spirit of love. He explores the process by which people are unified with God, initially through a commitment of faith, and then through spiritual and moral growth. And he tries to define who exactly Christ was—and is.

Writing at a time when Christianity was both new and numerically small, Paul was profoundly concerned with the philosophical status of Christian teaching: how it relates to other religions and philosophical traditions; and whether it marks the completion of all spiritual and intellectual searching. From roughly the beginning of the third century to the seventeenth, when Christianity dominated European thought, these issues rarely surfaced. But in the past three hundred years these issues have again become central—so Paul, the first great Christian philosopher, is strangely modern.

RIGHT *Paul's defense before Agrippa. "King Agrippa, believest though the prophets? I know that thou believest." Then Agrippa said unto Paul, "Almost thou persuadest me to be a Christian."*

CHRISTIAN HUMAN AND DIVINE

From Paul, a servant of Christ Jesus, chosen and called by God as an apostle to preach the good news. This good news was promised long ago by God through his prophets, and is written in the sacred Scriptures. It concerns his Son, our Lord Jesus Christ. At the human level he was born a descendant of David. At the divine level he was revealed as the Son of God; this was done by an act of power, which raised him from the dead. Through him God gave me the privilege of being an apostle, with the task of leading people of all nations to believe in him and obey him—including you in Rome who have heard God's call and now belong to Jesus Christ.

And so I send greetings to you: may God our Father and the Lord Jesus Christ grant you grace and peace.

Romans 1

CHRIST'S RECONCILING DEATH

Now that we have been put right with God by faith, we are at peace with God through our Lord Jesus Christ, who has given us access to that divine grace in which we now live; and we boast of our hope of sharing God's glory. Let us also boast of our present sufferings, because we know that suffering produces endurance, endurance brings God's approval, and his approval causes hope. This hope will not be disappointed, because, through his gift of the Holy Spirit, God has flooded our hearts with his love.

When we were still helpless, Christ died for the wicked, at the time God chose. Few would be willing to die even for a righteous person, though for a truly good man one might lay down one's life. But the proof of God's love for us is that Christ died for us while we were still sinners.

By his sacrificial death, we have now been put right with God; thus we shall all the more certainly be saved through him from God's final retribution. If, when we were God's enemies, we were reconciled to him through the death of his Son, we can be all the more certain that being

now reconciled, we shall be saved by Christ's life! But that is not all: we also rejoice in God through our Lord Jesus, who has reconciled us to God.

ROMANS 5

DYING AND RISING WITH CHRIST

What are we to say, then? Shall we remain in sin, so that God's grace will increase? Certainly not! We have died to sin; so how can we go on living in it? Surely you know that when we were baptized into union with Christ Jesus, we were baptized into his death. By our baptism, then, we were buried with him, sharing his death, in order that, as Christ was raised from death by the glorious power of the Father, so also we might begin a new life.

Since we have become one with him in dying as he did, so we shall be one with him in being raised to life as he was. We know that our old self has been crucified with Christ, in order that the power of sin might be destroyed; thus we are set free from slavery to sin. Death, of course, breaks the chains of sin. In dying with Christ, we believe we shall also live with him, because we know that Christ has been raised from death and shall never die again.

ROMANS 6

FRUITS OF THE SPIRIT

Christ has set us free, so let us remain free. Stand firm, refusing to submit again to the yoke of slavery. My brothers and sisters, you have been called to freedom, but do not use your freedom as a license to indulge your desires. Instead serve one another in love. I tell you, let the Spirit direct your lives, and then you will no longer yield to self-indulgence.

The behavior that results from self-indulgence is plain; jealousy, anger, and selfish ambition; division into parties and factions; mutual envy; drunken orgies and the like. I warn you, as I have warned you before, that those who behave in this way will never inherit the kingdom of God. But the fruit of the Spirit is love, joy, peace, patience, kindness, goodness, fidelity, humility, and self-control. We who belong to Christ Jesus have crucified our old nature, putting to death its passions and desires. And the Spirit has given us new life. So let the Spirit direct our lives.

GALATIANS 5

SONS AND DAUGHTERS OF GOD

Through faith all of you have become children of God, in union with Christ Jesus. You were baptized into union with Christ, clothing yourselves with Christ like a garment. Among you there is no difference between Jew and gentile, slave and freeman, male and female; you are all one in Christ Jesus.

The son who inherits his father's property is treated like a slave while he is still young; although the whole estate belongs to him, guardians take care of him and manage his affairs until the date set by his father. In the same way, while we remained spiritually immature, we were slaves of the ruling spirits of the universe. But at the right time, God sent his Son, giving him a human mother and putting him under the law; and this Son has brought us freedom from the law, so that we can become God's sons and daughters. And since we are God's sons and daughters, God has sent into your hearts the Spirit of his Son, crying: "Father, my Father." You are therefore no longer slaves, but sons and daughters, and as such you have become God's heirs.

GALATIANS 3

Justin

Having been a respected philosopher before his conversion, Justin was the first Christian to present the faith as the fulfillment of classical thought. Around 155 he wrote an Apology, addressed to the Roman emperor, defending Christianity against its detractors. He argued against the law that made it a criminal offense to call oneself Christian, saying that people should be judged by their conduct, not by the name ascribed to them. The Christian faith, he maintained, makes its adherents highly virtuous, and hence upholders of the social order.

ABOVE The Madonna and Child with St. Clement and St. Justin. (Fifteenth century fresco by Master of the Castello Nativity, Museo dell'Opera del Duomo, Prato).

Justin was born around the year 100. His parents were pagan and probably highly educated. He spent his early years wandering from one philosopher to another in search of truth. But none of the ideas he learned satisfied him. Then he decided to investigate the new faith of Christianity, and quickly realized that it answered his deepest questions.

At about the age of thirty he received baptism. He taught Christianity for a time at Ephesus, and he then moved to Rome, where, with great courage, he opened a school of Christian philosophy, inviting pagans to attend. He soon gained respect, even from among philosophers who disagreed with him; he thus made Christianity a credible religion for educated people to adopt. He was executed for his faith in about 155.

DEFENCE OF FAITH

Reason requires that philosophers, and all those who are truly pious, should honor and cherish only the truth: they should not merely accept old opinions if these are shown to be worthless. Reason does not merely require us to avoid bad behavior and false teaching; those who love truth must on every occasion, even at the cost of their lives, say and do what is right.

Thus, since you are known to be pious and wise guardians of justice and lovers of truth, we ask you at least to give us a hearing—that will prove your piety and wisdom. I do not come before you with flattery, nor do I want to win your favor with eloquence. I ask you to judge what I say according to the strict and precise application of reason.

Do not be moved by prejudice or superstitious sentence, or by irrational impulse, or by familiar evil rumors; to be influenced by these things would be a betrayal of yourselves. We for our part are convinced that no real harm can come to us, unless we are guilty of some kind of evil or crime. You may kill us, but you cannot destroy us…. The mere ascription of a name to people implies nothing about their moral standing: what matters is the behavior associated with that name. We are charged with being Christian.

To us the name Christian sounds gracious. But we do not ask to be pardoned on account of a name. If we are criminals, we should not be pardoned. On the other hand, if neither our name nor our conduct shows us to be wrongdoers, this punishment would be unjust— and in meting out punishment, you would be wrongdoers. Neither reward nor punishment should result from a name, but rather from the good or evil actions associated with that name.

Among yourselves you do not assume that defendants are guilty prior to their trial. But with us, our very name is taken as proof of guilt. In fact, in this respect you should punish our accusers: they accuse us of being Christians and it is not right to hate graciousness. If one of the accused denies the charge, saying he is not a Christian, you dismiss him, on the grounds that you have not proof of misconduct. Yet if he confesses that he is a Christian, you punish him because of his confession. Instead, you ought to investigate the lives of both those who confess and those who deny the Christian faith, judging them according to their actions....

We are called godless. We certainly admit to being godless with reference to the false gods which people commonly worship. But we are not godless with reference to the most true God, the Father of righteousness and self-control and all the other virtues—the God who is untouched by evil.

We are not godless in relation to the Son, who came from the Father, and taught us about the Father—and also taught us about the army of good angels who follow him and are made like him. And we are not godless in relation to the prophetic Spirit, whom we worship and adore, who guides our thoughts toward the truth, and who transmits the truth to others.

Some people will point out that a number of Christians have been arrested and convicted as criminals. It may be true that, if one were to examine the conduct of these Christians, a few would indeed turn out to have been criminals. But you should not condemn all Christians because of the crimes of a few.... We are happy that all those who have been denounced to you as Christians should be investigated. Those who are found guilty of some crime should be punished for that crime, and not as Christians. And those who are shown to be innocent should be set free, for it is no crime to be a Christian.

We shall not ask you, however, to punish our accusers, because their own wickedness and ignorance of the truth will cause them enough suffering. Please believe that I am speaking for your sake. When we are put on trial, we could deny that we are Christians. But we do not wish to survive by telling a lie.

We yearn for the life which is eternal and pure; we strive to dwell with God, who created and fashioned all things. Thus we are eager to proclaim our faith. We are certain in our belief that those who follow God in their actions, and who long to dwell with him in heaven where no evil can disturb their bliss, shall indeed go to heaven....

Specimen Codicis Argentoratensis.

ABOVE *Justin introduced the idea of Christianity as the fulfillment of classical thought. He invited his Roman detractors to "judge what I say according to the strict and precise application of reason."*

When you hear that we are looking for a kingdom, you rashly presume that we mean a merely human kingdom. But we speak of God's kingdom. This is why we are happy to proclaim our faith when we are brought to trial, even though death is the penalty.

If we were looking for a human kingdom, we would deny our faith in order to save our lives, or we would at least try to keep our faith secret. But since we do not place our faith in the present order, we are not troubled at the prospect of being put to death. Besides, we all have to die sometime. We are in fact, of all people, your best helpers and allies in securing good order.

We are convinced no form of malice or wickedness, nor any kind of virtues, escapes the attention of God; and that all people are punished or rewarded by God according to their actions. If everybody knew this, nobody would act sinfully, even for a short time, aware that eternal punishment could be the result; everyone would be self-controlled, orderly, and virtuous, in order to receive God's blessings and be spared his wrath.

We worship the creator of the universe. We declare that he has no need of animal sacrifices, libations, and incense. Instead he wants us to speak to him, praising him for all he has given us. He wants us to honor him, not by burning on the altar the food he has given us, but by nourishing ourselves with it, and by sharing it with those in need.

APOLOGY 2, 4, 6, 8, 11, 12, AND 13

Irenaeus of Lyons

*I*n the second century Gnostic ideas gained growing popularity with the churches. Gnostics made a sharp division between spirit and matter, condemning all bodily needs and desires as corrupt. In its extreme form it taught that Christ's body was an illusion, and that he was pure spirit.

Irenaeus vigorously opposed Gnosticism, stressing that God created both spirit and matter. He believed that God's glory is made manifest in every living creature; and thus the whole natural order should be cherished. And he taught that Christians should not try to suppress their bodily desires, but rather allow God to transform them, so that they can imitate Jesus Christ in their daily lives. In his theology, Irenaeus constantly identified Christ with the Word of God; and, following the New Testament teaching of John, he emphasized the role of the Lord as the agent of creation.

Irenaeus was born in Asia Minor (modern Turkey), and studied under Polycarp, the bishop of Smyrna. Irenaeus continued his studies in Rome, and was then invited to Gaul to serve as a priest under the first bishop of Lyons. He himself was appointed bishop of Lyons in about 173, remaining there until his death two decades later. Although under constant threat of persecution, he had no doubt that the greatest danger to the church was heresy within its own ranks. His book, Against Heresies, in which he opposes Gnosticism, remains the classic statement of the relationship of religion and nature.

RIGHT *Irenaeus of Lyons opposed Gnosticism and preached that bodily desires and needs should not be suppressed.*

CREATION AS GOD'S SELF-REVELATION

Through the creation, the Word reveals the Creator. Through the world the Word reveals the Lord who made the world. Through the infinite beauty of the world's design, the Lord reveals the great Designer. In this way the Word, who is the Son of God, reveals God the Father. Every creature testifies, by its very existence, to the power of God; but not every creature believes in God.

Through the Word and through the teaching of the prophets, the Lord proclaimed himself and the Father. The whole people heard; but not all believed. The same Word became visible and tangible in Jesus Christ. All saw the Father in the Son; but not all believed.... The Word, who is the Son, was the divine agent of creation from the beginning. And the Word reveals God to everybody, because that is what the Father wishes.

AGAINST HERESIES, BOOK 4

THE SINGLE TRUTH

The truths of the gospel are gradually spreading across the world. Yet despite the great distances between groups of believers, it seems as if they all occupy one house. Their common faith draws them together in heart and soul. They speak the same words, and they proclaim the same message. There are many different languages in the world; but one Christian doctrine is conveyed in all of them. Thus the church in Germany believes and proclaims exactly the same message as do the Spanish and Celtic churches; and it is the same message as that preached by Christians in Jerusalem, which is the center of the world. Just as the sun, which was created by God, is the same throughout the world, so the same truth now shines in every nation, and enlightens all those who respond to it in a spirit of faith. Those who are eloquent speakers cannot add to the truth; and those who are stumbling speakers cannot diminish the truth. Since truth is one and the same, regardless of who expresses it, no one can improve on it or undermine it.

AGAINST HERESIES, BOOK 1

THE WORD AS GOD'S AGENT OF CREATION

God's Word sustains the universe in being. His nature and his greatness cannot be seen or described by any of the creatures he has made. Yet he is known to all of them. The Word proclaims to all that there is one God the Father, who holds all things in being, and gives being to all creation. We are told that no one has seen God the Father except his Son, who is the Word; and it is through the Son that we know the Father.

The Son has revealed the Father from the beginning, because he was with the Father from the beginning. At appropriate times he gave to humanity prophetic visions and spiritual gifts of all kinds; and then he came in the flesh to serve humanity directly. The Son reveals the Father in an orderly manner, at opportune moments, when humanity can derive the greatest benefit, and where there is order, there is harmony.

Thus the Word is the dispenser of the Father's grace to humanity; and he never fails to be generous. He has revealed God to humanity, and raised humanity to God. He shields the Father from human sight, so that human beings will never undervalue God through familiarity, but will always have to reach out to God. Yet on the other hand, he reveals God to humanity in so many ways that human beings have no cause for ignoring God. God's glory is most fully revealed when ordinary human beings are transformed in the image of his Son.

AGAINST HERESIES, BOOK 4

BEING TRANSFORMED IN GOD'S IMAGE

There is one God, who by his Word and in his wisdom made and ordered all things. In these final times God's Word became a human being, to live among human beings, in the person of Jesus Christ, in order to reconcile humanity with God.... I acknowledge that no human being can see the greatness and the stupendous glory of God and live; God the Father in himself is beyond human comprehension.

SERVICE TO GOD

Those who live in the light do not themselves cause the light, but rather they are lit by it. They do not help the light, but are helped and illuminated by it. Similarly, our service to God does not provide him with anything, because he does not rely on us in any way. He bestows eternal life and glory on those who follow and serve him. He does this for their sake, and receives nothing in return. He is wholly self-sufficient, and so requires nothing from us. The reason why God wants people to serve him is that he wants to bestow blessings on those who persevere in his service. God does not depend on human beings; but human beings depend totally on God. Thus if you want to share God's glory, remain steadfast in his service.

AGAINST HERESIES, BOOK 5

But every human being can experience the love, the kindness, the mercy, and the power of God. All who turn to God in love receive his love—as the prophets have always testified. Human beings can never attain true and lasting joy by their own efforts; but through God this can be attained. Human beings cannot see God through their own powers. But God by his own choice has revealed himself to humanity.

God the Son appeared in human flesh, and now he manifests himself by his Spirit—when he wishes, to whom he wishes, and as he wishes. Those who perceive God's self-revelation, and respond by putting their whole trust in him, become his sons and daughters.

The Spirit transforms them in the image of God the Son, that in the fullness of time they may enjoy eternal life in the presence of God the Father. God's sons and daughters see the light and live in the light, and they reflect its splendor.

AGAINST HERESIES, BOOK 4

Tertullian

ertullian was the most prominent member of a movement that taught that the Holy Spirit guides and teaches each person individually—and therefore Christians have no need for priests and bishops to act as mediators between God and humanity.

Tertullian acknowledged that Christian communities need leaders to preserve order; but they should be accorded no special honors. Tertullian believed that the Spirit gives to each person a rule of life, appropriate to that person's spiritual state and circumstances; and the Spirit will adapt this rule as the individual grows in spiritual grace and as circumstances change. He embraced the doctrine of the Trinity, but was eager to put a little distance between the Spirit and God, in order to show how the Spirit can be active in the world, while God himself remains transcendent.

Not surprisingly, the spiritual movement to which Tertullian belonged—known as the New Prophecy— was bitterly opposed by many bishops, and eventually declared heretical.

Tertullian was born in Carthage, North Africa, in about 155. His father was a centurion in the Roman army. As a young man Tertullian went to Rome, where he became a successful lawyer, renowned for his sharp and eloquent tongue. He converted to Christianity at the age of about forty and returned to Carthage. He was offered, but seems to have refused, ordination. Instead he applied his intellect and wit, honed by the law, to Christian polemics, producing over twenty theological books.

Though the subjects varied, the underlying theme was always the relationship of the Spirit to the individual believer.

THE SPIRIT OF GOD

The term "Spirit of God" is at first sight confusing. It seems to imply that the Spirit is not God, but an agent of God. In truth the Spirit of God is God. The term is used to indicate that the Spirit is a part of the godhead, not the whole godhead. There is a further potential confusion, concerning the Spirit and the Word. The Word of God, the second person of the godhead, is made flesh in Jesus Christ. The Word is the activity of the Spirit in the world. And the Spirit is the substance of the Word.

AGAINST PRAXEAS, SECTION 26

THE WORD AND THE SPIRIT

The Word of God is not the totality of God; nor is the Spirit of God the totality of God. It is wrong to identify the Word or the Spirit wholly with God. We can say that the Word and the Spirit come from God, and so we can be sure that they have the same qualities and properties as their source. We can say that the Word and the Spirit belong to God; and so we can be sure that they have the same qualities as their possessor.

AGAINST PRAXEAS, SECTION 26

THE SPIRIT'S ROLES

The Holy Spirit teaches many things that Jesus himself did not teach; this is God's plan. The Spirit teaches us who Jesus Christ is. The Spirit enables us to appreciate the beauty and intricacy of God's creation. The Spirit inspires us to glorify God. The Spirit constantly reminds us of God. And the Spirit shows us how to behave, giving to each person a set of rules appropriate to their nature and situation.

How does a person know the Spirit's rules? Firstly the person will feel prompted consistently to act in particular ways. Secondly the person will find these rules at times hard to keep. This indicates that they are not based on the person's own selfish desires, but are divine in origin.

ON MONOGAMY, SECTION 2

CHANGING THE RULES

The Lord through the Spirit progressively revises the rules and standards by which he requires each person to live, in order gradually to bring each person to perfection.... Indeed, the formulation of a rule of life for each individual, and the adaptation of that rule as the individual grows in the image of Christ, is the primary function of the Holy Spirit. The second function is to reform and guide the intellect, to enable the intellect to interpret correctly the Scriptures. The Spirit enables each person to understand the Scriptures to the level that person needs.

THE VEILING OF VIRGINS, SECTION 1

SPIRITUAL ECSTASY

Lifted by the Spirit, each of us can enter a state of ecstasy. In such a state we go out of our minds, and we are no longer aware of what we are saying. Indeed, it is inevitable that when we behold the glory of God, and God begins to speak through us, we lose normal consciousness. We are overwhelmed by the power of God.

AGAINST MARCIOS, SECTION 4

RIGHT *The Effusion of the Holy Spirit (1604–14, El Greco, Museo del Prado, Madrid). Tertullian held that each individual is guided by the Holy Spirit, with no need for a mediating clergy.*

Origen

 native of the bustling cosmopolitan port of Alexandria, Origen was the most exciting writer of the early Church, possessing intellectual acumen, spiritual passion and mystical insight. The abiding interest was the relationship of the Creator with his creation, which for Origen posed two major problems.

First, how can such diversity as we see around us have emerged from a changeless, eternal Being? Second, if that Being is good, how can evil have entered the world? In answering the first question he developed a view of nature as a single organism—a view now shared by many ecologists. In answering the second, he tried to show how human freedom and divine providence, far from being at odds, are complementary.

Origen's parents were Christian; in fact, he is the first major Christian writer to have come from a Christian home. His father was martyred in 203 and Origen was only prevented from seeking the same fate by his mother hiding his clothes. He supported his mother and siblings by teaching, and at the age of eighteen became head of a small school of Christian philosophy.

At around this time he gave a literal interpretation to the words of Jesus about eunuchs, and had himself castrated. Under his leadership the school grew rapidly and he began to write prolifically. His daring theological speculations induced more pedestrian minds to accuse him of heresy. He was severely tortured during the Decian persecution of 249, and, weakened by the ordeal, he died four years later.

DIVERSITY AND HARMONY

Although the world is very diverse, it should not as a whole be regarded as disharmonious or incoherent. A body is a single organism made up of many parts, held together by one soul. In the same way, the whole world is a kind of immense and vast living creature which is united by one soul, namely the power and reason of God.

ON FIRST PRINCIPLES, 2.1.3

FREE WILL

The Creator granted to all human beings the gift of intelligence and the power of free will. His purpose was to give them the opportunity to do good on their own, using their own will. But laziness and distaste for the effort involved in doing good, and even dislike and disregard for goodness, cause human beings to stray from goodness. Straying from goodness means becoming established in evil. Evil is indeed the lack of goodness. The result is that people advance in wickedness to the precise extent that they stray from goodness.

ON FIRST PRINCIPLES, 2.9.2

THE USES OF FREEDOM

When in the beginning God created all beings which he wished to create, including rational beings, his only purpose was to satisfy his own nature—which is pure goodness. Since God, the creator of all things, has no variety, and cannot change or grow, there could be no diversity or variety in his creation; all things were equal and the same. But he gave those rational beings free will; and this freedom was used by some to imitate God, and by others to repudiate God. And this was the cause of diversity among rational creatures....

But God decided it was just to deal with his creatures according to their deserts. Just as a house contains vessels of gold and silver, wood and clay, and of good and bad quality, so God drew together those diverse beings into one world; the different vessels equipping a house correspond to different characters and minds.

This in my view is the reason for the diversity which the world displays.

Divine providence deals with individuals according to their different inclinations and characters. On this principle the Creator does not seem unjust in assigning different status to different people; nor should the differences in talents which individuals have at birth be regarded as accidental.

ON FIRST PRINCIPLES, 2.9.6

THE END OF EVIL

In the final consummation the devil in himself will not be destroyed, because he is created by God. But his hostile purpose will perish—because this does not come from God. Thus the devil will not cease to exist, but he will cease to be an enemy, and he will cease to destroy people's souls. Nothing is impossible to the omnipotence of God; there is nothing that cannot be healed by its Creator. The Creator made all things in order that they might exist; and if things were made to exist they cannot become nonexistent.

ON FIRST PRINCIPLES, 3.6.5

RESTORATION TO UNITY

The restoration to unity must not be imagined as a sudden event. Rather it should be thought of as a very gradual process, passing through countless ages. Little by little each individual will be corrected and purified. Some will lead the way, making rapid progress up the height of perfection; some will be just behind them; others will be far behind. Multitudes of peoples and groups, who were once enemies of God, will reconcile themselves to him.

ON FIRST PRINCIPLES, 3.6.6

GOD'S PROVIDENCE

It is our fixed and unchangeable belief that God is incorporeal, omnipotent, and invisible; and at the same time that he cares for our mental affairs, and that nothing takes place in heaven or on earth outside his providence. But note that we had said "outside his providence," not "outside his will." Many things take place outside God's will; but nothing takes place outside his providence.

Providence is the process by which God administers, orders, and watches over events as they happen. His will is the process by which he decides what should or should not happen.... Our belief that God administers and orders all things implies that he should reveal his will, showing human beings how to behave. If he did not reveal his will, he would not be expressing his concern for human beings; so we would not be able to believe that he cares for our mortal affairs.

HOMILY ON GENESIS, 3.2

WHOLE AND PARTS

God is concerned not just with the whole, but with every rational being individually. It is true that his care for the whole never fails. Thus, if the whole deteriorates through the activities of particular rational creatures who are part of the whole, God takes corrective measures, bringing the whole back to himself. He is never angry with animals and insects. But he will punish and rebuke human beings when they fail to fulfill the purposes for which they were made.

AGAINST CELSUS, 4.99

ABOVE *St. Mark preaching in Alexandria, Egypt (15th-century, Bellini and Giovanni, Pinacoteca di Brera, Milan Italy). Origen's revolutionary theories were considered heretical and he was tortured by his accusers.*

Basil of Caesarea

At a time when growing numbers of men and women were seeking spiritual fulfillment as hermits, Basil taught that the solitary life was both unnatural and dangerous. Yet he admired the courage of these hermits, and urged them instead to join monastic communities.

He is regarded as the founding inspiration of monastic life in the Eastern Church, writing two rules. The Longer Rule sets out a monastic philosophy, seeking to show that a properly organized community can fulfill both our natural instincts and our spiritual aspiration. The Shorter Rule contains practical guidance on how to live in harmony with others.

Basil was born in 330 into a distinguished Christian family in the cosmopolitan city of Caesarea. He received the finest education in schools in Constantinople and Athens, and returned home to pursue a legal career. But, under the influence of a devout sister, he decided to give up his worldly ambitions and dedicate himself to God. After visiting a number of hermits, some of whom were beginning to form loose-knit communities, Basil set up a monastery on his family's estate. In 370 he was appointed bishop of his native city, and died prematurely nine years later.

THE SEED OF LOVE

You cannot teach anyone to love God any more than you can teach someone to appreciate beauty or to cherish life. No one taught us to love our parents, or whoever brought us up. Similarly, and more emphatically, we do not learn to love God through a course of instruction. We love God because the seed of love has been sown in every human being. Those who have enrolled in the school of God's love are those who acknowledge and rejoice in this seed, cultivating it with care, nurturing it with knowledge, and in every way fostering its growth....

Thus the commandment that we should love God is like water on the seed of love. The proof of this is not external; we can discover the proof by looking inside ourselves. We naturally desire beautiful things, although we may differ as to what we regard as beautiful. And without being taught, we naturally have affection toward our relatives and close friends, and we feel gratitude toward those who show us kindness. What is more beautiful than the beauty of God? What is more captivating than the glory of God? What desire within the soul is keener and sharper than the desire to be close to God? What gratitude is fuller than our gratitude to God for all his blessings?

THE LONGER RULE, 2

COMMUNITY AND SOLITUDE

I believe that living in a community is more natural, and more likely to prove spiritually valuable, than living in solitude. None of us is self-sufficient. We depend on one another for the material necessities of life. And the body itself is an image of mutual dependence. The foot may be able to do certain things by itself; but separated from the rest of the body, its activities would be useless, and it would soon wither and die.

Those who live in solitude can be likened to feet divorced from the body: their efforts are useless to anyone apart from themselves; and they can wither in both body and spirit. God our creator has ordained that we need one another; he has bound us together....

How can you grow in humility, if there is no one against whom you can compare yourself? How can you express compassion, when there is no one to evoke that noble feeling? How can you understand and apply the teachings of the Scriptures without others to guide you?…

Living in community is like life in the arena: you are being continuously stretched in order to perform better.

THE LONGER RULE, 7

HARMONIOUS RELATIONSHIPS

We should be patient, whatever trials we have to endure. Even though we have the right to rebuke a person who has wronged us, we must not do this out of anger for having been wronged, but in the hope of teaching the wrong-doer the ways of God. We should not say anything against an absent brother, even if what we want to say is true.

We should turn away from someone who is speaking against a brother. We should not indulge in idle talk, which is useless to the listener and offensive to God, nor should we deliver speeches of exhortation, unless we are authorized to do so.

Instead we should apply ourselves quietly to the tasks we have been set. We should not aspire to an honored place in the community. We should regard others as more worthy of honor than ourselves. We should not shift from one task to another without the permission of those in authority—unless we are called urgently to help someone.

We should congratulate others for what they do well. We should never hold grudges against those who have done wrong and repented. Forgiveness should be total. When we find ourselves disliked by others, we should heal the rift with special acts of kindness. When we realize that we have done wrong, we should not wait; we should make amends at once.

THE SHORTER RULE

ABOVE *"I believe that living in a community is more natural, and more likely to prove spiritually valuable, than living in solitude. None of us is self-sufficient."* St. Basil, Archbishop of Caesarea, 379 C.E.

John Chrysostom

J ohn, the patriarch of Constantinople, was given the name "Chrysostom," which means "golden mouth," because of the eloquence of his sermons. Yet if the language and delivery were enthralling, the content was disturbing.

He set out to challenge wealthy Christians, whose generosity was confined to donating precious objects for display in their churches. He told them that, since their wealth came from God, their duty was to distribute it to the poor and needy. He also taught people that, instead of striving for personal riches, they should learn to value the common richness of nature, which God has created for all to enjoy.

He urged people to look carefully at their own mental attitudes, rooting out selfish and greedy desires, and developing a spirit of joyful compassion, which takes pleasure in the happiness of others.

John Chrysostom converted to Christianity in 368 at the age of twenty-one. He renounced a large inheritance and a promising legal career, and went to live in a mountain cave as a hermit, devoting himself to the study of the Bible. He eventually emerged and was ordained priest; his sermons were soon attracting huge congregations.

In 389, on the death of the old patriarch of Constantinople, the common people urged the emperor to appoint John. Despite opposition among the wealthy citizens, the emperor consented. John stripped the patriarch's palace of its treasures and used the money to build schools and hospitals. Eventually the emperor's wife led a group of aristocrats and senior clergy against John and succeeded in forcing him into exile, where he died.

ABOVE *John Chrysostom saw through the hypocrisy of some wealthy Christians. "The gift of a chalice may be extravagant in its generosity; but a gift to the poor is an expression of love."*

GIVING WISELY

W e should honor Christ in ways of which he would approve. He does not want golden chalices, but he does want golden hearts. I am not saying that you should not donate golden chalices, and other precious objects, to your church; but they are no substitute for giving to the poor. The Lord will not refuse your gift to your church, but he prefers a gift to the poor. In the case of a gift to the church, only you the donor benefit; in the case of a gift to the poor, both the donor and the receiver benefit. The gift of a chalice may be extravagant in its generosity; but a gift to the poor is an expression of love.

SERMON 50

GIVING JOYFULLY

I t is not enough simply to give to the poor; we must give with a generous spirit, and without grumbling. It is not even enough to give without grumbling; we must give with glad and willing hearts....

When you help the poor, two attitudes should always be manifest: generosity and joy. Why do you moan about the duty to give to the poor? Why do you express such resentment at having to share your wealth with those in need? If you resist giving to the poor, you are showing no mercy; you are merely exposing your callousness and lack of compassion. If you are full of resentment, how can you help someone who is in the depths of misery?

In fact, giving to others in a spirit of resentment only demeans and humiliates them, because it makes them feel beholden to you. But if you give to others in a spirit of joy, you create no sense of debt, because the receiver can see that you too are benefiting from your gift. Your resentment depresses the spirit of the receiver; your joy uplifts the receiver's spirit. If you give gladly, even if the gift is small, it will be munificent. If you give resentfully, even if the gift is substantial, it will be a pittance.

DIVINE PROVIDENCE

God made this world beautiful, glorious, varied, and abundant. He has given it the capacity to meet your every need; to nourish your body, and to uplift your soul by leading it toward knowledge of himself. For your sake, he has made the sky radiant with stars, and adorned it with the moon at night and the sun by day.

Everything in this world has been fashioned to give you joy. In every corner of the earth, trees are growing. It is impossible to know all the different species. One can simply marvel at the varied fruits, fragrances, barks, shapes, leaves, colors, and dimensions one encounters. And you rejoice in the healing properties that many of the trees possess.

God has made all these trees for your sake. In the same way God has inspired you to build cities, filling them with works of art, for your sake. He has made roads out of the cities, so you can enjoy the countryside. He has given you the ability to sleep, in order to refresh your body and mind. And, above all, he has given you life, so that you can appreciate the magnificence of his creation. The world will still exist for you when you awake tomorrow—and by then it will be even better....

The providence of God shines in every object and every creature in the world. Do not try to scrutinize God's motives in acting so generously toward you. The thoughts of God are impossible to fathom. All you need to know is that the world has been given to you out of pure generosity. God does not need or require anything from you in return. Just be grateful—and give God the glory.

ON PROVIDENCE, CHAPTER 7

EXAMINING OUR ATTITUDES

Let each of us frequently review our actions. We should try to bring every aspect of our lives before our minds, assessing whether we deserve correction or punishment. When we are indignant that someone guilty of various crimes escapes punishment, we should reflect on the magnitude of our own faults; then perhaps our indignation will cease.

A crime committed by someone else may appear great, because it involves some great or notorious matter. But when we look honestly at our own actions, we find misdemeanors of equal concern. Take, for example, stealing and fraud. The gravity of the offense is not affected by the value of what is stolen—whether it is gold, or merely silver. The root of the crime lies in the mind.

> *The providence of God shines in every object and every creature in the world. Do not try to scrutinize God's motives in acting so generously toward you.*

Thus a person who is capable of stealing something small will not balk at the chance of stealing something larger. And if he does not steal for a time, it is probably because no opportunity has arisen. A poor person who steals from a poorer person would not hesitate to rob from a richer person, if he could get away with it. Forbearance comes from weakness, not from choice.

SERMON 3

Pelagius

nderlying many of the doctrinal disputes in the early centuries was the issue of Christianity's relations with other religions and philosophies. Many church leaders wanted to assert that God saves people only through Christianity. But this raised two difficult questions: how does God decide which people to make Christians; and, how is it that many people who are not Christian display such goodness and holiness?

Pelagius answered that people are saved through choosing goodness and rejecting evil; and that all people have the freedom to choose goodness. The purpose of Jesus Christ, Pelagius thought, was not to save people directly, but to show them by example how they could save themselves.

As Pelagius' ideas grew in popularity, the church leaders became frightened that their own authority as purveyors of truth and mediators of divine grace would be undermined; and so he was declared a heretic.

Pelagius was born in Britain, and came to Rome in about 390, where he became a spiritual adviser to a number of wealthy women. His writings were mainly in the form of letters and treatises composed for these women; but some of them circulated these works more widely. Pelagius himself was renowned for his self-discipline and personal generosity, and even his opponents praised his exemplary way of life.

After the fall of Rome, he was forced to flee to North Africa, along with some of his disciples. The bishops there condemned him in 418, and he was driven into the desert, where he died two years later.

FREEDOM OF CHOICE

It is ignorance that makes people regard humanity as inherently evil. They point to the capacity of human beings to do evil; they even observe that human beings do not have an overwhelming urge to do good. They conclude that human beings are morally corrupt. But if you consider the matter carefully, you realize that a quite different conclusion should be drawn.

Humans are neither inherently evil nor inherently good; they do not have an overwhelming inclination in either direction. The special and unique feature of human beings is their power of rational choice: they are free to choose good or evil. People win praise and honor when they persistently choose good over evil. Indeed, true virtue consists in persevering in the path of goodness, knowing that at any time you could cross to the path of evil.

This capacity for rational choice has been implanted by God. At any moment we can choose good or choose evil quite naturally, and bend our will in the direction we have chosen. If we had an innate inclination toward evil, we would not be free. Our most excellent Creator wants us always to choose good; but he bestowed upon us great dignity, by allowing us—if we choose—to defy his will.

By making goodness a matter for voluntary and independent choice, it is even better than it would have been if God had imposed it. At every moment and in every situation we choose or oppose, approve or reject. Other creatures act as their instincts and circumstances direct; we act as our reason decides.

While some claim that human beings are inherently evil, others in their ignorance and lack of faith say the opposite. They criticize the Lord's work by asserting that he should have created human beings as perfect creatures, without any capacity for evil. They are like pots saying to the potter: "Why have you made us as we are?"

Some people who think in this way are merely foolish; they ignore the fact that they themselves are choosing to live good lives. Others are morally decadent: they refuse to correct their own lives, and instead blame God for letting them choose evil. This capacity for free choice is amply demonstrated by the behavior of pagans who do not worship God.

We have all heard, read, and even met pagan philosophers who are chaste, tolerant, generous, self-controlled and gentle; who reject the world's honors as well as its delights; and who love justice as much as they love knowledge. What, I ask you, is the origin of those good qualities? Is it not astonishing that people who are strangers to God nonetheless lead lives that are so pleasing to him?

The origin of those qualities is the inherent awareness, which each person possesses, of goodness as well as evil. And pagans can act in a manner pleasing to God because God has given them the freedom to do so.

Freedom of choice can be demonstrated in another way. Look for several individuals of similar temperaments and characters. Yet in a similar situation some will choose to do good, while others will choose to do evil.

Once you recognize that each person has perfect freedom of choice, the value of Christ's teaching becomes manifest. If people ignorant of God often choose goodness, how much more likely are Christians to do the same! Christians have not only been instructed by Christ in the path of goodness; they also receive divine grace, giving them greater strength to follow it.

LETTER TO DEMETRIAN, SECTION 3

THE PURPOSE OF THE SCRIPTURES

God, in his majesty and power, has sent us the holy Scriptures, in order to instruct us how to behave. Yet we fail to receive the Scriptures with unrestrained joy and reverence. And we forget that commandments contained in the Scriptures are given by God not for his own benefit, but for ours.

On the contrary, we are liable to be rather casual in our attitude to the Scriptures, and too proud to submit to their instructions. We are like lazy, haughty servants, protesting to God: "Your commands are too hard and difficult for us—we are just frail human beings."

What blind madness! What corrupt folly! We are accusing God of ignorance—of twofold

ignorance. Firstly, we are telling him that he does not understand our weaknesses, even though he himself created us. And secondly, we are chastising him for cruelty to us, by imposing on us impossible demands.

LETTER TO DEMETRIAN, SECTION 16

ABOVE *The Sermon on the Mount. Pelagius believed that Jesus Christ's purpose was to show people, by the example of his own life, how they could save themselves.*

CHRISTIAN BEHAVIOR

Christians are those who follow the way of Christ, imitating Christ in all things. They show compassion to all. They do not retaliate when wrong is done to them. They resist those who oppress the people. They encourage those who are sad, and feed those who are hungry. They mourn with those who mourn, and feel the pain of those who suffer. They are moved to tears by the tears of others. Their homes are open to all, and they close their doors to no one. All are welcome to eat at their tables, so no one starves in their vicinity.

ON THE CHRISTIAN LIFE, SECTION 14

Leo of Rome

In the first five centuries the main focus of doctrinal debate was the person of Jesus Christ. Influenced by Greek philosophy, many were unable to believe that God, who is eternal and unchangeable, could have become a finite and active human being. Some asserted that he was not truly divine, in any unique sense, but he was a perfect human being who enjoyed complete harmony with God. Others responded that his humanity was some kind of illusion.

In 451 a Council of bishops was called in Chalcedon to resolve the dispute. Leo, who was the pope in Rome, read out his solution. He proclaimed that Jesus Christ had two distinct natures, divine and human, which coexisted in unity, but never became confused. After the bishops heard this document, which became known as the Tome of Leo, they declared that "the apostle Peter has spoken through Leo." His ideas were distilled into the Nicene Creed, which continues to be said each week in Catholic, Protestant, and Orthodox churches.

Leo was born in Rome, and after his ordination he served in Gaul, where he successfully acted as peacemaker between warring tribes. His reputation spread, and he was elected pope in 440, serving until his death in 461.

In addition to restoring doctrinal unity, he strove to prevent Rome from being attacked by barbarians. On one occasion he persuaded Attila the Hun to refrain from ransacking the city, in return for a large tribute.

ABOVE *Leo declared that "While the Holy Spirit put fruitfulness into the virgin's womb, the body of Christ came from the virgin's own body."*

CHRIST HUMAN AND DIVINE

The whole body of the faithful acknowledges its belief in God the Father almighty, and in Jesus Christ, his only Son, our Lord, who was born of the Holy Spirit and the Virgin Mary. This simple statement of faith confounds all the heretics and their wicked devices. God is believed to be both almighty and Father.

It follows that the Son is coeternal with him, differing in no respect from him. The Son is God, born of God; he is almighty because his Father is almighty; he is eternal because his Father is eternal. He is not later in time, not inferior in power, not dissimilar in glory, not divided in essence. This same only-begotten, eternal Son was born of the Holy Spirit and the Virgin Mary.

But this birth in time has taken nothing from, and added nothing to, his eternal divinity. Its effects have been entirely on humanity, who had been deceived by the devil and placed under the power of death. Human beings could not, by their own efforts, overcome the devil, the author of sin and death. Victory was only possible by the Son taking our nature and making it his own. Sin could not defile him, nor death enslave him, because he was conceived of the Holy Spirit, in the womb of a virgin, whose virginity remained unblemished throughout her pregnancy....

That birth, which was uniquely marvelous and marvelously unique, should not be understood as constituting a new mode of creation, which precludes the distinctive nature of humanity. While the Holy Spirit put fruitfulness into the virgin's womb, the body of Christ came from the virgin's own body....

Thus the properties of both divinity and

humanity were fully preserved, and came together within a single person. Humility was assured by majesty, weakness by strength, mortality by eternity. To pay the debt which humanity had incurred, a nature free from sin and suffering was united to a nature capable of sin and suffering. And in order to heal our sinful natures, Jesus Christ as man was able to die, while Jesus Christ is God and unable to die.

Thus true God was born in the form and nature of true man. This person Jesus Christ was fully divine and fully human. His body had the same nature and properties as human bodies have had since the creation of the world. And he took on a human body in order to restore humanity to the same relationship with God that it had at the creation of the world. In the Savior there was no trace of the evil properties with which Satan had infected human flesh.

Thus although he shared our humanity, and understood our weaknesses, he was not stained by our sin. He became human without detracting from the divine; and in this way he lifted humanity toward divinity. He made the invisible visible; he made the immortal mortal. This act of condescension was prompted by compassion for humanity's plight. The Son of God emptied himself of power, in order to reassert God's power over humanity.

The devil boasted that humanity, deceived by his guile, had been deprived of divine grace, and thus lost the gift of immortality, and in this way the devil believed he had won for himself a great victory. The devil boasted too that God, bound by his own laws of justice, had been forced to alter humankind's destiny. God had created men and women with great honor; but now, owing to this disobedience, they were under sentence of death....

The only means of redeeming the situation was for the Son of God to come down from his throne in heaven, and, without losing his Father's glory, to enter this lower world. He could only do this through a new mode of birth, by which he made his invisible divine nature visible in human flesh. Although he had existed before all time, he now began to exist within time; although he had existed outside all physical boundaries, he now began to exist within finite space....

From his mother he took on human nature, but not human sin. He was truly God, and also truly human. This unity of the divine and the human is not some fantasy. The humility of being human and the majesty of being divine existed alternately. Just as God is not changed by having compassion for human suffering, so human nature is not swallowed up by the dignity of the godhead. Each nature, divine and human, performs its proper functions in communion with the other; the Lord performs what pertains to the Lord, and human flesh performs what pertains to human flesh. The one shines gloriously through miracles; the other submits to insults. The Lord retains equality with the Father; the human flesh retains equality with humanity....

THE TOME OF LEO

SLEEPING ARRANGEMENTS

The brethren are to sleep each in a single bed.... If possible, they should all sleep in one place. But if their numbers do not permit this, they should sleep in groups of ten or twenty, with senior monks who are entrusted with their care. A candle should burn continuously in the room until dawn. They should sleep clothed, with their girdles tied, but not with their knives at their side for fear that they might wound themselves.

So let the monks always be ready. When the signal is given, they should get up without delay. Each should try to arrive first for worship, moving in a gentle and orderly fashion. The younger brethren should not have their beds together, but be dispersed among the senior monks. They should encourage one another quietly in rising from their beds, since the sleepy are liable to make excuses.

CHAPTERS 39 AND 40

Benedict of Nursia

For a thousand years, from the middle of the first to the middle of the second millennium, the main centers of Christian scholarship were the monasteries. The greatest monastic founder was Benedict of Nursia; for much of that period the majority of monasteries in Western Europe followed his Rule. This Rule is not itself a scholarly or philosophical document but a practical guide to community life, blending tolerance of human weakness with firmness of common purpose. Benedict saw the monastery as a school whose members learn to serve God; and his successors recognized the importance of scholarship, as well as worship and acts of charity, in this divine service.

Born in the small town of Nursia in about 430, Benedict traveled south to Rome to study. But he was so appalled by the decadence there that he withdrew to a cave in Subiaco, about thirty miles away. After three years as a hermit, he was joined by others, and quickly established a network of monasteries. Jealousy and intrigue eventually forced him to leave, accompanied by a small band of disciples. He created a new monastery at Monte Cassino, writing his Rule to prevent the earlier problems from being repeated.

LEFT *St. Benedict prays with his monks (Fresco by Sodoma (Vercelli), 1477–1549, Abbey of Monteoliveto Maggiore, Siena). Benedict of Nursia was one of the greatest monastic founders.*

SCHOOL OF THE LORD'S SERVICE

We propose to establish a school of the Lord's service. In founding this, we intend that the rules shall not be harsh or burdensome. But if for the good of all, for the correction of faults or the preservation of charity, some degree of discipline is laid down, do not be immediately daunted, and run away from the way of salvation. The entrance is inevitably narrow. But as we make progress in the monastic life, which is a life of faith, our hearts will open wide, and we shall obey God's commandments with a sweetness of love that is beyond words. Let us never swerve from his instructions, but persevere in his teaching within the monastery until death. Thus through our patience we shall share in the sufferings of Christ, and deserve also to share in his kingdom.

The Prologue

"It is the Spirit who holds people together in their common faith. Indeed it is the Spirit who initially confers on people the gift of faith, and hence brings them together to form a church."

COMMUNITY MEETINGS

When anything important has to be decided in the monastery, the abbot should call together the entire community, and explain the issue under consideration. When he has heard the advice of the community, he should reflect on it carefully, and then judge what seems to be the best course of action. The reason everyone should be summoned is that often God reveals the best course to a younger brother. The brethren should give this advice with respect and humility, and not defend their opinions stubbornly. The decision rests with the abbot, and the brethren must be united in obeying it.

Chapter 3

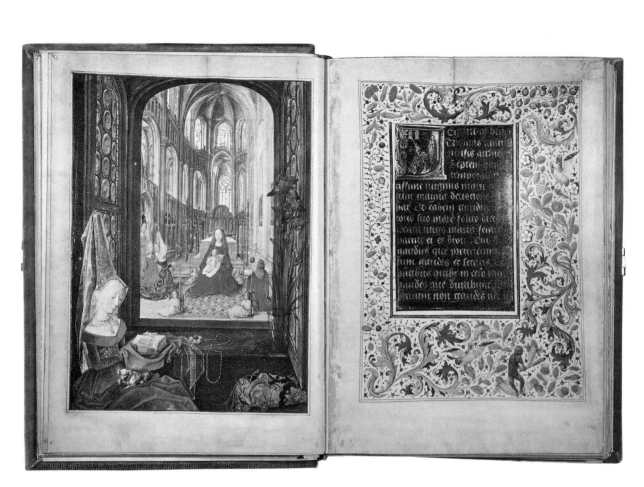

ABOVE *Hours of Mary of Burgundy. St. Thomas à Becket of Canterbury
in pictorial initial (Flanders, c.1477, National Library, Vienna).
Benedict recognized the importance of Christian scholarship.*

THE QUALITY AND QUANTITY OF FOOD

There should always be two cooked dishes at meals, to allow for the preference of different brethren; so if someone cannot eat one of the dishes, he may satisfy his hunger with the other. Two cooked dishes should be enough for everyone. But if fruit or tender vegetables are available, a third dish may be added. A full pound of bread should be enough for the day. God has made each person different, so it is with some diffidence that we fix the quantities of food and drink the monks should consume. But deferring to the frailty of the weaker brethren, we think that half a pint of wine each day is sufficient. But those to whom God grants the capacity to abstain will have their due reward.

CHAPTERS 39 AND 40

Anselm

nselm treated philosophy as an adjunct to prayer; and his most famous theological work, the Proslogion, is a mixture of philosophical discourse addressed to the reader and prayers addressed to God. In an opening prayer, he pronounced that we believe in order to understand—that belief in God comes prior to understanding God, rather than the other way around. This premise leads to his famous "ontological" proof for the existence of God, which, unlike other proofs offered by medieval theologians, continues to stimulate debate.

God, according to Anselm, is the highest entity our minds can conceive; therefore it is impossible to conceive of him not existing. Much of the rest of the book is devoted to dealing with the apparent paradoxes in God's nature, which had always disturbed Christian thinkers.

He was born in the Alpine town of Aosta and he went in 1056 to be a monk at the abbey of Bec in Normandy. There he was taught by Lanfranc, one of the greatest scholars of his day. When William, the Duke of Normandy, became king of England in 1066, he summoned Lanfranc to be archbishop of Canterbury.

In 1089 Anselm was summoned by William II to be Lanfranc's successor. To the king's chagrin, Anselm proved a powerful advocate of the independence of the church, defending both its wealth and its organization from royal interference. But he remained preoccupied with theological problems; on the day of his death in 1109, he was, puzzling over the origin of the soul.

ABOVE *St. Anselm's religious theories are still debated among theologians today.*

BELIEF AND UNDERSTANDING

I give you thanks, Lord, that you have made me in your image, so that I can remember you, think of you, and love you. But that image is worn, scarred by faults, and darkened by the smoke of sin. It cannot do that for which it was made, unless you renew and refashion it. Lord, I am trying to attain your level of knowledge, because I am not capable of that.

But I desire to understand a little of your truth, because my heart already believes in you and loves you. I do not seek to understand, in order that I may believe. I believe, in order that I may understand. Moreover, I believe that unless I do believe, I shall not understand.

PROSLOGION, CHAPTER 1

THE EXISTENCE AND NATURE OF GOD

Lord, you add understanding to faith. Therefore let me understand, as well as you think fit, that you exist, as we believe you do; and that your nature is what we believe it to be. We believe that you are that, above which nothing greater can be thought. The fool believes in his heart that there is no God. Is the fool correct?

But when the fool hears me use the phrase, "above which nothing greater can be thought," he understands what he hears. And what he understands is in his mind, even if he does not understand that it exists. It is one thing to have something in the mind; it is quite another to understand that it actually exists.

It is like a painter who, when he thinks out beforehand what he is going to paint, has it in his mind; but he does not yet understand that it exists, because he has not painted it. But when he has painted it, he knows both that it is in his mind and that it actually exists, because he has created it. So the fool has to agree that the concept of something above which nothing greater can be thought, exists in his mind, since he understood the concept when he heard it, and everything understood is in the mind.

But something above which nothing greater can be thought cannot exist only in the mind. For if it exists in the mind, it is possible to think of it existing in reality; and that would be greater. Therefore there is a contradiction in the fool's thought....

ABOVE *St. Anselm declared: "God is the highest entity our minds can conceive. Those who truly understand this understand that he must exist; it is impossible to conceive otherwise."*

Thus no one who truly understands that which God is, can think that God does not exist. A person may say in his heart that God does not exist, but the words have no meaning. God is the highest entity our minds can conceive. Those who truly understand this understand that he must exist; it is impossible to conceive otherwise. Those who grasp the nature of God cannot think of him as not existing....

What are you, Lord God, above whom nothing greater can be conceived? You exist alone above all things, and you have made everything else out of nothing. Whatever is not like is something less than the highest entity that can be conceived; and you, therefore, are greater than it. What good quality can be lacking in you, who are the highest good—and through whom all goodness exists? Thus you are just, true, generous, and whatever else it is better to be than not to be.

PROSLOGION, CHAPTERS 2, 4 AND 5

COMPASSION AND TRANSCENDENCE

Lord God, how can you be both compassionate and above passion. If you are above passion, you cannot suffer with anyone; but if you cannot share suffering, you cannot be compassionate—you cannot be made miserable by the misery of others. If you are not compassionate, from where can we derive consolation at times of misery? The answer must be that you are compassionate in your own manner, not according to ours. When you look upon us in our misery, you experience the effect of compassion, but not the emotion. You demonstrate compassion when you heal the sick and pardon the sinner; but you do not feel their suffering within yourself.

PROSLOGION, CHAPTER 8

OMNIPOTENCE AND POWERLESSNESS

How can you be omnipotent, O God, if you cannot do all things? How can you do all things if you cannot sin—if you cannot lie, if you cannot make false what is true? If you are unable to sin, you cannot claim to be able to do all things. Or is it that sin stems not from power, but from powerlessness? For those who commit sin have so little power over their own natures that they actually harm themselves. They are at the mercy of forces which they cannot oppose....

The more people have power to commit sin, the more they are powerless. So, Lord God, you are in fact more truly omnipotent because you cannot act through powerlessness.

PROSLOGION, CHAPTER 7

Bernard of Clairvaux

From his remote monastery Bernard exercised huge influence on ecclesiastical and political affairs, writing stern letters to kings and popes, and even intervening in the selection of a new pope. His enduring importance, however, was as a thinker who provided the theological basis for the great flowering of mysticism in the medieval period.

His primary focus of interest was how knowledge relates to love. He sought to show how ignorance of God is the cause of sin; yet he also believed that knowledge derived purely from theological speculation is even more dangerous. He concluded that only knowledge that comes directly from God, through prayer and contemplation, can conquer sin and engender love. In his famous commentary on the Song of Songs, he compared this kind of knowledge with a love song, sung by God to the soul.

Born near Dijon in 1090 to a noble family, at the age of twenty-one Bernard entered the monastery at Cîteaux, the center of the new Cistercian order. Four years later he led a dozen monks to form a second Cistercian monastery at Clairvaux in the Champagne region. Here he imposed on himself the most rigorous austerities, which made him permanently ill. He remained at Clairvaux for the rest of his life, dying in 1153.

ABOVE *St. Bernard writing the praises of the Virgin (illustration from St. Bernard of Clairvaux).*

SELF-KNOWLEDGE

There are two things you need to know: first who you are; and second who made you what you are. If you know both these things, you will exist—but not in yourselves and your own power. If you do not know who you are, let your friends teach you. If you do not know who made you what you are, this ignorance puts you on the same level as an animal.

Some people ignore the gift of reason within them, and behave like animals. They turn away from the glory inside themselves, and are slaves to their own senses. They are carried away by their own desires, and fail to realize that they possess something which puts them above animals; thus they become animals. We should be terrified by this kind of ignorance, which makes people undervalue themselves. But we should be equally terrified of the ignorance which makes people think too highly of themselves.

This happens when people think that they are the source of the good within themselves. But there is something even more detestable than ignorance. This is the pride by which people, in full knowledge of the truth, dare to boast of their own goodness. Even though they know that we are not the source of the good within themselves, they pretend that they are. They are thus stealing the glory which belongs to God. The first kind of ignorance has no glory. The second kind of ignorance has glory, but not in God's sight. Knowledge combined with pride is an act of treason against God.

On Loving God, Part 2

THE PURPOSE OF SUFFERING

This is how God causes you to love him. God not only created nature; he also protects it. Indeed, he created nature in such a way that it depends on his protection. To ensure that human beings recognize God's protection—and hence to prevent them imagining that they do not need him—God decided that human beings should endure suffering. When they suffer, human beings naturally turn to God for help, and thus honor God as he deserves.

ON LOVING GOD, PART 8

THE ENTRY OF GOD'S WORD

The Word of God has come to me many times. Yet I have never been conscious of the moment of his coming. I perceive his presence, and I remember afterward that he has been with me. Sometimes I even have an inkling that he will come. But I am never conscious of his coming or going. And where the Lord comes from when he visits my soul, where he goes after he leaves, and by what means he enters and withdraws, I admit I cannot say....

The coming of the Lord is not visible to my eyes, since he has no color; he is not audible to my ears, since he makes no sound; I do not sense him in my nostrils, since he mingles with the mind, not the air. Indeed, he does not make himself known through space, since he created space. I cannot taste him, because I cannot eat or drink him; I cannot touch him, because he is not tangible.

How then does the Word of God enter? Perhaps he does not enter because he does not come from outside. Indeed, he does not exist outside us, like a material object. Yet nor does he come from inside me; he is good, and there is no good in me. Even if I reach up to the highest spiritual level of which I am capable, he is still towering above me. In my curiosity, I have descended to the deepest level of understanding of which I am capable; and he is even more profound.

If I look outside myself, he is stretching far beyond the horizon. If I look within myself, he is further inside me than I can see. The truth is contained in the phrase: "In him we live and move and have our being." Blessed are those in whom the Word of God has his being, who lives for him, and is moved by him.

SERMON 74, ON THE SONG OF SONGS

ABOVE *Bernard of Clairvaux was the strength behind the resurgence of mysticism in medieval times.*

THE PURPOSE OF SUFFERING

This is how God causes you to love him. God not only created nature; he also protects it. Indeed, he created nature in such a way that it depends on his protection. To ensure that human beings recognize God's protection—and hence to prevent them imagining that they do not need him—God decided that human beings should endure suffering. When they suffer, human beings naturally turn to God for help, and thus honor God as he deserves.

ON LOVING GOD, PART 8

Aelred of Rievaulx

Christian philosophy has been mainly concerned with God's relationships with his creation. But Christian monasteries provide an ideal context for developing a philosophy of human relationships. And this is what the abbot of one of the great English monasteries sought to provide. His central theme was friendship, which he saw as our central emotional need, and also as a vital aid to spiritual development.

While he recognized that universal love is the goal to which Christians should aspire, he believed that friendships with particular people are the means by which this is attained. Aelred was born in northern England in about 1110, and as a young man served as steward to King David of Scotland. In 1134, visiting his home territory on royal business, he called at the newly formed monastery at Rievaulx in Yorkshire. He was captivated by its way of life, and joined at once. He became abbot in 1147.

ABOVE *Rievaulx Abbey, from the Liber Studiorum engraved by Henry Dawe, 1812 after J. M.W. Turner. On visiting Rievaulx Abbey in 1134, Aelred joined at once and became abbot in 1147.*

A BOND OF SWEETNESS

Friendship is a virtue by which two hearts are united and made one, in a bond of sweetness and love. For this reason, the philosophers of the world have classed friendship not with the perishable and transient things of time, but with the virtues that last forever....

A man that could bring himself to injure a former friend was never a friend at all. Equally, a man who withdrew his friendship when he suffered injury from a friend had never experienced the joy of true friendship. Friends love one another at all times. Whether a person is rebuked, injured, burned at the stake, or nailed to a cross, that person's true friends remain loyal.

SPIRITUAL FRIENDSHIP, CHAPTER 1

FRIENDSHIP AND CHARITY

There is a difference between friendship and charity. God has taught us that charity has universal application, whereas friendship is particular. Charity means loving all people, including enemies. But the name "friend" is applicable only to those whom we can fully trust, and with whom we can share our secrets; and in friendship, this trust is vital, so friends can depend on one another completely.

SPIRITUAL FRIENDSHIP, CHAPTER 1

SENSUAL, WORLDLY, AND SPIRITUAL RELATIONSHIPS

Men may be attracted to one another by passion; but this is not friendship in the true sense. Friendship is based on love; and a friend who does not love is not a true friend....

To make things clearer, let us distinguish three types of relationship. There are sensual relationships, based on the gratification of the bodily instincts. There are worldly relationships, stimulated by the expectation of material gain. And there are spiritual relationships, based on similarity of outlook and common ideals. Only the last type of relationship may properly be called friendship....

Genuine friendship is always spiritual. It is not motivated by earthly considerations or self-seeking. It is cultivated for its own intrinsic worth, and because it satisfies the deepest needs of the human heart.

SPIRITUAL FRIENDSHIP, CHAPTER 1

HUMAN AND DIVINE LOVE

The transition from human friendship to divine love is neither difficult nor unnatural. Christ inspires us to love our friends; and Christ then offers himself as a friend. In this way, human love becomes divine love; emotional pleasure becomes spiritual pleasure; affection for people becomes affection for God. The bond of human friendship becomes the bond between Christ and the soul. We move upward through the different degrees of love until we attain perfect friendship with Christ; and that friendship is sealed with a divine kiss.

SPIRITUAL FRIENDSHIP, CHAPTER 2

THE SPIRITUAL KISS

It is quite proper for two friends to kiss. In giving and accepting the touch of the lips, two spirits mingle and two hearts are joined. In such a kiss, the Spirit of God is present, so everything connected with the kiss is chaste; the joy of the kiss derives directly from God. It is as if Christ is offering his kiss, through the lips of another person. Between true friends, a kiss creates such a holy feeling of delight that there seems to be one soul in two bodies.

SPIRITUAL FRIENDSHIP, CHAPTER 2

THE CONSOLATION OF FRIENDSHIP

The sweetness of God that we taste in this life is given us, not so much for enjoyment as for a consolation and encouragement for our weakness. That is why it is such a great joy to have the consolation of someone's affection—someone to whom one is deeply united by the bonds of love; someone in whom our weary spirit may find rest, and to whom we may pour out our souls… someone whose conversation is as sweet as a song in the tedium of our daily life.

He must be someone whose soul will be to us a refuge to creep into when the world is altogether too much for us; someone to whom we can confide all our thoughts. His spirit will give us the comforting kiss that heals all the sickness of our preoccupied hearts. He will weep with us when we are troubled, and rejoice with us when we are happy, and he will always be there to consult when we are in doubt. And we will be so deeply bound to him in our hearts that even when he is far away, we shall find him together with us in spirit, together and alone.

The world will fall asleep all round you, you will find, and your soul will rest, embraced in absolute peace. Your two hearts will lie quietly together, united as if they were one, as the grace of the Holy Spirit flows over you both. In this life on earth, we can love a few people in this way, with heart and mind together, for they are more bound to us by the ties of love than any others.

THE MIRROR OF LOVE

THE MEDICINE OF LIFE

No one can be truly happy in this world without a friend. A man who has no friend to share his sorrows and his joys cannot truly live. Each person needs someone to relieve his mind of the thoughts that trouble him and to complete the happiness he derives from his spiritual experiences. What can be more glorious than the union of two hearts and two minds? In such a union there is no fear of rivalry, no grounds for mutual distrust. If one corrects the other, there is no misunderstanding; and praise is never flattery. A friend is the medicine of life; and no medicine is more efficacious, more valuable, in curing all our temporal ills.

SPIRITUAL FRIENDSHIP, CHAPTER 2

Thomas Aquinas

In his day, Thomas Aquinas was highly controversial, criticized for diluting the Christian faith with the secular philosophy of Aristotle. But he came to be regarded as the greatest of the medieval theologians; and to this day his thought remains a major pillar of Roman Catholic teaching, studied in depth by those training for the priesthood.

His central concern was the way in which human beings can know divine truth. Following Aristotle, he emphasized that all human knowledge originates in the senses, and that reason must assert mastery over the senses. But he also recognized that through contemplation, individuals can have a direct encounter with God, which transcends rational thought.

Thomas Aquinas also entered the controversy, which raged through the medieval period, over the means by which Christ's death reconciles human beings with God. He did not directly refute the notion that Christ acted as a substitute, taking on himself the punishment that humans deserve. But he preferred the idea of the crucifixion exemplifying every virtue to which humans should aspire.

Born in 1255 to a noble family in the Italian town of Aquinas, Thomas was from boyhood fat, slow, and somber, earning the nickname "dumb ox." He studied at Naples University under a Dominican teacher, who inspired him to join the Dominican order. His family, who had secular ambitions for him, tried to dissuade him by tempting him with a prostitute, and even by kidnapping him. But he remained unmoved, and went to continue his studies at Paris University, where he spent most of the rest of his life.

DOUBT, OPINION, AND BELIEF

When we are faced with a contradiction, in which there are two opposing views, our understanding can respond in different ways. Sometimes it does not incline one way or another, either because of lack of evidence, or because of the apparent equality of evidence for both sides. Thus the understanding wavers between two views, and is in a state of doubt. Sometimes the understanding is inclined more to one side than the other; yet the evidence is not of sufficient weight to demand complete assent. Thus the understanding is in a state of opinion....

Sometimes the understanding is immediately convinced that one view is right, because it conforms to fundamental axioms; thus it is in a state of knowledge. Sometimes the understanding does not incline one way or the other, because neither view is obviously in conformity with fundamental axioms. But the will chooses to assent to one view, definitely and positively, through some influence which can move the will, but not the intellect. This influence is such that the will regards it as good and right to assent to one view.

This is the state of belief. We believe in the words of someone, because to believe seems proper and advantageous. In particular we are moved to believe in certain sayings when it seems that eternal life depends on belief.

De Veritate, Question 14

THE RELIGION OF CONTEMPLATION

Contemplation can cause delight in two ways. Firstly by exercising the faculty of contemplation we feel pleasure, since contemplation is natural to us. We are rational animals, and contemplation is the fullest application of our rationality. All of us naturally desire to know the truth, so we take delight in seeking it. And when we acquire the habit of contemplation, so that we can contemplate the truth without difficulty, this delight is even greater.

Secondly the object of contemplation causes

delight, because we love the object. To gaze on another person, who is an object of love, gives great pleasure. The pleasure is far greater when the object is God, since God is the source of love, as well as its supreme object.... Although contemplation is chiefly an act of the intellect, its origin lies in the human desire for love. It is because we yearn for love that we want to contemplate God. Thus we can say that the end of contemplation corresponds to the beginning.

DE VERITATE, QUESTION 180

KNOWLEDGE AND HAPPINESS

In what kind of knowledge of God does ultimate happiness consist? Almost all people possess a general and confused knowledge of God. This is partly because the existence of God is self-evident in the world around us.

There is another kind of knowledge, which is in one respect superior to this: knowledge of God through faith. This surpasses knowledge of God through evidence because through faith we know things about God which are too sublime for evidence. But not even in this kind of knowledge can our ultimate happiness consist....

Our ultimate happiness consists in our desire being satisfied in such a way that we desire nothing more. If there is still unsatisfied desire, we cannot be at peace. This complete satisfaction cannot happen in this life, since the more we understand, the more we desire to understand; the desire to understand being natural to human beings.... Therefore our ultimate happiness consists in the knowledge of God which we shall possess after death.

SUMME CONTRE GENTILES, PART 3

THE CROSS AS AN EXAMPLE

Was it necessary for the Son of God to suffer for us? It was very necessary, on two counts. Firstly, as a remedy for our sins; and secondly, as a model for us in our behavior. Through the death of Christ, we have the opportunity for our sins to be forgiven, and for us to be saved from the evil consequences of our sins. But the passion of Christ is no less useful to us as an example. Indeed it is sufficient in itself to instruct in life

ABOVE *Although condemned in medieval times as highly controversial, the teachings of Thomas Aquinas today form an important part of Roman Catholic beliefs.*

as a whole. If you want to live a perfect life, you need only despise the things which Christ despised on the cross, and to desire what Christ desires. The cross provides an example for every virtue.

If you are looking for an example of charity—Christ laid down his life for us on the cross.... If you are looking for an example of patience—Christ allowed himself to be led like a lamb to the slaughter.... If you are looking for an example of humility—Christ allowed himself to be judged by such a man as Pontius Pilate....

CONFERENCES ON THE CREED, 6

Eckhart

Eckhart taught that God can be born in every human soul, and thus every person can become an incarnation of God. He was condemned as a heretic for this view, because it gave such a high status to the individual Christian that bishops and priests seemed redundant. But, although many copies of his books were burned some survived and continued to circulate; and his ideas influenced the Protestant reformers.

He was born around 1260 and at the age of fifteen went to the Dominican school in Erfurt. He joined the order, and his superiors sent him first to Cologne and then to Paris to study theology. He soon gained a reputation not only for intellectual brilliance, but also for eloquence. So his order recalled him to teach and lead his brothers in Germany; he became superior of the order in Thuringia, and then was chosen to start a new branch in Bohemia.

When he preached in parish churches, he attracted huge crowds. His popularity evoked jealousy among other clerics, prompting them to make charges of heresy. He was sent to the pope for trial, but by the time he arrived he was too ill to defend himself; he died a few weeks after his condemnation in 1327. He wrote a number of academic books in Latin. But his most powerful works are in his native German, and were originally produced in talks and sermons.

RIGHT *Early German illuminated text, from Decretum Gratiani, Mainz (Peter Schoffer) 1473. A brilliant academic, Eckhart wrote many books in both Latin and his native German text.*

THE BIRTH OF GOD IN THE SOUL

Inward work—work within the soul—is godly because it is aimed at making the soul more godlike. Outward work, regardless of its quality and magnitude, its length and its breadth, does not in any way increase the value of inward work. Even in a thousand lifetimes outward work cannot make a person more similar to God.

Inward work is good in itself. If our inward work is feeble and worthless, our outward work will be feeble and worthless too. If our inward work is great, it will make our outward work great as well. If our inward work draws its goodness from the heart of God, and from nowhere else, it receives the Son into the soul; and the soul is born as a son in the bosom of the heavenly Father. Outward work does not draw goodness directly from God, but receives its goodness from inward work. Outward work is complex, and its value is measured by its quality; in these respects it is foreign and alien to God. Outward work clings and adheres to inward work, and thus finds serenity and light; but in itself it is blind, without purpose.

Through inward work, God's Son is born in the soul; and the soul is born as a child of God. The Son of God in the soul is the spring and source of the Holy Spirit; and, since God himself is Spirit, the Holy Spirit brings to birth God's Son in the soul. God's Son is the origin of all who are children of God; only they are born of God, and transformed in his image. Those in whom God's Son has been born are estranged from all quantity and complexity, including the complexity of the orders of angels.

Indeed it is true to say they are estranged from goodness, truth, and everything which allows any shades of difference or distinction. They are entrusted to God, who cannot be received and has no complexity—in whom the Father, the Son, and the Holy Spirit are stripped of all differences and attributes, and are totally unified. This unity blesses us. The further away we are from the writing of God, the less we are children of God, and hence the less perfectly the Holy Spirit springs up in us and flows from us.

The nearer we are to the unity of God, the more fully we are children of God and the more perfectly the Holy Spirit flows from us.

Book of Divine Consolation, Chapter 2

GOD IN ALL PEOPLE AND THINGS

If God is in you, then he remains in you wherever you go. When you walk down the street, or visit friends, God is in you—just as much as when you are in church, in the desert, or in a monastic cell. So long as God, and God above, is in you, nothing and no one can hinder you. Why? Because when the mind is totally fixed on God, then all things become nothing but God. You carry God wherever you go, and in every action you perform. Indeed, all your actions are performed by God; this is because he is the cause of your actions and is responsible for them.

Thus when you concentrate your mind purely and simply on God, he is working in and through you; so neither your circumstances, nor the people around you, can hinder you. You will aim for nothing and seek nothing except to unite your endeavors to God's; and you will have no reward except the knowledge of doing God's will. And just as God cannot be disturbed by complexity and difficulty, in the same way nothing will upset you or disturb your thoughts. In God all complexity is simplicity, all difficulty is blessing.

You should see God in all things; and you should constantly remind yourself that God is in your mind, in your actions, and in your heart. To do this you need to keep watch over your mind. When you go out into the crowd and into the clamor of the world, keep the same mood that you have in church or in your cell. You should not regard all activities and all places as equally noble or worthwhile. On the contrary, it is better to pray than to sin; and a church is an easier context for prayer than a road. But in all places and in all activities you should be tranquil and serene, and your mind fixed firmly in God. In fact if you are firm in this way, no one can take your mind away from God.

Talks of Instruction, Number 6

Desiderius Erasmus

While the Protestant reformers such as Luther and Calvin attacked the abuses of the late medieval church on theological grounds, the Dutch humanist Erasmus preferred satire. As his serious writings show, he was their equal in theological argument, and largely agreed with their views. But he rightly feared that direct confrontation would cause the church to split, and this in turn would lead to long and bloody conflict. Thus he worked to reform the church from within, and used his sharp wit in order to promote this.

His greatest work, In Praise of Folly, is written from the perspective of Folly herself; and she rejoices in the disciples she has recruited. Her particular praise is directed to philosophers and theologians, whose futile arguments successfully prohibit honest thought. But she also takes delight in the madness of religion itself, caused by intense love for God.

The illegitimate son of a priest, Erasmus went to Rome as a young man, where he immersed himself in classical literature, learning to emulate the elegant Latin of Cicero. In 1492, after ordination as a priest, he became secretary to a wealthy bishop. After three years, the bishop awarded him a small stipend, to enable him to become a wandering scholar and writer.

He made England his second home, where he formed a close friendship with Thomas More. At the height of the Reformation in the 1520s, both sides called for his support; and both regarded his pleas for compromise as betrayal.

PHILOSOPHERS AND THEOLOGIANS

The philosophers, wearing cloaks and beards to command respect, insist that they alone possess wisdom, and that the ideas of the common people are mere fleeting shadows. They have a pleasant form of madness, which causes them to create models of the universe with bits of string, and to measure the sun, the moon, and the stars; and they love to speculate on the causes of thunderbolts, gales, and eclipses.

They never pause for a moment, as if they were private secretaries to nature, architects of the heavens, or members of a great council of angels. In the meantime, nature laughs at them and their ideas, mocking them for their endless disagreements among themselves, which demonstrate their own lack of certainty. In truth, they know nothing at all, yet they claim to know everything.

Their minds are so absorbed by all their abstract concepts—their notions of essences, universals, prime matters, quiddities, and the like—that they sometimes cannot see a ditch or a boulder lying in their path. Then there are the theologians. They are a remarkably supercilious and touchy lot. I might do better to pass over them in silence, rather than stir the mud of their thoughts or grasp the poisonous plant of their emotions.

If I attack them, they will denounce me as a heretic, using all sorts of spurious arguments to put me in the wrong; that is what they do to anyone they dislike. There is no group so unwilling to recognize my service to them as the theologians; in fact they are indebted to me on several counts. I have nurtured within them self-love, which enables them to dwell in an illusory heaven, looking down with pity on the rest of humanity as mere cattle crawling across the earth.

I have fortified them with an army of scholarly definitions and conclusions, propositions and corollaries, both explicit and implicit. I make little holes in the arguments of their opponents, so when their arguments close around them like a net, they can slip out. I mint for them all sorts of new and strange-sounding words and expressions, which they can exchange like coins. The theologians like to interpret the mysteries of faith in order to suit themselves.

These mysteries include how the world was designed and created; through what channels sin is handed down from one generation to another; by what means Christ was formed in the Virgin's womb; and how in the Eucharist bread and wine are turned into the body and blood of Christ. They wrap their mysteries in such complex arguments and such subtle definitions that no one can escape.

They then add moral maxims that are utterly amazing: that, for example, it is a lesser crime to butcher a thousand men on a weekday than to repair a poor man's shoe on the Lord's day; or that it is better to allow the whole world to starve than to tell a single insignificant lie. Such is the erudition and intelligence of these theologians that the apostles themselves would require the special assistance of the Holy Spirit to understand what they teach.

IN PRAISE OF FOLLY, CHAPTER 3

THE FOLLY OF CHRISTIANITY

It is quite clear that the Christian religion is akin to folly in some form, and it has nothing at all to do with wisdom....

When the mind makes proper use of the organs of the body, it is called sane and healthy. But when it begins to break its bonds with the body, with the intention of setting itself free— as if it were trying to escape from prison—then people call it insane. The mind that is becoming detached from the body is able to foretell the future, can easily learn the languages of other nations, and acquires other divine faculties. This is because the mind is liberating itself from the contamination of the body and exercising its true powers.

And for the same reason, people as they are dying often speak words of supernatural grace. Yet those who have these wonderful faculties are regarded as mad; and since these numbers are so small this adverse judgment seems justified....

Yet truly pious people devote their lives to detaching themselves from the body and its desires, and to attaching themselves to that which is eternal, invisible, and spiritual. Consequently,

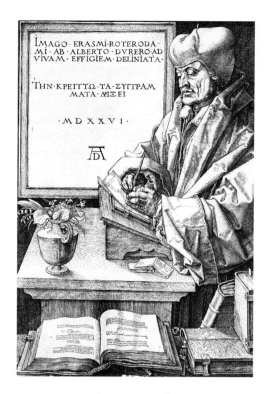

ABOVE *Desiderius Erasmus chose to use wit rather than anger as a means of fighting for reform of the medieval Church.*

there is total disagreement between a person who is pious and one who is not, and each regards the other as mad—though in my view, the epithet is more properly applied to the former.

IN PRAISE OF FOLLY, CHAPTER 4

THE HAPPINESS OF LOVE

Those who love intensely exist not in themselves, but in the object of their love; and the more they can abandon themselves, and live within that object, the happier they are. This is the state of a soul who loves God intensely, and hence wishes to leave its body, to live wholly within God.

The popular expressions "he is beside himself," or conversely "he is himself again" refer to the soul abandoning the body, and then returning to it. And these expressions concern madness and the recovery from it. Thus the more perfect the love, the greater the madness— and the greater too the happiness.

IN PRAISE OF FOLLY, CHAPTER 4

Martin Luther

A man who combined spiritual passion with intellectual brilliance, Martin Luther led the Protestant Reformation in northern Europe. As a young monk he was wracked with guilt, struggling vainly to win God's approval through strict conformity to the monastic rules. But by reinterpreting the epistles of Paul, he came to believe that faith alone justifies the individual soul before God—and that good works are the natural expression of faith. Since faith, in Luther's eyes, is a direct gift of God, he asserted that the ministry of priests as intermediaries between God and humanity was redundant.

Born in 1483, he entered a monastery in Erfurt at the age of twenty-two, and was ordained priest two years later. After his theological conversion he became openly hostile to many catholic practices, pinning his famous Ninety-five Theses on the church door at Wittenburg. He was excommunicated in 1521, and after refusing to recant, he was condemned by the Diet of Worms. He hid in Wartburg Castle, where he translated the new testament into German. Under his influence many of the German states, and eventually much of scandinavia, seceded from rome.

ABOVE *Martin Luther as a young monk.*

THE RIGHTEOUSNESS OF GOD

I hated that term "righteousness of God." Following the common interpretation, my teachers had defined this as an active righteousness, whereby the righteous God punishes the unrighteous sinner. Though I lived blamelessly as a monk, my conscience was deeply disturbed. I felt that I was a sinner before God, and I could not believe that he was placated by my good behavior.

The truth is that I did not love God. I hated the righteous God who punishes sinners; and secretly and inwardly, if not blasphemously, I was angry with God. I cried out to myself: "Surely it is enough that miserable sinners are eternally damned through their original sin, and are crushed by their inability to keep God's love. Yet God adds to our pain by the gospel which threatens us with his righteous wrath!"

Thus I raged with a fierce and troubled heart. Nevertheless I continued to grapple with Paul, struggling to understand what he really meant. At least, by the mercy of God, meditating night and day, I reflected in the words that follow the phrase I hated: "Those who through faith are righteous shall live."

I began to understand that the righteousness of God is a gift of God, granted by faith. This is Paul's meaning: the righteousness of God revealed by the gospel is a passive righteousness, with which by faith, God justifies us. As it is written: "Those who through faith are righteous shall live."

I felt that I was completely born again, and had entered paradise itself, through open gates. A quite different face of the Scriptures showed itself to me. I ran through the Scriptures in my mind, and found other phrases which affirmed what I had discovered.

"The work of God" is what God does within us. "The power of God" is the means by which God makes us strong. "The wisdom of God" makes us wise.

THE AUTOBIOGRAPHICAL FRAGMENT

FAITH AND GOOD WORKS

Faith is not the human idea and feeling that some people call faith. People hear and speak a lot about faith. Yet when they see someone whose life is not improving and who performs few good wishes, they are apt to say quite erroneously: "Faith is not enough; a person must do good works in order to be righteous and be saved." They make this error because, when they hear the gospel, they work hard to generate within themselves a mental state in which they can say, "I believe." And they take this to be true faith.

But this kind of belief is a human attitude which can never reach the depths of the heart; so nothing comes of it, and it leads to no improvement of life. True faith is a divine work, by which we are born anew. It kills the old self, and transforms us in heart, soul, mind, and faculties; and it brings with it the Holy Spirit. This faith is a living, busy, active, and powerful thing. It expresses itself constantly in good works.

It does not stop to ask whether good works have to be done; before there is time even to ask the question, it has already performed the good works. Those who do not do good works show that they do not have faith....

Faith is a vibrant and courageous confidence in God's grace. It is so sure and certain that believers would stake their lives on God's grace a thousand times. This confidence makes people joyful, bold, and happy in their relationship with God and with other people.

PREFACE TO THE EPISTLE TO THE ROMANS

FREE IN CHRIST

A Christian is a perfectly free lord of all, and subject to no one. A Christian is a perfectly dutiful servant of all, and subject to all.... Although Christians do not have to prove themselves through good works, they should freely empty themselves and behave like servants. Just as Christ in human form served humanity in every way, so should Christians serve their neighbors....

Just as our heavenly Father in Christ came to our aid, so we ought freely to help those around us, both materially and spiritually. We should, as it were, become Christs to one another, that Christ may be seen in all. We are called Christian not because Christ is absent from us, but because he dwells in us. He transfigures us in his image, that we may act toward others as he acts.

THE FREEDOM OF A CHRISTIAN

RIGHT *Martin Luther nails his Ninety-five Theses to the church of Wittenberg on October 31, 1517. (Painted in 1872 by Ferdinand Pauwels, Eisenach, Wartburg.)*

John Calvin

*C*alvin tried to do for Protestantism what Thomas Aquinas had done for medieval Catholicism: to produce an entire theological system covering every aspect of faith and morality. The book in which his system appears, The Institutes, was written, revised, and enlarged over a decade, and remains the supreme statement of Protestant doctrine.

He also tried to apply the Protestant vision to an entire city, Geneva, preaching to the citizens daily, and imposing laws that demanded the highest standards of behavior; and he had no compunction about burning as heretics those who would not accept the Protestant faith. Despite his stern rule, many were inspired by him, taking his ideas and practices to other parts of Europe. His theological writings are at times surprisingly tender.

He was educated in Paris, where he encountered the teachings of Luther; in 1533, at the age of twenty-four, he experienced a sudden conversion to Protestant beliefs. Four years later he was invited to Geneva, to help consolidate the Reformation there. He met furious opposition from many of the townspeople, who expelled him.

But in 1541 the Protestant leaders asked him to return, and he now prevailed. He made no distinction between religious and civic offices, seeking to impose God's laws— as he understood them—on the political and economic life of the city as well as its religion.

ABOVE *John Calvin's The Institutes remains the supreme statement of Protestant doctrine.*

THE WORD AND THE SPIRIT

By a mutual bond the Lord has joined together his Word and his Spirit, so that the perfect religion of the Word may dwell in our minds when the Spirit, who enables us to contemplate God's face, shines. We, for our part, are able to embrace the Spirit with no fear of being deceived, because the Word enables us to recognize the Spirit—the Lord and the Spirit being reflections of one another. God did not reveal his Word to the world for some momentary display, with the intention of withdrawing his Word when the Spirit came. Rather he sent down his Spirit by the same power with which he had revealed his Word, in order to complete the work of the Word.

THE INSTITUTES, PART 1

THE SEAL OF THE SPIRIT

The Word of God is not received by faith if it flits about in the top of the mind. It must take root in the depth of the heart, and hence become an invincible defense against temptation. Without the Word the heart's distrust of God is far greater than the mind's blindness; hence it is far harder for the heart to learn to trust God than for the mind to understand God. When the Spirit comes, the mind is enlightened by the truth; and then the power of the truth must take hold of the heart. The Spirit thus serves as a seal, confirming within the heart those divine promises which the mind has already accepted....

The memory of the first coming of the Spirit is constantly renewed by experience. Faith is often tossed about by various doubts, so the minds of the devout are rarely at peace—or rather, inward peace is intermittent rather than continuous. But when temptation besieges those who are faithful, they rise up in resistance; and when confusion attacks them, they stand firm at their watch.

THE INSTITUTES, PART 1

FELLOWSHIP IN CHRIST

Christ has made himself known to you, blessing you with numerous gifts, and making you a member of himself, so that you can live in unity with him. Thus his righteousness overwhelms your sins, his salvation wipes out your condemnation; in his worthiness he intercedes that your unworthiness may not be brought to God's attention.

We should never separate Christ from ourselves, or ourselves from Christ. Rather, we should bravely hold fast with both hands to that fellowship by which he has bound himself to us....

Christ is not outside us, but dwells within us. Not only does he tie us to himself with an unbreakable bond of love; but in his wonderful grace, he enters us ever more fully, until he becomes completely one with us.

THE INSTITUTES, PART 3

JUSTIFIED AND SANCTIFIED

Why, then, are we justified before God by faith? Because by faith we grasp Christ's righteousness, through which we are reconciled to God. Yet you could not grasp this righteousness without at the same time grasping sanctification.... Christ justifies no one who he does not also sanctify.

These benefits are joined together by a permanent and indissoluble bond, so that those whom he illumines with his wisdom, he also redeems; those whom he redeems, he justifies; those whom he justifies, he sanctifies. But since our question concerns only righteousness and sanctification, let us dwell on these. Although we may distinguish them, Christ contains both of them inseparably in himself.

Do you wish to attain righteousness in Christ? You must first possess Christ. Yet you cannot possess Christ without first sharing his sanctification, because Christ cannot be divided into pieces. Christ sacrificed himself that we might enjoy his benefits; hence he bestows both of them at the same time, never giving one without the other. Thus it is clear that we are justified not without good works, yet not through good works. By becoming part of Christ, we are justified before God; and in the process we are sanctified also.

THE INSTITUTES, PART 3

SLOW PROGRESS

The stimulus for right living is spiritual, where the emotions and desires are totally directed toward God, in order to cultivate holiness and righteousness. No one who is imprisoned in the body has sufficient strength to press ahead rapidly. Most people are weighed down by weakness; they waver, and limp, and even crawl along the ground. But each of us proceeds according to our feeble ability, living the journey we have begun. All of us will make some headway, however small.

Let us not cease our efforts; then we shall make increasing progress in the way of the Lord. Let us not despair at the slowness of our progress; even though our attainment falls short of our desire, each step is worthwhile—all that matters is that today we are further forward than yesterday. We should keep watch over ourselves, to ensure that we remain sincere in our desire to reach the goal. We should avoid flattering ourselves at our spiritual achievements, and we should honestly admit our errors and sins.

Then, little by little, we shall surpass ourselves in goodness. This journey will last the entire span of our lives; and it is only complete when we cast off our feeble bodies, and enter total union with God.

THE INSTITUTES, PART 3

Jacobus Arminius

he reformed churches that had been inspired by Calvin found themselves in the early seventeenth century divided on the issue of human freedom. Basing themselves on Calvin's own teachings, many Protestants claimed that God alone can choose who shall be saved; thus some are predestined for salvation, while others are doomed to condemnation. Jacob Arminius led the opponents of the rigorous position.

He believed salvation is a matter of free choice: the individual can decide whether to accept the gospel or reject it. And the consequence of accepting the gospel is to attain a higher form of liberty—freedom from sin, and freedom to love. Nonetheless, Arminius recognized the central importance of divine grace, both in alerting the individual to the nature of the choice to be made, and in giving strength to implement the right choice.

Arminius was ordained a minister in the Dutch Reformed Church in 1588 at the age of twenty-eight, and went on to become professor of theology at Leiden. A modest and self-effacing man, he felt compelled to engage in a public debate with the leading proponent of predestination. The debate caught the public imagination, and was attended by all the leading political and academic figures in Holland.

In preparation, Arminius formulated his beliefs in a series of "disputations." The debate was inconclusive, and Arminius died a year later. But his views were discussed widely in Western Europe, and influenced the Evangelical revival in the following century.

CHOICE AND FREE WILL

Human beings possess the faculty of choice and free will. This is the ability of the mind to make judgments about things proposed to it; and the ability to transmit these choices to the will, so that they are enacted. Choice and free will have their roots in the human capacity for rational thought....

To understand the nature of choice and free will, we must look at the stages in the moral development of humanity.

Firstly there is the state of primitive innocence, when the human mind had a clear understanding of God's truth and glory; when the human heart loved God's righteousness....

Secondly, there is the state of darkness of mind and perverseness of heart. The darkness of mind is when humanity chooses to ignore God and his righteousness, in favor of Satan's notions of goodness—notions which we call sin. Perverseness of heart occurs when these sinful notions are regarded as the only means to happiness, and hence the object of human desire....

This gradually weakens the powers to perform that which is truly good; human beings become morally impotent.

Thirdly, there is the renewed state of righteousness in which the mind and the heart are transformed. This can be achieved by knowledge of God in Christ. The mind once again understands the true nature of goodness; and this in turn rekindles in the emotions and affections a desire for goodness. But the renewal does not occur instantly. It takes place gradually over a long period. And it depends on the daily effort of the individual.

Each day the individual must make a choice in favor of true goodness; and this choice must be transmitted to the will. The mind, the heart, and the body struggle against this choice; and the will resists its transmission. Thus the process of renewal is a series of battles—and some of these battles will be lost.

DISPUTATION 11

CHRISTIAN LIBERTY

Liberty in the general sense is the state in which people are free to act as they wish, and are not bound to act in particular ways. The opposite of liberty is bondage or slavery, in which people do not have control over their own actions, but are subject to the commands and prohibitions of others. Christian liberty is the liberty which Christ procured.

This liberty belongs to those who believe in Christ because as true believers in Christ, individuals must first recognize their servitude; they must acknowledge that they are in bondage to sin, and hence to death. There are four stages by which human beings are freed from this bondage.

The first is freedom from the guilt of sin, and the punishment which it deserves. This is purchased by the blood of Christ on the cross.

The second is deliverance from the tyranny of sin within the mind and the heart. This is attained by the mind and heart freely choosing to be open to the power of the Holy Spirit.

The third is obedience to the moral laws of God. Although he could demand obedience, God simply invites us to obey his laws, leaving us free to accept or reject that invitation.

The fourth is freedom from external rules of worship, through having direct access to God in prayer. The individual who trusts in Christ can speak to God and listen to God, without the mediation of priests and their ceremonies.

DISPUTATION 20

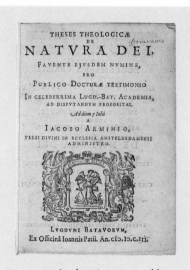

ABOVE *Jacobus Arminius, unlike many of his fellow Protestants, believed that the individual could choose to be saved and that salvation was not God's choice alone.*

DIVINE PROVIDENCE

The nature of God, the nature of the creation, the testimony of the Scriptures, and the testimony of human experience all indicate the benign providence of God.

Providence is not an intrinsic quality of God; nor is it some kind of divine habit. God does not need to express providential care for his creation, in order to be God. Providence is an expression of divine choice. Providence may be defined as God's continual care for the world, and for every creature that lives in the world. God watches over every creature's feelings and actions. And especially he watches over men and women who have put their trust in him. God in his providence works for the good of all creatures.

The good of a creature is defined by the nature of the creature, and by the relationship between the creature and God. Divine providence is the process by which God ensures good relations with all creatures, in order that their natures might be fulfilled. The actions of God in his providence demonstrate his wisdom. In his wisdom he is sometimes severe, and sometimes merciful; but always he is just.

We may distinguish two aspects of providence. The first is preservation, by which God sustains all creatures. The second is government, by which God guides their feelings and actions.

We may also distinguish four ways in which providence operates. The first is motion, by which God prompts creatures to feel and act in a particular fashion. The second is assistance, by which God strengthens the good inclinations of creatures. The third is concurrence, by which God supports and opposes the feelings and actions of creatures. And the fourth is permission, by which God allows his creatures to feel and act in a particular fashion.

DISPUTATION 28

Blaise Pascal

ne of the leading scientists of his day, Pascal turned his intellect to the central spiritual dilemma of the modern world: that people continue to have a very strong need and desire for religion, yet religious beliefs are unprovable and for many people implausible. His answer was that religion alone can bring deep and lasting happiness to people; thus the rational person should gamble on the truth of religious faith.

He was, however, critical of forms of religion that exploited people's fears and sense of guilt, and he wanted to discredit these. Instead, he believed that religion should stir the imagination, in order to carry the mind and heart above the confines of reason.

Pascal was a child prodigy, producing at the age of sixteen a geometrical theory that astounded mature mathematicians. When his father and sisters joined a Roman Catholic revivalist movement, Pascal was initially skeptical. But in 1654, at the age of thirty-one, he experienced his own conversion when, without warning, he felt the love and joy of God penetrate his entire being.

He now devoted his scientific genius to charitable purposes, designing a drainage system to turn marshland into farmland for the poor; he also worked out the first bus timetable in history, for a Paris service whose profits were given to widows and orphans. He wrote his religious ideas in the form of short thoughts, which were collected and published after his death under the title Pensées.

ABOVE *Portrait of Blaise Pascal, from an engraving by Edelinck.*

CONTEMPLATING NATURE

Contemplate the whole of nature in its dazzling beauty and complexity. Contemplate the universe in its awesome vastness, with the earth as a mere speck within it. Then realize that your rational mind cannot comprehend the complexity of nature or the vastness of the universe. Yet where reason must stop, imagination can proceed.

The imagination can rejoice in its own simplicity, as compared with nature's complexity; and it can thus find peace by resting in nature's ample bosom. The imagination can rejoice in its own smallness, recognizing that within the infinity of space everywhere is the center.

PENSÉES 72

THE PARTS AND THE WHOLE

If we look honestly at ourselves, we recognize the severe limitations of our knowledge. We cannot possibly comprehend the whole of God's creation. Yet we aspire to comprehend those parts to which our mental capacity bears some proportion. Then we begin to realize that every part of God's creation is connected and linked together; so that by understanding what we can, we have an inkling of the whole.

PENSÉES 72

DISAGREEMENTS POINTING TO TRUTH

Let us see how people define the greatest good, and find out the extent to which their definitions agree. Some say the greatest good consists in virtue; others in obedience to the laws of nature; others in truth; others in total ignorance; others in indolence and self-indulgence; others in abstinence from superficial pleasures; others in serenity and in never being surprised; others in doubt and skepticism. And there are some very wise people who say that the greatest good can never be defined, however strongly we want to define it. That is the finest answer—the agreement to which our disagreements point.

PENSÉES 73

REASON AND IMAGINATION

Imagination is the dominant faculty in human beings. It sometimes leads the mind toward truth, and sometimes toward falsehood. And since there is no means of telling the direction in which it is leading, it is a most unreliable and deceptive master. Not only fools, but wise people also, are led by imagination. And even when reason objects, imagination usually proves too strong. Indeed, imagination in its arrogance treats reason as its enemy, and takes pleasure in demonstrating its power over reason.

Imagination can make people sad or happy, sick or well, rich or poor. It can make people believe or doubt. It can deaden the senses or arouse them. It can raise people's understanding, or it can plunge them into ignorance. It can give far greater pleasure and satisfaction than reason, entertaining the mind with wonderful pictures and sounds. Those who have lively imaginations regard themselves as far superior to those who possess rational intelligence.

They are bold and confident in conversation, whereas rational people are cautious and hesitant; thus they win the trust and admiration of their listeners.

PENSÉES 82

TERROR AND GRACE

The way of God, who is gentle in all things, is to instill religion into our minds through reasoned arguments, and into our hearts with grace. But if we attempt to instill it into people's minds by force, with threats of retribution, we instill only terror. Indeed much of what passes for religion is terror.

PENSÉES 185

HATRED OF RELIGION

Many people hate religion. And hatred is deepened because they are afraid it might be true. The cure for this is first to show that religion is not contrary to reason, and thus should be taken seriously. Secondly, make religion attractive, so that good people want it to be true. Thirdly, explain to them that religion can help them to understand themselves, and in this way, bring them many blessings.

PENSÉES 187

THE GAMBLE OF FAITH

I would be much more afraid of rejecting religious faith, and later finding out it were true, than of embracing religious faith, and later finding out it were false.

PENSÉES 241

WAYS OF FAITH

There are three ways of having faith: reason, habit, and inspiration. Christianity will not accept people as its true children unless they have inspiration. This does not mean that Christianity excludes reason and habit. Indeed it requires that we open our minds to the rational foundations of its teachings, and allow our habits of thought and behavior to be changed. But this charge can only be achieved if God inspires it.

PENSÉES 245

FAITH AND THE SENSES

Faith tells us what the senses cannot; but true faith does not contradict the senses. Faith is above, not against, the senses.

PENSÉES 265

REASON AND RELIGION

If we make reason the only judge of truth, our religion will become devoid of mystery. But if we ignore reason, our religion will become absurd and ridiculous.

PENSÉES 273

William Penn

lthough most famous for founding the colony of Pennsylvania, William Penn also expressed in vivid and robust terms a particular kind of attitude to religion and morality, which has remained remarkably strong in the Anglo-Saxon world. He was suspicious of all theological speculation, even opposing the doctrine of the Trinity as intellectual self-indulgence. He was also suspicious of excessive public worship, since it encourages the notion that God is only present in religious buildings and rituals.

The essence of both theology and worship, in Penn's view, is a continuous sense of God's presence in every situation and within every creature. And this must find expression in honest speech and generous actions. He was also a strong proponent of religious tolerance, allowing people to worship God as they wish; this belief formed the basis of his government in Pennsylvania.

The son of a distinguished naval commander, Penn became a Quaker as a young man. In 1681 he founded a small colony on the banks of the Delaware River, which later expanded. In 1688 the new king, William III, took the colony from his control. William Penn used his enforced retirement to write a book of reflections, Some Fruits of Solitude, in which he expressed his religious and moral convictions.

THE FOLLY OF PRIDE

A las! When all is done, what folly, as well as irreligion, is there in pride! It cannot add one cubit to any man's stature: what crosses can it hinder? What disappointments help, or harm frustrate? It delivers not from the common stroke: sickness disfigures, pain misshapes, and death ends the proud man's fabric. Six feet of cold earth bounds his big thoughts; and his person that was too good for any place, must at last lodge within the strait limits of so little and so dark a cave: and he who thought nothing well enough for him, is quickly the entertainment of the lowest of all animals, even worms themselves.

No Cross, No Crown

THE TRUE PILGRIM

T he true, self-denying man is a pilgrim; but the selfish man is an inhabitant of the world: the one uses it, as men do ships, to transport themselves or tackle in a journey, that is to get home; the other looks no further, whatever he prates, than to be fixed in fullness and ease here, and likes it so well, that if he could, he would not exchange. However, he will not trouble himself to think of the other world, till he is sure he must live no longer in this: but then, alas! It may prove too late.

No Cross, No Crown

RIGHT *William Penn's treaty with the Indians when he founded the province of Pennsylvania, 1661.*

THE RELIGIOUS PERSON

Religion is the fear of God, and its demonstration in good works, and faith is the root of both; for without faith we cannot please God, nor can we fear what we do not believe. The devils also believe and know abundance, but in this is the difference: their faith works not by love, nor their knowledge by obedience, and therefore they are never the better for them.

And if ours be such, we shall be of their church not of Christ"s, for as the head is, so must the body be. He was holy, humble, harmless, meek, merciful, etc., when among us to teach us what we should be when he was gone. And yet He is among us still, and in us too, a living and perpetual preacher of the same grace, by His spirit in our consciences.

A minister of the gospel ought to be one of Christ's making, if he would pass for one of Christ's ministers. That minister whose life is not the model of his doctrine is a babbler rather than a preacher; a quack rather than a physician of value. The humble and true teacher meets with more than he expects. He accounts contentment with godliness great gain, and therefore seeks not to make a gain of godliness.

As the ministers of Christ are made by Him, and are like Him, so they beget people into the same likeness. To be like Christ then is to be a Christian. And regeneration is the only way to the Kingdom of God, which we pray for. Let us today, therefore, hear His voice, and not harden our hearts, who speaks to us many ways in the Scriptures, in our hearts, by His servants and His providences.

And the sum of all is holiness and charity. Amuse yourself not, therefore, with the numerous opinions of the world, nor value yourself upon verbal orthodoxy, philosophy, or your skill in tongues, or knowledge of the church Father— too much the business and vanity of the world. But rejoice in this, that you know God, who is the Lord, who exercises loving kindness and judgment and righteousness in the earth. Public worship is very commendable, if well performed.

We owe it to God and good example. But we must know that God is not tied to time or place, who is everywhere at the same time. And this we shall know, as far as we are capable, if wherever we are, our desires are to be with Him. Serving God, people generally confine themselves to the acts of public and private worship, which the more zealous do oftener repeat, in hopes of acceptance. But if we consider that God is an Infinite Spirit, and as such, everywhere, and that our Savior has taught us that He will be worshiped in Spirit and in truth, we shall see the shortness of such a notion.

Serving God concerns the frame of our spirits in the whole course of our lives, in every occasion we have in which we may show our love to His law. For as men in battle are continually in the way of shot, so we in this world are ever within the reach of temptation. And herein do we serve God, if we avoid what we are forbidden, as well as do what he commands. God is better served in resisting a temptation to evil than in many formal prayers.

ABOVE *William Penn wrote down his beliefs in a book of reflections,* Some Thoughts of Solitude.

SOME FRUITS OF SOLITUDE

THE MORAL PERSON

A right moralist is a great and good man, but for that reason he is rarely to be found. There are a sort of people who are fond of character, but who in my opinion have but little title to it. They think it enough not to defraud a man of his pay or betray his friend. But certainly he that covets can no more be a moral man than he that steals, since he does so in his mind. Nor can he be one that robs his neighbor of his credit. The complete moralist begins with God.

He gives Him His due—his heart, his love, his service. He that lives without a sense of this dependency and obligation cannot be a moral man, because he does not make his returns of love and obedience, as becomes an honest and sensible creature.

SOME FRUITS OF SOLITUDE

Friedrich Schleiermacher

*S*chleiermacher moved the focus of theology from the objective nature of God and his actions, to our subjective religious feelings. In an age when science was apparently discrediting many traditional Christian doctrines, Schleiermacher remained convinced that religious experience was both authentic and vital to human well-being.

He thus redefined religious concepts such as miracle, revelation, inspiration, grace, and faith, in terms of human perception and emotion. He was frequently accused of trying to destroy Christianity by undermining the system of beliefs; his ideas are still opposed by many Christian leaders today. He responded by saying that religion is not a matter of belief, but of discerning the divine dimension in everyday events. Although few would acknowledge their debt to Schleiermacher, this view of religion is now widely held in the Western world.

The son of a Prussian army chaplain, in 1796, at the age of twenty-eight, he became chaplain to a hospital in Berlin. He read widely in philosophy, and set out his ideas in his most famous book, On Religion, *published in 1799.*

In 1804, he became a professor of theology and remained in academic life until his death in 1834. He was an early proponent of ecumenism, striving to reduce the hostility between different Christian denominations.

LEFT *Friedrich Schleiermacher regarded religion as a matter of discerning the divine dimension in everyday events, rather than simply a belief in God. This view is still widely accepted today.*

POINTS OF BEGINNING

From time to time, every person is overwhelmed by a feeling of unity: an intermingling of the self with all the objects of the senses. These moments come and go, they fade and return, indeed, they can pass so swiftly that they seem scarcely to have occurred in the realm of time. I only wish they would last long enough that they could inform and guide all our activities from the mundane to the most elevated. I cannot directly describe these moments, so I must use metaphors.

They are like dew on blossoms and berries; they are like the modest and tender kiss of a maiden; they are sacred and fruitful like a bride's embrace. They are the initial encounters of the individual with the universal—although they fill no span of time, and have no tangible consequences. They are the marriage of divine and human reason; they transcend all errors and mistakes; they consummate all creative passions.

When they happen, you lie, as it were, in the bosom of infinity. You feel as if infinite power and eternal life are your own possessions. Your body, its every organ and muscle, is penetrated by divine energy. These moments are points of beginning, when life itself is reborn. These moments truly belong to you; and from them religion arises.

MIRACLES

What is a miracle? In the religious it is a sign or intimation. Thus to speak of an event as a miracle is to describe the observer as well as the event itself. A miracle is an event which both draws attention to itself, and points beyond itself. Yet in this respect, every event is miraculous, because everything that occurs in this finite realm points toward the infinite realm; all that is finite is part of the infinite whole.

Does the fact that we refer to some events as miracles, while other events are not given this description, imply that some events have a more direct relationship with the infinite? No; "miracle" is simply the religious term for an event. Every event, even the most mundane, is seen as a miracle once the religious perspective becomes predominant. For many people, only strange and inexplicable events are miraculous. But for me all events are miracles. And the more religious you become, the more miraculous the world around you appears.

REVELATION

What is meant by divine revelation? Every new and original communication to human beings of the universe and its meaning is a revelation. Thus, every moment is potentially revelatory, if you are properly conscious of its inner character. And every consequence of every moment adds to the revelation. We cannot logically demonstrate that this is the case, because it lies beyond conscious observation. Yet we must not simply speak about revelation in general terms.

We must assert that individuals must judge for themselves whether an event is merely normal, without any revelatory character, or whether it is new and original. Have you never experienced the originality and newness of an event? If not, then I urge you to make yourself open to the possibility that events are not mere repetitions of similar events in the past, but are fresh disclosures of the meaning of the universe.

PROPHECY

Prophecy is the religious anticipation of the latter half of an event. Prophecy is not concerned with accurate predictions of the future; it is concerned with how we should react to future events, and thence how our reactions shape future events. Individuals may be said to have a prophetic gift if they are able to grasp the religious dimension of events—if they are able to see the miraculous and revelatory character of events.

INSPIRATION

When we speak of inspiration, what do we mean? Imagination is simply the religious term for a sense of true morality—which is also a sense of true freedom. By morality I do not mean merely those occasions when we make deliberate choices about right and wrong. No; by true morality I mean the connection between the inner heart and outward action. If this connection is made, individuals act justly, regardless of external pressures and influences. And this connection engenders freedom because it frees individuals from slavery to worldly demands and attachments.

GRACE

Religious people often speak about the operation of grace.
It is nothing other than a general expression for revelation and inspiration—for that interplay between events as the senses perceive them, and their meaning as the heart understands them. To be aware of the operation of grace is to recognize the divine creativity in events. Thus for the religious person the whole of life is a series of operations of grace.

FAITH

True faith is to know oneself to be in possession of religion. In contrast, what people normally call faith—to adapt someone else's thoughts and feelings, and apply them to oneself—is both undignified and burdensome. Some people say that faith in this sense is the apex of religion. Actually it should be spurned by anyone wanting to move into the real sanctuary of religion. Such faith is nothing but an echo.... Religion is no kind of slavery, no kind of captivity. It is the place where you can be yourself. And the desire to be yourself is the beginning of faith.

ON RELIGION, CHAPTER 2

Søren Kierkegaard

For Kierkegaard, any attempt to prove the existence of God, or to determine the objective truth of any Christian doctrines, is fruitless. He believed that the starting point of religion is resignation, in which the individual renounces all temporal desires and ambitions, recognizing that they cannot bring lasting happiness. This is followed by faith, which is a subjective moment of decision.

Having renounced the temporal, the individual experiences a growing passion for the infinite and eternal—and yet is uncertain whether the object of this passion, whom Christians call God, truly exists. Thus faith is a risk, in which the individual makes a leap into the unknown. Kierkegaard's ideas were too strange and disturbing to gain popularity in his own time, and he was regarded with suspicion and contempt by many of his contemporaries. But in the century and a half since his death, his influence has steadily grown, and he is now widely regarded as one of the prophets of the modern world.

The son of a small businessman, Kierkegaard entered Copenhagen University in 1830 at the age of seventeen. His intention was to train as a Lutheran pastor. But he soon gave up his course and became an intellectual socialite, running up huge debts for drink and clothes. By 1840, the combination of boredom and poverty compelled him to withdraw from social life.

He devoted the remaining fifteen years of his life to writing, publishing a series of books on religious philosophy. He wrote exclusively in Danish; and it was only in the early twentieth century, when his works began to be translated into English, that his genius was recognized.

RESIGNATION AND FAITH

Faith, therefore, is not an esthetic emotion, but something far higher. It is based on resignation, on renunciation. It is not an immediate instinct of the heart, but is a paradox at the heart of life....The act of resignation is the foundation of faith, but does not require faith. Through resignation, I gain an awareness of eternity; this is a philosophical change in my attitude, which I can train myself to make. Whenever I seem overwhelmed by finite concerns, I deliberately draw back from them and turn my mind and heart toward God, who is eternal and infinite.

As I say, faith is not required for the act of resignation, but it is needed for going beyond an awareness of eternity. And this is where things become paradoxical. Resignation and faith are frequently confused, because it is said that people need faith to renounce their claim to worldly things. Indeed one hears a stranger thing than this.

People lament their loss of faith; but when one looks closely at them, one sees that they never had faith, but had merely made an act of resignation. In the act of resignation I renounce everything. This is a movement I make by my own effort. If I fail to make it, this is because I am cowardly, weak-minded, and apathetic and thus do not feel the great responsibility which has been given to all human beings to be their own censors—a far greater responsibility than that of being Censor General to the whole Roman Republic.

Having made this movement myself, I gain awareness of eternity, and thus enter a loving relationship with the Eternal Being, whom we call God.

FAITH AND RESIGNATION

SUBJECTIVE AND OBJECTIVE TRUTH

Christianity is not concerned with objectivity; it wants individuals to be wholly concerned with themselves. Subjectivity is the concern of Christianity; it is only in subjectivity that truth exists—if it exists at all. Objectively, Christianity has no reality. If the truth of Christianity existed subjectively in only one person, Christianity would thereby be true—in that person alone. And there is greater Christian joy in heaven over this one individual than over any number of universal theories and theological systems....

Those who choose to follow the objective way find themselves in a process of continuously trying to improve their knowledge, in the hope that this virtually proves God to exist. But this is an impossible quest, because God is a subject, and therefore exists only in terms of subjective awareness. Those who choose the subjective way see instantly the difficulties of finding God objectively, and a recognize the vast amount of time this quest would use.

They sympathize deeply with those pursuing the objective way because they know for themselves how painful it is to be separate from God: every moment without God is a moment lost. The subjective way leads people directly to God. They are not required to engage in any kind of intellectual reflection. Rather, they must have an infinite passion for subjective truth....

In the objective way, there is never a moment of decision. The objective way involves spending great effort in trying to define the difference between good and evil, in eliminating all contradictions, and thus delineating clearly the distinction between truth and falsehood. Only in this subjective way is there a moment of decision—a decision which recognizes that the objective way is mistaken. Passion for the infinite is the decisive factor, not the content of the infinite. Subjectivity, and the subjective "how," constitute the truth....

I contemplate nature in the hope of finding God. I see within nature omnipotence and wisdom; but I also see much else which disturbs my mind and causes anxiety. For this reason, inwardness—the subjective way—becomes acutely intense; it embraces objective uncertainty with the same passion that it has for the infinite. In the case of a mathematical proposition, the objectivity is irrefutable; but for this reason the truth of such a proposition is of no consequence. The above definition of truth is also a definition of faith.

Without risk there is no faith. Faith is that contradiction between subjective passion for the infinite, and objective uncertainty. If I were capable of grasping God objectively, I would not have faith. It is because I cannot do this that I require faith. If I wish to retain my faith, I must constantly hold fast to the objective uncertainty.

SUBJECTIVE-OBJECTIVE TRUTH

THE RELIGIOUS DECISION

Objectively becoming or being a Christian is defined as accepting the doctrine of Christianity. But this begs the question: what is this doctrine? And in seeking an answer to this question, your attention is instantly turned outward. You try to learn, down to the last detail, the various orthodox propositions, in order to determine not merely what Christianity is, but whether you are a Christian. You begin the erudite, anxious, fearful, and contradictory process of pinning down religion.

This process can be protracted indefinitely, so that the decision about your own religious position is relegated to oblivion. Subjectively, becoming a Christian is about making a personal decision. The adoption of the Christian faith involves a strange spiritual process which is quite different from any other. Being a Christian is not defined by what Christianity is, but by how a person exists as a Christian.

This points to an absolute paradox. If it were possible for us to gain some higher degree of knowledge so that we could perceive the infinite directly, then we would cease to have faith. Yet faith can never rest content with lack of knowledge; on the contrary, it is from our discontent with ignorance that the passion of faith stems.

CONCLUDING UNSCIENTIFIC POSTSCRIPT

ABOVE *"Whenever I seem overwhelmed by finite concerns, I deliberately draw back from them and turn my mind and heart toward God, who is eternal and infinite."* Søren Kierkegaard.

Albert Schweitzer

amous for his work as a doctor in equatorial Africa, Albert Schweitzer was motivated by his conviction that reverence for life is the basis of all true morality. He applauded compassion and love as emotions that can inspire moral behavior. But all emotions are volatile; and compassion in particular is narrow, focusing on the suffering of particular individuals.

Ethics, he believed, must consist in a mental attitude that affects the entire way in which we think and act; and this attitude is to regard all life, down to the tiniest insect, as sacred. He recognized that human beings are sometimes compelled to inflict injury; but we should never cause pain beyond what is strictly necessary.

The son of a Lutheran pastor in Alsace, by his mid-thirties Schweitzer had become renowned both as a theologian and an organist. Then in 1913, at the age of thirty-eight, he went to Lambarene in Gabon, where at his own expense he founded a hospital. He spent most of the rest of his life there, returning to Europe occasionally to raise money by organ recitals and lectures. Ten years after arriving in Gabon, he published Civilization and Ethics, in which he propounded the principle of reverence for life.

THE NATURE OF ETHICS

Ethics consists in a compulsion within me to treat the will-to-live in other creatures with the same reverence as my own will-to-live. This basic moral principle has been given to us; it has been implanted within our minds. It may be stated even more simply: that it is good to maintain and encourage life, and bad to destroy and obstruct it.

THE BASIC MORAL PRINCIPLE

The basic moral principle, that it is good to encourage life and bad to destroy it, both deepens and widens current ethical attitudes. People are truly ethical only when they obey the compulsion to help all living creatures they are able to help, and shrink from injuring anything that lives. They do not ask how far this or that life derives sympathy or should be regarded as valuable; nor do they ask whether, or to what degree, it is capable of feelings.

Life in all its forms is sacred to them. They tear no leaf from a tree, pluck no flower, and strive to avoid crushing any insect. If in summer they are working by lamplight, they prefer to keep the window shut and endure a stuffy atmosphere, rather than to see one insect after another fall with singed wings onto the table. If they walk on the road after a shower of rain, and they see an earthworm that has strayed onto the road, they will lift up the worm and put it in the grass—for fear that it would soon become dried up in the sun.

If on the same walk they find an insect that has fallen into a puddle, they hold out a leaf or a stalk on which the insect can save itself. They are not afraid of being mocked as sentimental. It is the fate of every truth to be laughed at until it is widely acknowledged.

Once white people who treated black people as humans were considered foolish; but that folly is now an accepted truth. Today it is thought extreme to respect as sacred everything that lives, down to the lowest manifestation of life. But the time will come when people will be astonished to learn that it was once acceptable to inflict injury on other living creatures.

LOVE AND ETHICS

When we define ethics as responsibility without limits to all that lives, people may regard that definition as impossibly wise. Yet it is the only complete definition. They may want to make compassion the basic ethical principle. But this is too narrow, because it denotes only concern for the suffering of other creatures. Ethics should embrace all the circumstances and aspirations of other creatures. The ethical person wants other creatures to live their lives to the full, and thence to take pleasure in all they do.

Love means more than compassion. It implies solidarity, not only in suffering, but also in joy and in effort. But it is really a simile for ethics—albeit a very profound and natural simile. The fullest expression of love is when two creatures are joined, both physically and emotionally, in sexual intercourse. Yet this illustrates that love, as the word is normally understood, is always particular and always temporary. Ethics must exist as constant and general habits of thought. Thus the principle of reverence for life must lead to an attitude of mind in which all life is regarded as sacred.

The phrase "reverence for life" may sound so general as to be almost meaningless. Yet once it has entered people's minds and molded their thoughts, it will never let them go. It includes compassion and love, and every other positive emotion. It operates like a living force within the brain. It prompts a feeling of responsibility for other living creatures in every place and at every moment. Just as the propeller churning in the water drives the boat along, so reverence for life drives the individual who holds it.

HUMANS AND OTHER CREATURES

What does reverence for life say about the relationship between human beings and other living creatures? Whenever I injure life of any sort, I must be sure that it is necessary. I must never inflict greater injury than circumstances demand. The farmer, who has mown down a thousand flowers in his meadow as fodder for his cows, must be careful on his way home not to strike the heads off any of the wildflowers on the roadside—that would be a sin, because it would not be under the pressure of necessity....

Whenever an animal is forced into the service of human beings, we should all be concerned about the suffering which that animal may undergo. We should feel responsible for preventing any pain which can be avoided. We should not soothe our conscience with the idea that the suffering of animals is beyond our sphere of concern. Even if we do not witness the pain which our society inflicts on animals, we remain responsible for it. Let the moan of thirsty animals in railway trucks not go unheard. Let the misery of animals in slaughterhouses, dying at the hands of unskilled butchers, not go unseen.

CIVILIZATION AND ETHICS

ABOVE *Albert Schweitzer. "Ethics consists in a compulsion within me to treat the will-to-live in other creatures with the same reverence as my own will-to-live."*

Dietrich Bonhoeffer

waiting death in a Nazi prison, Bonhoeffer looked forward to an age when Christianity would be freed from the trappings of religion. In his view, religion in the conventional sense was simply the garment that Christianity had worn for the first nineteen centuries of its existence; it was now being forced to strip naked, becoming "religionless." God should no longer be encountered solely on the boundaries of human existence in times of failure; but he should be experienced in the midst of life. And the Christian should no longer be bound up with the Church as an institution, nor even strive to become someone special, like a saint. We are called, Bonhoeffer taught, to follow Christ in the world, sharing his sufferings.

The son of a professor of psychiatry, Dietrich Bonhoeffer trained as a Lutheran pastor in New York. When Hitler came to power in 1933, Bonhoeffer had returned to Berlin as chaplain at the university; he took a leading role in the Christian resistance to Hitler's policies.

In 1939, he rejected the offer of a job in the United States, believing that he had to remain with his fellow Christians in Germany. Serving as a double agent, he vainly tried to persuade the British government to support a conspiracy to assassinate Hitler. He was arrested in 1943 for smuggling fourteen Jews into Switzerland, and hanged on April 9, 1945, at the age of thirty-nine. His Letters and Papers from Prison, published after the war, have inspired numerous movements across the world striving to reform and renew Christianity.

RELIGIONLESS CHRISTIANITY

I find myself incessantly asking: what is Christianity, and who is Christ, for people today? In the past, a set of doctrines, combined with pious advice, was sufficient. But that time is over. So too is the time for trying to reduce Christianity to a matter of inward experience and pure individual conscience. In fact, the time for religion, in the conventional sense, is over. We are moving toward a period when people will be religionless. Already many people find they simply cannot be religious.

And those who honestly describe themselves as religious do not act up to it—so presumably they mean something quite different by "religious." For the past nineteen centuries, since the Christian Church began, its teaching and theology have rested on the assumption that human beings are inherently religious. Christianity has put itself forward as one form—the true form—of religion.

But it is now becoming clear that religion is a transient form of self-expression, conditioned by particular historical circumstances; and that humanity today is becoming radically religionless. Take, for example, this present war: unlike all previous wars, it is not evoking a religious response. So what does this mean for Christianity? It means that the foundation of the edifice, which we have called Christianity, is being taken away.

There are a few survivors of the earlier religious age, and a few intellectually dishonest people, whom we can still call religious. Are these the chosen few?…Or should we recognize that the form of Christianity which we have known was only a preliminary stage toward a complete absence of religion? And if religion is disappearing, where does that leave the Church and its members? Can Christ be the Lord of religionless people, as well as those who are religious? Can there be religionless Christians?

It must be admitted that the outward forms of Christianity have changed greatly from one century to another. But if religion itself is only a garment in which Christianity has been clothed, what becomes of Christianity as the garment is removed?…

ABOVE *Dietrich Bonhoeffer. Bonhoeffer wanted Christianity to become "religionless" and free from the trappings of the first nineteen centuries. His writings from jail, before he was hanged, have breathed new life into modern Christian renewal.*

I find myself intuitively drawn more to religionless people than to those who are religious. I don't approach religionless people with any evangelizing intention; I feel closer to them in spirit. Among religious people, I am often reluctant to mention God by name, because that name does not seem to ring true with them. Indeed, to talk of God with religious people seems rather dishonest, as if one were simply using religous jargon—so the word itself makes me feel awkward and uncomfortable.

Yet to religionless people, I can on occasions mention God quite calmly and plainly. Religious people speak of God when human knowledge has come to an end, or when human resources fail, or even when they are too lazy to think. They bring God onto the scene as the apparent solution to insoluble problems, or as strength in human failure—they want God to help them at the boundaries of their lives.

And the further that people can push out these boundaries by their own efforts, the more superfluous God becomes. I am very doubtful of this talk of human boundaries. We are striving anxiously in this way to reserve some space for God. Yet I should prefer to speak of God, not on the boundaries, but at the center, not in weakness but in strength—and so not in death and guilt, but in human life and goodness.

As to boundaries, it is better to remain silent, and to leave the insoluble unsolved. Belief in the resurrection does not solve the problem of death. God is not beyond our normal perceptions and thoughts. God is in the middle of life, here and now.

LETTERS AND PAPERS FROM PRISON, APRIL 30, 1944

THE TRUE CHRISTIAN

We are called as Christians to live in a godless world, without attempting to gloss over or explain its ungodliness with religious ideas. In this way, we are called to share the sufferings of Christ—the sufferings of God. We should be free from fake religious obligations and inhibitions. To be Christian does not mean to be religious in a particular way. It does not mean turning oneself into some category of person, such as a repentant sinner or a saint, by following some special spiritual method. It simply means being a person—the person that God creates in us. It is not religious activity that makes us Christian; participation in the sufferings of God in the world is the mark of true Christianity.

LETTERS AND PAPERS FROM PRISON, JULY 16, 1944